Benjamin Franklin
and His Enemies

Benjamin Franklin and His Enemies

Robert Middlekauff

University of California Press

Berkeley   Los Angeles   London

University of California Press
Berkeley and Los Angeles, California

University of California Press, Ltd.
London, England

Library of Congress Cataloging-in-Publication Data

Middlekauff, Robert.
Benjamin Franklin and his enemies / Robert Middlekauff.
p.   cm.
"A Centennial book."
Includes bibliographical references (p.   ) and index.
ISBN 0-520-20268-6 (alk. paper)
1. Franklin, Benjamin, 1706–1790. 2. Franklin, Benjamin,
1706–1790—Friends and associates. 3. Statesmen—United States—
Biography. I. Title.
E302.6.F8M644   1996
973.3'092—dc20
[B]   95-30917

Printed in the United States of America
9 8 7 6 5 4 3 2 1

For Beverly

Contents

Preface

enjamin Franklin in the pages that follow is not the "harmonious human multitude" depicted in Carl Van Doren's great biography. Franklin certainly possessed a multitude of talents, and his achievements in a variety of fields were enormous. But though his psyche had its harmonies, he was sometimes out of tune with himself and his world.

This book seeks to see him under the pressure of enemies, several of whom were deeply interesting men—and one, John Adams, a good and, perhaps, great man. It is, in a sense, also about the force of the passions in history, including love and friendship, but mostly hatred, anger, scorn, the feelings enemies have for one another. It looks at a man, Benjamin Franklin, and at others around him in crisis, entangled in the affairs of eighteenth-century government and the diplomatic relations among nations. The American Revolution plays an important part in this story, but so does the politics of a British colony, Pennsylvania, before the Revolution.

Revolutions and politics, primarily public events (upheavals of masses of people, wars) are made by organized institutions, factions, interest groups, leaders and led. In analyzing them, historians usually resort to studying their "objective" circumstances—their sources in society and economics, the ideas that draw their support, the resources that make possible the movements that shape them, and the wars that the participants fight. This book makes use of such accounts, for they are the stuff of written history. But its central assumptions are that emotions are as important as objective circumstances and that they are usually inseparable from what can be counted and measured and seen. It seeks to demonstrate that even in Benjamin Franklin, a rationalist and the preeminent American philosophe, the affective side of life throbbed and influenced virtually all that seemed so rational.

I trust that this book also says something about Franklin's time. The era of the American Revolution, after all, was a period of enormous passion, and its politics translated into intense, galvanizing, organizing animosities. The study of these animosities—which often became passionate hatreds—can be made into an important device for viewing the era and its issues. Franklin and many of those he dealt with in America and Europe translated their political beliefs, hopes, and fears into intensely personal terms. This process of translation may not have been admirable, but it was a form of acting on principle. The passing of English power in America, with all that meant for English aristocratic and gentry classes, generated passions of extraordinary power in England and America. Franklin and his enemies shared these feelings—and acted on them.

Franklin responded unevenly to crisis—sometimes calling on his intellectual resources, which were of a very high order, and sometimes ignoring reason and fact in favor of giving expression to a dark side of his passions when fear and anger took over. He lost his political equilibrium when he was in middle age and behaved foolishly, persuading a good many others, mostly in Pennsylvania, to behave in a similar way. But he was at his best as an old man, his good judgment restored, in the service of his country in Paris.

Franklin's enemies were of several sorts. I have tried to be fair to them and to Franklin. One of them, John Adams, has always seemed to me admirable, even though he was sometimes foolish and vain; but then so at times was Franklin. My comments about two of Franklin's modern enemies in the Prologue are meant to be suggestive and to point up the ironies of perception in the eighteenth and twentieth centuries.

R.M.

Acknowledgments

In the course of writing this book, I called upon many friends and institutions for help. I began it while I was director of the Henry E. Huntington Library and Art Gallery and finished it as a member of the faculty of the University of California, Berkeley. Both institutions support scholarship in a variety of ways. I wish to thank President Robert Skotheim of the Huntington and Martin Ridge, then Director of Research there, for a Fletcher Jones Fellowship in 1990–91, and for a variety of kindnesses. My own university provided stimulation and tangible support, especially through the Preston Hotchkis Chair.

Claude-Anne Lopez and I originally planned to write the book together. Not long after we began our collaboration, Mrs. Lopez decided not to proceed. But she has remained an interested party, and she has been an inspiration to me. Her own books on Franklin, one co-authored with Eugenia W. Herbert, set a high standard. *The Papers of Benjamin Franklin,* to which Mrs. Lopez contributed for many years, has been the most important source for my study. I wish to acknowledge, however inadequately, its great distinction and the superb scholarship of its editors over the years: the late Leonard Labaree and William Willcox, Claude-Anne Lopez, and the present editor, Barbara Oberg. Dr. Oberg and her colleagues, especially Jonathan Dull and Kate Ohno, were wonderfully helpful to me when I worked in the unpublished papers in the Franklin collections at Yale University.

I owe much to Michael Zuckerman, who invited me to try out several ideas in 1991 in his Philadelphia seminar; to Leo Lemay, who provided a similar opportunity at the conference "Reappraising Franklin: A Bicentennial Perspective," held in Philadelphia in April 1990; and to The [San Francisco] Bay Area Colonialists, who commented helpfully on a part of Chapter 4 in 1993.

Librarians at the American Philosophical Society, in particular Ted Carter; the Historical Society of Pennsylvania, especially in the manuscripts room; and the Huntington Library, in particular Mary Robertson and Alan Jutzi, eased my way. John Van Horne of the Library Company of Philadelphia and Mark Lloyd of the Pennsylvania Archives provided valuable information about sources.

I am very grateful to colleagues who read all or parts of this study, much to its profit: James Thorpe, the former Director of the Huntington and Paul Zall, a Research Scholar there; Gunther Barth, James Kettner, Lawrence Levine, Nicholas Riasanovsky, and Irwin Scheiner of my department. Several students also helped in various ways—Mark Cachia-Riedl, Jacqueline Frobose, Brian Gregg, and Ralph Squillace.

My greatest debt is to my beloved wife, Beverly.

Prologue: The Modern Enemies

There were those in Franklin's time who thought virtue and morality fell too easily from his tongue. The aphorisms he made famous in *Poor Richard's Almanac* frequently advise good conduct. They urge restraint in eating and drinking, caution in choosing friends; and they suggest that a man should select his wife with his eyes wide open and when the deed is done, close them. They also more commonly praise hard work, saving time, frugality. Not content to give such counsel, Franklin lived a life that exemplified the virtues he advocated and then wrote his *Autobiography* telling about his success in practicing what he preached.

Franklin did much more of course. Almost any of his major achievements would have satisfied an ordinary man. He was a successful businessman, retiring from business when he was forty-two; in retirement he turned his attention to electricity and dazzled the learned of the century with his experiments. While he did such things, and sat in the legislature at the same time, he served his city in various ways, getting its streets paved and lighted and establishing a fire department, a lending library, schools, and a hospital among other useful institutions. He represented his province in Britain and, a little later, his country in Paris. And through it all, he wrote essays, doggerel, letters, reports of great interest and sometimes of distinction.

A later age celebrated his achievements, admired his virtues, and wrote his biography over and over again. There is no state named after him, but just about every other sort of institution has been—schools, towns, cities, hospitals, colleges, a mint, and many children as well. All the celebration and honor seem just and appropriate given his achievements.

But such a paragon makes many uneasy. Franklin has too many accomplishments, and he has perhaps received too much commendation. This age in particular seems put off by all that has come to him by way of praise. For Franklin's virtues are those not prized in our time, a period of slack, an age that has made leisure an occupation, one that celebrates the liberated spirit—and flesh—not the disciplined mind.

Even in the nineteenth century, a sterner time than our own but also a century much given to moralism not far different from Franklin's, there were skeptics or critics fond of mocking the high-mindedness of Franklin and his apparently ceaseless efforts to do good. Mark Twain, for example, took him on, though in a light-hearted way. Twain admired technological genius, and that side of Franklin did not draw his disdain. But Franklin's apparent pleasure in work, pursued early and late, his desire to get something done, and his habit of telling the world about his achievements did—and in Twain's sights loomed as large targets.

"The Late Benjamin Franklin," Twain's memoir, begins in a way characteristic of some of his best humor: "This party was one of those persons whom they call Philosophers." It is clear from that point in the sketch that Twain has little use for those bearing such a designation. For Twain explains that Franklin's philosophy was simply a screen for ideas and conduct calculated to make miserable the lives of boys, "boys who might otherwise have been happy." Twain's Franklin acted with "a malevolence which is without parallel in history"—he "would work all day and then sit

up nights, and let on to be studying algebra by the light of a smoldering fire, so that all other boys might have to do that also, or
else have Benjamin Franklin thrown up to them." As if the hard
work were not enough, the Franklin of malevolence also led an
ascetic life: "He had a fashion of living wholly on bread and water,
and studying astronomy at mealtimes—a thing which has brought
affliction to millions of boys since, whose fathers had read Franklin's pernicious biography." Asceticism extended to early rising in
the morning, with a boy "hounded to death and robbed of his
natural rest because Franklin said once in one of his inspired
flights of malignity—'Early to bed and early to rise / Makes a man
healthy and wealthy and wise.' " The cost to Twain of his parents'
experiments on him with this maxim were, he reported, "my present state of general debility, indigence, and mental aberration."
Forced to rise before nine o'clock in the morning, he experienced
"sorrow" so deep as to defy description. Where, he asks, would he
be now had his parents "let me take my natural rest." The answer—"Keeping store, no doubt, and respected by all." [1]

This final line suggests several meanings, and Twain's ostensible complaints turn upon themselves. Left to his own devices, including getting up after nine in the morning, he would have attained respectability. But of course he never really had much use
for the conventional middle-class life, and his jabs at Franklin's
moralism expressed his convictions about its worth. He announced these conclusions in a light spirit, but they reflected the
way he felt. The Benjamin Franklin who advocated a regular life,
which in its own way was intended to make a man out of a boy—
"respected by all"—was not for him.

Twain's demolition of the virtues Franklin advocated depended
upon an ironic appreciation of what might happen if Franklin's
life was not taken as a model. There is a sense of the grotesque in
Twain's little sketch, for all its apparent simplicity and indirect-

ness. Such tactics have not served others critical of Franklin in the modern period.

D. H. Lawrence's essay in *Classic Studies in American Literature* uses a direct attack.[2] Lawrence presents Franklin as a "snuff-coloured little man," a bourgeois, self-satisfied man and a threat to the imagination and the spirit. Lawrence seems to have read only Franklin's *Autobiography* and not to have understood that deceptive book. He begins by proclaiming that Franklin believed in the perfectability of man, an erroneous assumption about Franklin that is followed by many others. Clearly what Lawrence despised most in Franklin was the order he represented and exemplified. Franklin, he writes, was good at setting up barbed wire fences, within which "he trotted . . . like a grey nag in a paddock." The worst of it was that Franklin wanted a barbed wire fence around everyone, and he wanted everyone to emulate the "pattern" American, a peculiar creature recognizable in his materialism, conventional behavior, and complacency.

The essay Lawrence wrote about Franklin does not really argue a thesis about the great man, the snuff-colored automaton, the enemy of man's mysterious depths. Rather it erupts with anger and violence and makes its point through its explosiveness. There is no joy in Lawrence's demolition of Franklin, no happiness, and his essay's errors and misunderstandings are not really important. What is important is the expression of Lawrence's animus against both Franklin and America as enemies of Europe.

Franklin, Lawrence wrote, "knew that the breaking of the old world was a long process. In the depths of his own unconsciousness he hated England, he hated Europe, he hated the whole corpus of the European being. He wanted to be American." And what was an American, besides an enemy of Europe and the unfettered spirit? Lawrence's America was materialistic and repressive, "tangled in her own barbed wire, and mastered by her own machines.

Absolutely got down by her own barbed wire of shall-nots, and shut up fast in her own 'productive' machines of squirrels running in millions of cages. It is just a farce." Franklin more than personified all of this. As far as Lawrence was concerned, he had helped produce it.

Franklin's eighteenth-century enemies would not have recognized either Twain's or Lawrence's portraits. To be sure, they shared some of Twain's distaste for Franklin's advocacy of the virtues we have come to associate with the Protestant ethic, Max Weber's term for work, striving, frugality, and asceticism. But most of these enemies, especially in America, believed Franklin lived rather well; and after all, he had retired from the printer's shop when he was only forty-two years of age.

What really called into being Franklin's enemies in his own day was the danger he embodied. To his enemies he was a threatening man—to some a democrat and an egalitarian in an aristocratic age, to others an advocate of change when stability was needed, and finally a libertine given to a dissolute life when self-control and severe morality were required. He was, for these men, anything but the tight little defender of the middle-class world evoked by Twain and Lawrence.

If Franklin could be summoned from his grave, he would surely find the differences in these perceptions interesting, though perhaps he would offer a joke about them. While he was alive, however, he rarely joked about these men—his enemies demanded that he take them seriously. The record shows that he did.

CHAPTER I

The Friends of Benjamin Franklin

A few days after Franklin's death, Thomas Jefferson wrote Ferdinand Grand that "the good old Doctor Franklin, so long the ornament of our country and I may say of the world, has at length closed his eminent career." In suggesting that Franklin belonged not just to America but to the world, Jefferson sounded a theme that echoed throughout Europe and America. The next year he sent a few lines to William Smith, once Franklin's enemy but now his eulogist, in which he referred to Franklin "as our great and dear friend, whom time will be making greater while it is spunging us from it's records." Time has not erased Thomas Jefferson from its records, though it has not been so kind to William Smith. But Jefferson was right about Franklin, who seems even larger now than he did in his own century.[1]

Fame of the sort Franklin enjoyed, even in his own day, is uncommon. It commonly prevents friendship because it keeps men at a distance. George Washington was as well known as Franklin from the Revolution on, but those who knew him—and those who did not—spoke of him in a language different from what they used in describing Franklin. Washington was a remote figure, a legend, a monument while he lived. To most men he appeared great and mighty—and a little cold. Franklin was great, all agreed, but though he had enormous intellectual and moral power, no one thought of him as mighty, and only rarely did anyone think him cold.

Joseph Priestley, the great English chemist, noted that strangers sometimes found Franklin reserved, but such reactions were not common enough to evoke frequent comment. Not that Franklin was a hail-fellow-well-met. He could keep himself at a distance, and in fact he never showed all of himself to anyone. But very few men do, and complete openness is not necessary for friendship—indeed it might discourage it (a genial hypocrisy has its uses)—and Franklin met everyone he was not bound to distrust with directness and honesty. He was a good judge of others and normally brought a friendly and warm spirit to his exchanges with them. His curiosity about virtually everything under the sun tended to draw others out, and he was notably successful in his attempts to learn about the human as well as the natural world.[2]

Franklin seems to have been born curious; his capacity for friendship, though appearing early in his life, was actually an acquired characteristic. He tells us in his *Autobiography* that as a youth he was "fond" of argument, was in fact of a "disputatious turn," a bad habit, he soon realized, "productive of disgusts and perhaps enmities where you may have occasion for friendship." He had "caught it by reading my father's books of dispute on religion. Persons of good sense, I have since observed, seldom fall into it, except lawyers, university men, and men of all sorts who have been bred at Edinburgh." Giving up his taste for argument, he next "put on the humble enquirer." This role he learned first from an English grammar and then from Xenophon's *Memorable Things of Socrates.* The Socratic method reinforced his natural hunger for trapping his adversaries in positions they really did not wish to defend—"entangling them in difficulties out of which they could not extricate themselves, and so obtaining victories that neither myself nor my cause always deserved." He liked to win—he gave no quarter even in chess—but he soon saw that scoring in this fashion was pointless. It convinced no one, and it cost him friends. He then adopted "the habit of expressing myself in terms of modest diffidence," a practice he followed all his life that, one suspects, allowed a freer expression of his own desire to learn. It also helped draw men and women as well as children to him. And in time it became his natural style; what began in artfulness led him to what he really was.[3]

Among other things he was a good friend to all sorts, ranks, and ages of people. He made friends all his life and with rare exceptions kept them. When he was young, they tended to come from his own class, though he soon attracted the interest of a number of men of the better sort—William Keith, for example, the governor of Pennsylvania. Shortly after he arrived in Philadelphia, Franklin formed the Junto, an organization of young craftsmen who had aspirations to rise, to talk with others of their own kind about business and public service, and to do good. The members included Hugh Meridith, like Franklin an apprentice in Samuel Keimer's print shop. The two soon left Keimer and with the aid of Meridith's father set up on their own. Meridith's fondness for strong drink and his aversion to work soon shattered this partnership. Franklin, however, did not abandon him but lent him money and for several years after their parting attempted to help him in business. The Junto and Franklin also attracted Joseph Breintall, a small merchant and copyist. Breintall worked on another of Franklin's favorite projects by serving as secretary of the Library Company of Philadelphia from 1731 until his death in 1746. There was also William Parson, a shoemaker by trade and an original member of the Junto, who as librarian guarded the books in the company. The others were not really different: Stephen Potts, from Keimer's shop; George Webb, once a scholar at Oxford;

William Maugridge, a joiner by trade; and William Coleman, a merchant's clerk.[4]

After Franklin became well known in Europe and America, he did not scorn such men. He considered himself a printer all his life, though he did not follow his calling. Artisans everywhere recognized that in some sense he was one of their own. A group of ship carpenters, the White Oaks, came to his rescue in Philadelphia in 1766 when for a time the public believed that he favored the Stamp Act, a notorious and hated measure of parliamentary taxation.[5]

In the years of fame and reputation, Franklin naturally found most of his friends in other circles. Many were in public life, and some had reputations that rivaled his own, Thomas Jefferson and James Madison, for example. But his closest friends, in England and France as well as America, shared more than political interests with him.

Margaret Stevenson, Franklin's landlady in Craven Street, London, for two extended periods was one. She did not have Franklin's interest in politics, but she offered a warm family life to him. Her daughter, Mary, usually called Polly, also became Franklin's friend. Mrs. Stevenson did much to make his life comfortable. She cooked and baked for him and saw to it that his clothes were cared for, his linen clean; she worried over his health and shopped for him and for his wife, though Deborah Franklin was three thousand miles away. Soon after Franklin first came to Craven Street, in 1757, he grew fond of Margaret Stevenson. He also loved Polly Stevenson, who was eighteen years of age when he first met her.[6]

Polly delighted him. With all the enthusiasm and happiness of the young, she displayed a lively spirit. She also impressed him with her fine intelligence, and he was soon acting as her tutor, giving advice on what to study and read and challenging her to use her gifts to the fullest. He wrote poems to her and letters when they were apart; he teased her and talked with her about things serious and frivolous. She returned his affection, responded to his questions with those of her own, teased him back, and knitted him garters. Thirty-two years later she would sit by his bedside in Philadelphia as he lay dying.[7]

For the most part, it was an interest in science, technology, and agriculture that brought Franklin and his English friends together. They often discovered that they shared other concerns; most, for example, were liberals in politics; many were dissenting in religion. They also had aversions in common. None of them had much use for superstition and prejudice; they preferred to trust reason and evidence. They respected authority, but they did not admire the socially powerful. The corruption in English politics offended them, and only a few served in Parliament or held offices in the government.

They differed in personality, but not so greatly as to divide them. Some were bold; some, rather quiet, even meek. Almost none tried to make a big splash in company; several bordered on the reclusive. They did enjoy spending time together, however, often in a London coffeehouse. They visited one another in their homes and businesses, and Franklin traveled with several of his friends. Perhaps most of their meetings were at supper time or at gatherings of the Royal Society.

A glimpse of Franklin's correspondence might lead one to conclude that he knew everyone in London and was friends with everyone worth knowing. But he did not consort often with literary people or with artists. He and Dr. Samuel Johnson met at least once, but Johnson, a Tory, had no desire to know Franklin better. Franklin, after all, brought a whiff of revolutionary, or at least radical, fervor with him to England. The artist Franklin knew best was Benjamin Wilson. The son of a well-fixed clothier, Wilson took surprising turns while he was still young. His father went broke, and Wilson took a place as a clerk in a business. He was frugal and he had a talent for painting. Hogarth, a much greater artist, gave him encouragement, and for a while Wilson enjoyed the patronage of several wealthy men. He became interested in electricity and published an account of his experiments in 1750. Not surprisingly, when Franklin arrived on the London scene in 1757, the two met and became friends. Wilson painted Franklin's portrait not long after their first meeting. It was one of the few friendships Franklin made that eventually failed.[8]

The successes were striking and much more common. Peter Collinson, born in London of Quaker parents, was one of them. Collinson, a mercer, ran a business with his brother and traded with American merchants. Business did not bring the two men together; science did. Collinson had an interest in natural history and collected American plants. Franklin seems not to have sent plants to him; he sent something even more interesting—descriptions of his electrical experiments, which Collinson read to the Royal Society. The next year he began their publication in London, and Franklin's name as a scientist was made.[9]

Franklin's friendship with William Strahan, a Scottish-born printer in London, may have been even closer. The two men took to one another as soon as they met; the year was 1757, and Franklin was on a mission for the Assembly of Pennsylvania. He spent his first night ashore with Peter Collinson and the next with Strahan. Shortly afterward Strahan was writing Deborah Franklin that "I never saw a man who was in every respect, so perfectly agreeable to me."[10] Franklin and Strahan talked and laughed together and for a time plotted the marriage of Franklin's daughter Sally, then six or seven years of age, to Strahan's son William, who was three years older.[11]

Strahan found Franklin agreeable. Most people did, including

Lord Shelburne, who headed the ministry that made peace with America in 1783. Few of Franklin's friends in England, however, were in the highest governing circles, or even in society. But several had great distinction, David Hume and Richard Price, for example. Most were people who are known today only because of their friendship with Franklin. One was Jonathan Shipley, Bishop of St. Asaph in Wales, who avoided his diocese like the plague, preferring the comfort of his family home at Twyford, near Winchester. The bishop's family took to Franklin immediately, and their warmth and admiration encouraged him to begin in 1771 to write his memoirs. The bishop and his wife had six children; the two younger girls, Georgiana and Catherine (Kitty), evidently charmed Franklin and he them. On a trip to London with Franklin by post chaise, Kitty Shipley confessed that she preferred old men to young ones and looked forward to marrying one. Franklin suggested that perhaps she should marry a young man and make him into someone she really wanted. Kitty, who was eleven years of age, replied that she did not want to follow this course and would marry an old general so that she could become a young widow. Fifteen years later Franklin wrote *The Art of Procuring Pleasant Dreams* for Kitty.[12]

Franklin's friendships with children were not uncommon. But his warm connection to a bishop in the established church—or to any churchman—was. His preference for nonconformists or dissenting clergy was clear in his choice of the Club of Honest Whigs. Religious opinion did not bring him to the meetings of this group, a supper club that met every other week in London at St. Paul's Coffeehouse, but anything that smacked of formalism, High Church, or anything similar would have kept him away.[13]

If the Club of Honest Whigs was not a religious club, neither was it a political group, at least in its beginnings. As the revolutionary crisis developed and reached a peak before independence, the group grew more political, supporting the American cause. But even as America was breaking away, and sympathies for it increased and anger at the ministry kept pace, the members continued to sup together, primarily because of their commitments to natural and moral science. Political agreement provided a comfortable atmosphere for meeting but not a rationale. For the members of the club had important matters to talk over, matters that stimulated their minds.

Although their conversations about science and politics were spirited and informative, they also simply enjoyed one another's company and the food and drink they consumed. Franklin was in his element in these meetings; he had long since learned the virtues of silence, but in these gatherings he spoke in a variety of ways. James Boswell, a member but not in constant attendance, remembered Franklin's asking a question that indicated how he sometimes took it upon himself to stimulate argument in the group: "Franklin asked whether infidels or Protestants had done the most to pull down Popery." [14]

The club numbered about twenty-five in all—the largest contingent composed of dissenting clergymen and schoolmasters. The most distinguished would have stood out in any gathering, for the Honest Whigs included John Canton, Richard Price, and Joseph Priestley. Franklin admired all three, valued their friendship, and gave each of them more than he received. He would have had reasons for friendship with these three—and many of the others—had the club never existed. He and John Canton came together through their fascination with electricity; both were, in the terminology of the day, electricians. Canton, the master of the Spital Square Academy in London, the son of a weaver, was self-made, a journalist in his earlier years, and during Franklin's English stay a supporter of Franklin's single-fluid theory of electricity. Franklin found Canton's own experiments stimulating and looked to him for ideas as much as for agreement. Two years before Franklin left Philadelphia for London on his first mission for the Pennsylvania Assembly, he remarked in a letter to Peter Collinson that he planned to write "the ingenious Mr. Canton."[15] He was delighted, he said, by Canton's discovery confirming his own that clouds carry both positive and negative electrical charges. Once Franklin reached England, the two men saw much of one another in the meetings of the Royal Society as well as the Honest Whigs, and they visited each other in the Spital Square Academy and at Franklin's house on Craven Street. Franklin served on the committee of the Royal Society that studied Canton's experiments on the compressibility of water and took the lead in persuading the society to award Canton the Copley Medal, given in recognition of an outstanding discovery or invention in science. In 1771, the year before Canton's death, he and Franklin went together to the Midlands, stopping to visit Joseph Priestley at Leeds.[16]

Canton has fallen into obscurity; Priestley's fame as a chemist—he was the discoverer of oxygen—and an enlightened thinker has grown. He was born in Fieldhead, West Riding, Yorkshire, in 1733. He attended a dissenting academy at Daventry; afterward he filled various pulpits and served as a schoolmaster. At the time he met Franklin in 1765, he was tutor in languages and belles lettres at Warrington Academy. His friendship with Franklin and Canton revolved around their interest in electricity. Priestley suggested that he might write a history of electricity and began when Franklin, Canton, and Richard Price gave him encouragement. Franklin did more by providing Priestley with books and suggestions, and Canton proved as helpful. Franklin was delighted by the result, three volumes called the *History and Present State of Electricity with Original Experiments* (London, 1767). Priestley carried out the original experiments of the title while he was writing his history. Writing about theory and finding unsatisfactory everything already done, he attempted to discover the truth for himself. Both the *History* and the experiments won Franklin's approval, and he, with others equally pleased, proposed Priestley for membership in the Royal Society even before the books were published. The next year, in a curiously ineffective attempt, Franklin proposed Priestley for the Copley Medal—ineffective because Franklin's written assessment of Priestley's scientific work scanted most of the experiments. Six years later Franklin and his friends did it right, and Priestley received the prize.[17]

Before returning to America on the eve of the war, Franklin spent his last day in London, March 19, 1775, with Priestley. The two men talked that day about the crisis and read recently arrived newspapers from America to find articles that might serve the American cause through their reprinting in London papers. Priestley remembered that Franklin wept when he read the messages sent by Massachusetts towns to Boston, which had been closed to all commerce by one of the Coercive Acts passed by Parliament as punishment for throwing the greatest tea party of the century.[18]

Priestley shared Franklin's grief at the prospect of war. Like many British intellectuals, including members of the Club of Honest Whigs, he had watched the crisis develop, and he had argued against parliamentary measures. The year before, at Franklin's suggestion, he had written *An Address to Protestant Dissenters of All Denominations*, in which he held that the American colonies had never been subject to the laws of England except voluntarily. By leaving England, the colonists had removed themselves from English control and had placed themselves under the English king only out of "their regard to the country from which they came."[19] This was radical doctrine in England, though not in America, where Thomas Jefferson had made a similar argument in his *Summary View of the Rights of British America*.[20] Priestley, however, was not all radicalism and seemed to concede that Boston should compensate the East India Company, which it had "injured" when it threw the tea overboard.[21]

At the end of the *Address*, Priestley quoted his friend Richard Price to the effect that war with America would lead to the "public bankruptcy" of England. Price was also Franklin's friend, and he regarded the conflict between England and the colonies just about as his two friends did. He had been born in Wales, the son of a Presbyterian minister, and was educated there and in London. When Franklin first met him he was preaching at Newington Green, a few miles north of London. Price was small in size but large in spirit. His friends seem not to have been simply fond of him; many loved him. He was a gentle man devoted to his preaching and to his books. Reports on his pulpit style indicate that he did not preach with great force—his voice was weak and he did not have much eloquence. Franklin liked preachers who spoke about how life should be led and what constituted morality. Price satisfied him on these grounds and in many other ways as well. His mathematical and scientific interests intrigued Franklin— Price wrote on what today would be called probability theory, and he also studied demographic projection. But for the most part it was Price's amiable character, his sweet personality, and his politics that drew Franklin to him.[22]

The two men never laid eyes on one another after Franklin's departure for America in 1775, but their correspondence did not flag. Price's calm spirit deserted him when he wrote about the American crisis, and the criticism he received in the newspapers for his attacks on governmental policy made Franklin fear that he might be prosecuted. Price attempted to help American prisoners held in England during the war, and he occasionally sent Franklin intelligence about the movements of ships. This action may have brought him close to treason.[23]

The war separated Franklin from his British friends, but it joined him to new ones in France. As in England, science provided the common ground, and as in England, several of these friendships were preceded by exchanges of letters. Condorcet, one of the great encyclopedists and a distinguished mathematician, wrote him first in 1773 with questions about subjects ranging from the performance of barometers in the New World to the condition of free blacks. Franklin asked the American Philosophical Society to reply to the scientific questions but commented on blacks himself, saying among other things that free blacks in America were generally "improvident and poor." He added his own opinion to the effect that "they make good Musicians." The two men met in Paris after Franklin's arrival as commissioner, and they maintained their friendship until Franklin's death. Condorcet eulogized Franklin before the Royal Academy of Sciences in November 1790.[24]

The great French chemist Lavoisier was also drawn to Franklin. The twenty-five-year difference in their ages did not keep the two apart; in fact, in France as elsewhere Franklin found friends of all ages. He saw Lavoisier in a number of settings—in the Frenchman's laboratory, where he conducted experiments on combustible materials; at meetings of the French Academy; on the commission that investigated Mesmer and animal magnetism (one of the fascinating fakeries of the century); on less interesting committees; and at the Lavoisier home. Madame Lavoisier shared her husband's affection for Franklin and painted his portrait while he was in France.[25]

The friendship might have foundered had either man been given to jealousy or other forms of pettiness. Lavoisier's interest in the chemical composition of air brought him into conflict with Joseph Priestley, who was an exponent of the phlogiston theory. Franklin kept Priestley informed of Lavoisier's experiments, but he did not reveal his own opinion on the scientific dispute that divided the two.[26]

Lavoisier and his scientific colleagues in and out of the Royal Academy of Sciences, which made Franklin a member, admired him and the Revolution he represented. Their sympathies were engaged, for they sensed that something fresh—even original—had appeared in the political world with the Declaration of Independence. They had spent much of their lives speculating on the meaning of liberty and hoping for the end of the tyrannies that disfigured European life. Now, with the American Revolution, an enormous change seemed in the making.

French merchants undoubtedly shared this hope, but, understandably, their own interests shaped their attitudes with even greater vigor. Franklin looked to them for arms and munitions, and for ships to carry these items and the clothing and equipment needed by the army. They looked to him with the gleam of profits in their eyes.[27]

Franklin's landlord, Chaumont, was one of them, a man genuinely fond of his tenant and genuinely fond of profit. Chaumont exuded charm and energy. He was generous, and he was eager to get into the American trade. The French government recognized his talents and seems to have kept its lines open to him, confident that he would keep it informed of Franklin's activities. Chaumont was more than an agent—it is not clear that he was paid—and he took to his opportunities to make money in the new trade with enthusiasm. This quality sometimes led him to overextend himself, as he did in a protracted effort Franklin made in 1779 to send supplies worth three million livres to Washington's army. Franklin first relied upon Chaumont to secure fifteen thousand uniforms; Lafayette, who became one of the actors in an affair that soon involved other French merchants, shipowners, and the French government, promised to find fifteen thousand stands of arms. Responsibilities in an effort of this sort, in which none of the participants had much experience, soon became entangled with promises and the uncertainties of war. Before the effort ended two years later, Franklin felt his patience fray and his temper rise, but he kept his head—and he kept Chaumont's friendship. The delay in shipping the supplies occasioned the strain between the two men. Franklin was not at fault; Chaumont was.[28]

An interest in America and a desire to help it to independence undoubtedly steadied Chaumont's course at those moments when his uncertain judgment and his greed threatened to throw him into an eccentric orbit. Franklin's solid presence in French society must have reminded Chaumont that he was dealing in no ordinary business when he contracted to deliver ships and goods to the Americans. He indicated his regard for Franklin soon after they met by having a medallion made with Franklin's head imposed. Then there were the meetings and parties at Passy or nearby where the talk and the wit were comfortable and exhilarating.

Chaumont was in fact part of a circle of friends revolving around Passy. Almost inevitably French ladies took an important part in making this circle work. They probably soon realized that Franklin liked them as people—and appreciated them because they were women.

Franklin had close female friends all his life. Some of these friendships began as flirtations, but something more than sexual tension soon appeared. Franklin's deep attachment to his neighbor Madame Brillon illustrates the major points of this pattern. Louis-Guillaume de Veillard, who lived near Madame Brillon, introduced Franklin to her. It was an encounter that intrigued them both and soon entered another phase. Franklin was at first the great man she wished to meet and to know. One meeting led to others, which soon became exercises in gallantry on Franklin's part. How an aging man, now seventy-one, played the part of gallant without appearing and feeling foolish is not clear, but Franklin evidently managed. Madame Brillon played, not the temptress, but the faithful wife and mother, flattered and pleased by his attentions, perhaps feeling sexual desire akin to his but determined to remain faithful to her husband.[29]

It was her talent and charm that held Franklin's attention after Madame Brillon made him realize that she would not fulfill his sexual demands. The talent lay in music and the fine arts: she was an accomplished harpsichordist and she apparently learned to play the piano well in that instrument's infancy. She also composed music interesting enough to be praised by Charles Burney, the well-known English music critic. Her drawing and painting, moreover, brought her praise from those who saw her work. She was, in short, a woman of sensibility and taste.[30]

Madame Brillon was also young—still in her thirties in 1777, when she and Franklin met—beautiful, and the mother of two attractive daughters. Her husband was twenty-four years older than she and did not mind the attention Franklin paid his wife. He may in fact have encouraged it. Brillon was a worldly man, unfaithful to his wife, though she had not learned of his behavior when she met Franklin. By the time she discovered her husband's infidelity, Franklin had become her *cher Papa*, someone to confide in, someone who listened to her recital of grief and offered comfort and wisdom.

The Brillons sometimes traveled for her health, and in these absences from Passy she poured out her heart to Franklin just as she did when they were together. He soon made it his practice to spend an evening or two a week with them and sometimes strolled in the gardens with his young friend. These visits provided moments he cherished. He wrote many of his most charming bagatelles under her tutelage—or with her interests in mind. She gave him encouragement, resisted whatever impulse she had to correct his French, and thoroughly enjoyed all that he did.

The awkward moments that every friendship of any length endures were rare after Franklin recognized that he would not become Madame Brillon's lover. Franklin entertained hopes for a time that his grandson, William Temple Franklin, who served as secretary for the American commission, might marry Cunegarde, the Brillon's seventeen-year-old daughter. Temple, as he was called, was twenty-one at the time, a handsome, rather lazy, and useless young man. The Brillons feared such a marriage would deprive them of their daughter, for they expected that Temple would eventually return to America. They accordingly refused, to Franklin's dismay, but this blow did not break their deep and abiding attachment to him.[31]

There were several other Frenchwomen who loved Franklin, none more interesting to him than Madame Helvetius. He met her early in 1778, at a time when he was on intimate terms with Madame Brillon. Madame Helvetius hardly knew Madame Brillon, and their paths rarely crossed; Madame Brillon's life centered on Passy, Madame Helvetius's on Auteuil. Madame Helvetius possessed a strong sense of herself, one of the ways she resembled Franklin. She took the world as it came and responded confidently, and sometimes, to Franklin's delight, with an earthiness verging on the coarse but without descending to the vulgar. Madame Brillon was much too interested in herself, much too concerned about her own reactions, given to moodiness and emotional swings from depression to delight, to be able to match Madame Helvetius's sure-footed march through life.[32]

Born Anne-Catherine de Ligniville d'Autricourt to a noble family, related to Austrian royalty, Madame Helvetius nevertheless was poor and at age fifteen was packed off to a convent. She was without a dowry and apparently without hope for an aristocratic life. She remained in the convent for fifteen years until she was forced to leave because her pension, granted her by a cardinal, expired when he died. There seemed no choice but to return home to a life of genteel poverty shared by fifteen brothers and sisters and a mother who was pregnant again. Her aunt Madame de Graffigny rescued her by taking her to Paris. This aunt, a successful novelist, presided over a salon where her niece, familiarly called Minette, was noticed for her beauty and her bright, lively mind. Suitors soon appeared, including Anne-Robert Turgot, who in a few years would become one of the powers in the French government as comptroller-general and minister of the navy. Turgot wanted to marry her, but she rejected him in favor of Claude-Adrien Helvetius, a wealthy man who at thirty-six was four years older than she.[33]

The marriage, ended by Helvetius's death, lasted twenty years, during which time Madame Helvetius's salon became famous in Paris. Who was the most distinguished among its members is not clear, but it drew Diderot, d'Alembert, Condorcet, and Turgot, among others, and occasionally a visitor from abroad such as David Hume.[34]

Fifty-two years of age in 1771 when her husband died, Madame Helvetius sold the Paris house after marrying off her daughter. Her new residence was a small estate in Auteuil, near Passy and the Bois de Boulogne. Here she turned to gardening—not the formal gardens with straight lines and disciplined beds so admired by people of her class, but a scattering of colorful plants, from rhododendrons and hortensias to gooseberry bushes. Madame Helvetius loved birds and animals, and the grounds were home to a profusion of ducks and deer, dogs and cats, and exotic species in aviaries.

At times Madame Helvetius must have entertained as many human visitors as animals and birds. Several from her Paris salon appeared, chief among them Turgot. But fresh faces appeared as well and now and then a great one, Voltaire, for example. Before long several of her favorites lived in the house or enjoyed temporary quarters there. The Abbé André Morellet, who lived in Paris, found the house in Auteuil so enticing that he often spent several days a week there. A short-term arrangement seemed to be all that the Abbé Martin Lefebvre de la Roche expected when he arrived to comfort Madame Helvetius in her widowhood and to prepare her husband's manuscripts for publication. He found a pavilion on the grounds for his books and went to work; thirty years later he was still there.[35]

The other long-term resident was a young man, Pierre Georges Cabanis, who soon became almost a son to Madame Helvetius. He was twenty-two when Turgot brought him to Auteuil. A brilliant young man, Cabanis, despite the differences in age, hit it off well with the two abbés and Benjamin Franklin. Cabanis's major interest was medicine—not its practice, but its theory. He was indeed, in the way of the eighteenth century, a philosopher of medicine. He was also deeply devoted to Notre Dame d'Auteuil, as Franklin dubbed Madame Helvetius, and a fully participating member of l'Académie d'Auteuil, as the group of intellectuals around her came to call itself.[36]

Turgot first brought Franklin to Auteuil. Soon he was a full member of the Académie—nourished by its intellectual vitality and delighted by the wit and fun he found in it. But as important as the group was to him, Madame Helvetius proved more important. She was in her late fifties by this time, no longer the great beauty, but handsome and attractive in ways difficult to grasp two hundred years later. She fascinated Franklin.

Part of the fascination arose from the easy equality she assumed. To Madame Helvetius Franklin was not *mon cher Papa* but *mon cher ami*. She was in certain regards a friend in the manner of his closest male friends. She treated him as they did, combining respect with a comfortable informality. Madame Helvetius was sometimes forgetful, perhaps distracted by the incessant comings and goings at Auteuil and by the changing mixture of old and new faces. She forgot about Franklin on occasion, once inviting him for breakfast and then forgetting that he was coming. When he arrived, there was little to eat. The Abbé Morellet, who apparently had eaten heartily, did his best, but Franklin went away hungry and consoled himself by writing a bagatelle—"Bilked for Breakfast"—on the incident.[37]

Madame Helvetius was not an intellectual and did not try to match the genius of her guests. But she was not a fool—she judged those who came to her with discernment—and fools did not receive invitations to Auteuil. Her wit and her delight in good conversation pleased Franklin enormously, and though he never neglected Madame Brillon, he seems to have preferred going to Madame Helvetius's.

In the end it was the lady herself who won his heart—not the menagerie of philosophes and the resident abbés. Late in the year 1779, Franklin asked her to marry him. His petition was serious and seriously made, though in the months of pursuit that followed lightness and wit did not desert their conversation. She was touched, even tempted to agree, but finally turned him down. Turgot, who had wanted to marry her earlier and who advised her to reject Franklin, was pleased. Franklin, who had never quite lost his head, perhaps had never come close, responded with an irony that revealed his courtship had not robbed him of his capacity for watching himself in action. Still, he was disappointed; he had wanted her badly and would have remained in France for the rest of his days had she married him. At first, indeed, he did not accept rejection, writing a bagatelle, "The Elysian Fields," in which he rehearsed her refusal to marry him and asked her again.[38]

Madame Helvetius disappointed Franklin with another rejection, but she did not fail him. Like Madame Brillon before her and, still earlier, Margaret Stevenson in Craven Street, London, she had made him a part of her family. Franklin seems to have needed the warmth and the comfort that such settings provided; and in fact he received the affection and the admiration of women all his life. There was sexual attraction in several of these friendships, and perhaps at times there was sexual fulfillment. Franklin and Margaret Stevenson lived in the same house for sixteen years, which included a long period during which both were healthy and vigorous. After a while their friends customarily invited them together on social occasions. The time and the setting were right for sexual relations, though no one knows if they occurred.

The emotional support that friendships provide was present in these connections and in many of the ties between Franklin and friends of all ages. With many of the men there was even more. Ideas joined affection in a number of these friendships, and Franklin surely gave much more than he received. In fact he proved to his friends, if any proof were needed, that he was a generous man. He gave of his purse, his mind, his affections—he gave of himself.

The reasons young and old were attracted to Franklin varied in the course of his life. When he was young, his friends were also young, artisans for the most part. They—and he—looked for ways to rise, to make money, and, in accordance with popular ideas about virtue, to serve the public. Franklin attracted these young men because he was curious about the world, curious about them;

he was also amusing, a good listener, and a good organizer. They sensed immediately that his intelligence was high and they soon discovered that he was genuinely interested in them. He brought people together, which was always his instinct.

Franklin was older when he became famous and wealthy and powerful. People then came to him because he was all of these things. But his friends were not simply people who wanted something from him. His friends continued to be drawn from all ages and kinds, children as well as adults, the weak as well as the strong. The qualities of his youth may have been somewhat tempered, but his curiosity had not diminished, nor had his sense of fun and the glee he felt in games and jokes. Perhaps more than anything else a current of passion ran deeply in the older man as it had in the younger. Its warmth appeared in various guises—in the public servant, in the eager listener to children's chatter, and surely most strongly in the scientist probing the secrets of nature. Whatever it was—and in Franklin this quality seems to have been a compound of emotion (bordering on piety) and intellect—it helped him make friends.

Franklin was a big man in every sense, and he possessed a splendid capacity for friendship. But despite his generosity and his largeness of spirit, he was not all sunshine and light. There was another, passionate, side that once aroused could attract enemies, even make them. And, of course, there are always men who need little or no reason to become the enemies of others.

CHAPTER 2

Making Enemies

Franklin's virtues and his strength made some men his enemies. These men disliked anyone larger than themselves.
Perhaps such men exist in every generation. From the time
that fame came to Franklin after his experiments revealed that
lightning and electricity were the same thing, he stood out as a
tempting target. As his fame increased, and as he showed his gifts
as a political leader, first in Pennsylvania, then in Congress, and
finally in Europe, his shadow lengthened. There was also his immense charm. People of all sorts took to him, liked and admired
him enormously. Wherever he was he played to this disposition in
others to find in him something attractive and reassuring. And
there was of course much that was attractive as well as remarkable
about him. The variousness of his talents and his careers, some
pursued simultaneously, aroused admiration when they did not
inspire awe.

Not all were charmed of course. Not all felt admiration, let
alone awe. Restless in his shadow, they could not wait to get at
him, to diminish him, to show that there were dark sides to his
character. Without realizing it, they really wanted to prove that
he was like them. To a certain extent these men were right, and
Franklin invited the hostility that came his way. He could be guile-
ful; his judgment, usually firm and good, sometimes failed him. At

times he himself yielded to ugly passion. Everyone knew that there was a powerful temperament beneath his placid surface. What they did not always recognize was that occasionally his sense of power led him into miscalculation and behavior unworthy of his standards.

The two men closely connected to the life of Pennsylvania most eager to believe the worst of Franklin, the two who proved his most serious antagonists in provincial affairs, were Thomas Penn, the proprietor of the colony, and William Smith, the provost of the Academy and College of Philadelphia, who was Penn's friend and agent. At first sight, Penn and Smith seem to have had little in common. Penn was twenty-five years older than Smith, of English background, and though he broke his ties with the Quakers, he was the son of one of the great men among them. William Smith was a Scot who left Aberdeen for London before he was twenty-five years of age and, soon after, came to America. A few years later he returned to England to take holy orders in the Church of England. Though he went to England for a second visit afterward, he spent most of his life in America. Thomas Penn, in contrast, lived for nine years in Philadelphia, from 1732 to 1741, and never returned. These were surface differences, for the two men worked closely together after Smith came to America and were tied to one another by interest, politics, and what became a passionate hatred of Benjamin Franklin.[1]

At the time Penn and Smith formed their alliance, in the early 1750s, the province of Pennsylvania was a little more than seventy years old. Its population, rapidly growing in size and variety, numbered around 120,000 in 1750. Ten years later that figure would

reach 185,000. The province had grown in almost every way during Franklin's life. When he had arrived in Philadelphia in 1723,
the Quakers ran the city and the colony; they continued to do so
at mid-century when Penn and Smith arrayed themselves against
him.[2]

Although the Quakers controlled the province, other religious
sects and peoples abounded, drawn to Pennsylvania by the political liberty and freedom of worship established by William Penn,
the founder. The Church of England took hold, especially in Philadelphia, as merchants made their fortunes and sought social eminence. The church was found elsewhere in the colony, though
it could not call for tax support as it did in other colonies. The
Presbyterians soon outnumbered both Quakers and Anglicans,
with the Scotch-Irish who poured in from Northern Ireland making up their ranks. The Germans, in flight from provinces along
the Rhine, founded Lutheran and Reformed churches and established sects—Moravians, Mennonites, Schwenkfelders, and Dunk-
ers, among others. There were also Swiss Mennonites, Dutch
Quakers, and a few Jews (mostly in Philadelphia). Besides all these,
there was a smattering of French Huguenots as well as a handful
of Catholics.[3]

Most of the Germans and Scotch-Irish, whatever their religion,
found their way to land west of Philadelphia, along the frontier.
Germans concentrated in upper Philadelphia County; in Berks,
Northampton, and York Counties; and in the Lebanon Valley of
Lancaster County. The Scotch-Irish settled in all these counties,
but their heaviest numbers were in Chester and Lancaster and
the two farther west—Cumberland and York. Chester and Bucks,
along with Philadelphia the oldest settled regions in Pennsylvania,
remained the preserve of the English and the Welsh.

Although national groups tended to settle together, none seems
to have sought a perfect isolation, which was unavailable in any

case. Even national and religious concentrations were broken up, to some extent, by other peoples. For example, Germantown, which took its name from the Germans who founded it and made up most of its inhabitants, almost from its beginnings received other nationalities, including Swiss, Swedes, Dutch, and French. The young in all these groups intermarried, even when separated by religion. Eventually wealth and poverty set people apart far more decisively than religion and nationality.[4]

Germantown has been called an urban village, and in such a community, where people lived fairly close together, mixing does not seem surprising. But most of the people of Pennsylvania lived on dispersed farms or in villages smaller than Germantown. There, in relative isolation, old-world culture—language, national feeling, religion, and kinship—held together longer.[5]

The Germans, Scotch-Irish, English, Welsh, and other farmers made the Delaware Valley the center for grain crops and the production of foodstuffs. Farmers supplied their own needs, but they were not simply subsistence or self-sufficient producers—they produced for the market, feeding the middle colonies, parts of New England, and western Europe. The grain went into bread and was shipped unrefined as well. Meat produced in Pennsylvania was also carried to outside markets, and horses and oxen were shipped to the West Indies.[6]

The bread, flaxseed, and meat that flowed out of Philadelphia were collected by merchants who knew the markets overseas. They were an enterprising lot, eager to do business with any-one having money or commodities to exchange. At home, in the province, they relied on a group of retailers, themselves eager to prosper and to become merchants. These shopkeepers sold an immense variety of goods, advertised in the local newspapers, and constantly replenished their stock by trading across the ocean.

Those who carried on the trade did so independently. They
made up a large group, with Quakers and Anglicans at the top and
small traders and a good many men on the make in the lower
ranks. Membership in the mercantile community shifted often,
with some merchants falling out altogether and new men making
their way to the top. The most cohesive elements among them
were the Quakers and the Anglicans. Religion and culture probably provided whatever social cement held these men together; it
was not the size of their firms, for many merchants operated alone,
without partners, and most partnerships never embraced more
than two or three members. Local business associations thus were
simple, and local ties limited; the average Philadelphia trader
dealt, not with another trader, but rather with European merchants and with provincial, usually city, retailers.[7]

Political power in the province did not find its way to the merchants, and not simply because they were fragmented. Rather the
structure of power had a complex base; merchants were only a part
of it, though many exercised considerable authority in determin-
ing how the colony was governed. In fact, a fairly broad elite ran
the colony, with no single group or interest, economic or other,
holding power to the exclusion of others.[8]

The Charter of Privileges of 1701, issued by William Penn,
provided the constitution for the colony. Under its terms a governor represented the proprietor, and an Assembly served as the
legislature representing the people. This body was popularly
elected under a franchise as liberal as any in the English colonies.
The Assembly could initiate legislation, and in fact thought of
itself as a parliament. The proprietors, William Penn and his son

Thomas, did not. That difference in perception made political life complex and almost naturally led to conflict.

Perception was one thing; interest, another. Throughout the history of Pennsylvania, from its founding to the Revolution, the Society of Friends understood their own interest as inseparable from that of the province. William Penn was a Quaker, and he always thought of the colony as a refuge for Quakers; more than that, however, he envisioned it as a society broadly tolerant of all religious persuasions and protective of the civil rights of those who came to it. Pennsylvania would be a holy experiment in religious and political freedom as well as a special place for the Society of Friends.

The Quakers who succeeded the founding generation, although they shared Penn's hopes, understandably felt that Pennsylvania was theirs, despite its openness to all faiths and peoples. For them it was a Quaker enterprise, not only in origin and spirit, but also in interest.

Implicit in this attitude was the belief that a Quaker party should exercise power. By the time Benjamin Franklin reached maturity, such an organization had existed for several years, and after William Penn's death in 1718 its dominance as a political organization was clear. Quaker supremacy in politics did not translate itself fully into government, for once the proprietary interest passed to Thomas Penn, some of the old idealism was lost. William Penn had often faced opposition in Pennsylvania, but he at least could feel that the local leaders who resisted his policies were men like himself who had been in on the beginnings of the holy experiment. Thomas Penn had no such assurance, and in fact he himself fell from the old faith. At best he was only a nominal member of the Society of Friends; he married an Anglican and soon after began worshiping in the Church of England.

The Quaker Party he faced defined its interests in complicated ways, in part because the Society of Friends that founded the province had long agreed on its social and economic purposes. Its best-known leaders lived in Philadelphia. They counted among their number the richest merchants of the city: Pembertons, Norrises, Whartons, Foxes, and others. By mid-century some of the great Quaker families no longer lived on the proceeds from commerce; they had invested in land, and they lent their money at a good return to those engaged in business. So Quaker economic concerns in Philadelphia extended into several sorts of activities. Most of the big fortunes lay in the established eastern counties when they were not concentrated in Philadelphia itself, but there were wealthy Quaker farmers elsewhere, even in the newer settlements along the frontier. Just about everywhere in the eastern counties the Quakers ran things, and in the West they or their allies among German and other pietists usually held control. Their organizations were not elaborate on the county level, or in the city and the Assembly for that matter. But when elections were held for the Assembly, informal collections of leaders of the Quaker Party met to prepare slates of candidates. The same men controlled the political life of the counties as well, and within the Assembly a cadre of Quaker leaders held the most important committee assignments year after year. Sometimes those leaders were not of the Quaker faith, but their political allegiance remained with the prevailing powers. They had been "Quakerized," in Richard Peters's tart term.

The supporters of the proprietor ought to have constituted a second political party in the first half of the eighteenth century— ought to have, but did not, even though they have been referred to as the Proprietary Party. They were a faction, lacking the organization of the Quaker Party and lacking the energy to take an active role in defense of proprietary interest. They were, in fact, curiously inert for much of the period before the Revolution, satisfied at the most to support the proprietor in a low-key way. Their most powerful members sat on the Governor's Council, but they did not really act effectively. The colony's constitution prescribed no role in legislation for the council, and its members demonstrated no eagerness to take on the Quakers in the Assembly in any case—at least not before the election of 1764.

During ten noisy years of strife, from 1754 to 1764, almost every member of the council served the proprietor in some public office. They sat as judges—one, William Allen, held the post of chief justice of the highest court in the province. Benjamin Chew, a power in this group, operated from his post as attorney general. Richard Peters was secretary of the province and secretary of the Board of Property, charged with looking after the proprietor's real estate, a vast amount of land. These men knew their way around in the highest political circles, and most belonged to the elite of Philadelphia society. Most of the remaining members of the council could hold their own with them and figured as big men in the eyes of the province. Below them were men in a variety of public offices—judges in lesser courts, quitrent collectors, tax assessors, tax collectors, excise collectors, provincial customs collectors, commodity inspectors, Indian agents, court recorders and clerks, registrars, and surveyors of the land office. These people, followers, were a part of the proprietary interest but did not weigh heavily in elections or even in the broad exercise of power.

The proprietary interest—the men of influence, councillors, and their friends—dominated other institutions in Philadelphia life. During the 1750s, years of unusual importance in Pennsylvania's politics, they controlled the College of Philadelphia, the Pennsylvania hospital, and the Library Company.

Whatever members of the Proprietary Party thought about

provincial politics, they repressed any inclinations they had to act. Before the election of 1764 they ordinarily did not count more than two of their number in the Assembly. They did not suffer defeats in running for Assembly seats because they did not stand for election, preferring to stay out of things. To be sure, the governor could call upon them for advice, and several wrote the proprietor about Pennsylvania's affairs. Others served the governor and the proprietor in the land office and in a variety of other ways. But they did not challenge the dominance of the Quaker Party in the legislature. Until the beginning of a prolonged crisis in 1755 they do not seem often to have even ventured into the newspapers. To be sure, the *Pennsylvania Journal,* one of the Philadelphia weekly papers, carried messages from the governor to the Assembly, and occasional essays appeared in the proprietor's interest. But even in these cases, despite occasional tracts defending his position, the proprietor could not depend upon the press to explain his side of an argument.

For much of the first half of the eighteenth century, political life was tranquil, compared with that of other, more faction-ridden, colonies like New York or Massachusetts. The century had not begun in tranquillity, and in its early years William Penn engaged in tumultuous disagreements with the Assembly. But even Penn enjoyed years free of strife; and after his death, though there were bursts of antagonism, politics in the hands of the governing oligarchy remained calm.

The reasons are not to be found in the underlying social circumstances of Pennsylvania. What was true of the economy in the 1730s, a period of peace, for example, was also true of the 1750s, a period of tension and struggle. Pennsylvania's economy grew in both decades—indeed throughout the century—as did its population. The economy was undeveloped, but undergoing development. Population doubled about every twenty-five years, as Franklin pointed out in his *Observations concerning the Increase of Mankind.*

Not everyone made money in the century, but the people who counted did—those who owned land and businesses—even as the number of urban poor increased. The poor had no voice and no influence in politics; monied people ran the province. Prosperous and unthreatened, the proprietor's supporters quietly went their own way, giving advice to the governor on occasion to hold firm against the Assembly's demands, but rarely doing much more than that.

The Assembly's demands grew more urgent in the 1750s. Underlying them were the old feelings about Pennsylvania as a special place, a holy experiment; but there was also an animus, usually quiet and sometimes asleep, against authority of any sort. The origin of this feeling lay in the religion of the Society of Friends. A people convinced that the Holy Spirit spoke within every man did not regard the requirements of the external world with undue respect. The Quakers had undergone an ordeal of persecution, and they arrived in Pennsylvania determined to resist should it reappear in America. Any external authority drew their suspicions, even when it was in the hands of someone with the vision and the nobility of William Penn. His sons, who lacked the aura of their father, soon proved that they lacked his idealism as well. Not long after Thomas Penn assumed the powers of the proprietorship, he was made to feel the opposition of the Assembly.

Opposition was in fact the policy of the Assembly. It was most often in evidence when questions of land, taxation, or public finance were aired. What was also in evidence, though never clearly announced, was the Assembly's desire to become an autonomous institution, one that, despite the presence of the proprietor's representative, would govern the province.

Franklin shared the Assembly's convictions that it should control provincial affairs, but his ideas about the province were always more complex than this simple proposition. They changed in the struggles with Thomas Penn from the 1750s on as Franklin came to realize how extraordinarily resistant to American demands the proprietary interest was. But the conflict with Penn did not lead Franklin to greater wisdom, or to an increased sensitivity to popular desires in Pennsylvania. Rather, the years of strife seem to have produced passion rather than understanding, and the passion proved to be the father of near-disastrous action.

On the face of things this is surprising, for Franklin seemed to have talents in abundance for playing the political game in Pennsylvania. He also had political experience. He began his career as a provincial politician at thirty years of age, when he was appointed clerk of the Assembly. The clerk's post was something of a plum. As clerk, Franklin did most or all of the Assembly's printing—the laws, its votes (as its records were called), and the paper currency that it periodically authorized. The remainder of his work amounted to a political apprenticeship, because he had to attend the meetings of the Assembly, write minutes of its deliberations, and sometimes prepare resolutions and messages under its direction. There is little doubt that Franklin used his opportunities to do more than act as a clerk in an ordinary sense. He was too able and shrewd, and much too engaged by public life, not to contribute to the Assembly's deliberations. He has left us a record in his *Autobiography* and in his letters of how he operated in other groups, and in the Assembly he had the opportunity to exercise his abilities. As the Assembly's clerk he could not have escaped learning all about Assembly business. It is not too much to say that Franklin never missed an opportunity to learn all he could about everything that came his way.[9]

During these years he also served in local offices, as a common councilman and alderman of Philadelphia. In these posts he worked with local worthies on matters close to his heart and home. As he told everyone who would listen, the city's business was important—its streets, its lighting, its fire protection, and its educational and cultural life. He acted on virtually all the needs he saw for improving city life, and in acting he added to his store of knowledge about men in the political arena.[10]

Nothing in Franklin's experience could fully prepare him for the politics of the 1750s. To be sure, he did become politically adroit as a clerk of the Assembly and in his city offices. But these years were calm compared to what came after them, and after Franklin joined the Assembly as an elected member from Philadelphia in 1751, the pace of change picked up. He was by this time familiar with the Assembly's disposition to oppose proprietary authority; and he understood the structure of politics and government. This knowledge and his experience stood him in good stead in the regular business of government. But it was less useful in the extraordinary period beginning in 1754 with the French and Indian War, and his relations with Thomas Penn and William Smith followed no predictable path.

Thomas Penn was the son of William Penn and Hannah Callowhill, William's second wife. He spent his early boyhood with his family in Ruscombe in Berkshire until his father apprenticed him to a London mercer when he was fourteen or fifteen years of age. William Penn suffered a near-crippling stroke in 1712, and Hannah Penn then assumed more of the responsibility for the family's welfare, including its finances. It was she who kept close watch on Thomas's life as an apprentice in London, worrying about his health, warning him to avoid the cold temperatures in the winter and recommending "a little moderate purge of Epsom waters" on occasion.[11] She also urged him to read the Scriptures and, since like her husband she was a Quaker, prescribed "the happiness of silence in meetings."[12]

The recipient of this loving advice did not protest and, as far as we know, faithfully went about his business. He also served his mother's and his family's financial interests whenever instructions arrived from Ruscombe. Hannah Penn, with a husband in a state of debilitation and the cares of the family on her shoulders, made Thomas her representative in London, young though he was. In London he could collect debts owed the Penns, fight off the family's creditors, buy supplies, and generally guard his mother's interests. He worked in London as an apprentice and then as a businessman until 1732, when he went to Pennsylvania. He remained in the province for nine years, returning to England in 1741. In these years in Philadelphia, he looked after the family's holdings, an immense amount of land, and at times engaged in overseas trading, sending flaxseed and flour to Britain, for example.[13]

Whatever the reasons—a peculiar nature, a depression of spirits brought on by the burdens Hannah Penn placed on him, or an apprenticeship that proved hard—Thomas Penn grew into manhood marked by a coldness and a formality of manners so pronounced that they were remarked upon in his own day, when restraint and correct behavior were expected of men of his station. Penn seems to have been able to soften his demeanor only when he was with his family, which he clearly cared deeply about. In the 1750s and 1760s he suffered terrible blows, for of his first five children four died in the early years of their lives.[14]

His dealings with the province that he inherited from his father were another matter. In 1746, with the death of his brother John, the proprietorship became his principal responsibility. Penn's attitude toward the province at that moment cannot be reconstructed. His knowledge of it, after his nine-year stay, from 1732 to 1741, was becoming stale, an important fact since the population and the economy of the province were both expanding. He had long felt an interest in the colony and sometimes showed an enlightened concern. In 1747, for example, he sent the Library Company what was described as "a compleat electrical apparatus," for which Franklin wrote him of the company's gratitude.[15]

On most matters concerning the province, however, Penn's initial responses expressed a sour spirit. He opposed most changes in the province and seemed to believe that every request for land grants concealed a design to rob him of family estates. He met with distrust the proposal to establish an academy in the city. The plan "for the education of youth is much more extensive than ever I had designed," he wrote the governor, "and I think more so than the circumstances of the Province require."[16] The circumstances he referred to apparently concerned economic development, for his real objection grew out of his belief that the "best of our people must be men of business which I do not think very great public schools or universities render youth fit for."[17]

Some peculiar, almost morbid, suspicion—similar to that evoked by the proposal for the academy—skewed Penn's reaction to one of Franklin's important services to the province when Pennsylvania faced simultaneously a military threat from the Iroquois and Spanish and French privateers in King George's War. Recognizing the dangers, Franklin tried to organize the defense of the province and earned Thomas Penn's hostility for his efforts. He did not learn of Penn's animosity at the time; indeed he seems to have acted in the expectation that the proprietor would approve of all that he attempted to do in establishing a military force in the colony. In 1747, when this affair began, Franklin was disgusted by almost all factions in Pennsylvania: the Quakers whose pacifist principles he understood but did not share, and certain wealthy merchants who opposed arming because of the expense.[18]

The war that Britain and France fought did not ravage Pennsylvania, nor did it tax the province's resources as it did those of the New England colonies. Still, by 1747 the war seemed about to spread to the Pennsylvania frontier, and the capture of merchant ships off the Delaware Capes was an ominous sign. The danger increased in July when a French privateer put a raiding party ashore near Bombay Hook in New Castle County, Delaware, a little more than fifty miles downriver from Philadelphia.[19]

Prudence required preparations to defend shipping and the city, and common sense suggested creation of a land force to protect the frontier. But neither prudence nor common sense seemed to have much of a chance. In the autumn the Assembly refused to do anything; and the governor, who was in bad health, was not even in America, having taken a ship to England to see his physicians.

No admirer of inertia or deadlock, Franklin resolved to do something on his own. He had little confidence in the Assembly at this time and probably even less in the governor. He had been disillusioned by both two years before, when the Massachusetts colony had requested Pennsylvania's aid in an expedition against Louisbourg, the French fortress on Cape Breton Island at the entrance to the Gulf of St. Lawrence, only to be turned down in political maneuvers that he called a "farce."[20] The governor and the Assembly, he said at the time, were simply "playing tricks to amuse the world."

Franklin kept these feelings to himself in 1747, or at least did not admit publicly to having them. Instead he went to the people with an appeal to form an association for the defense of Pennsylvania. He published *Plain Truth*,[21] a pamphlet advocating common action, on November 17, and spoke four days later at a public meeting of the tradesmen and mechanics in favor of the association and again two days afterward to "gentlemen" and merchants. There is evidence that he also used his powers of persuasion outside the public eye—in particular on the Philadelphia Corporation, the governing body of the city, and the Pennsylvania Council. Both endorsed the idea of private action by the association, as did many of the leading men in the colony.[22]

Plain Truth undoubtedly helped in these efforts. It contained several unappealing truths, and it apparently spared no one in its condemnation of sloth in getting ready for war. In the meetings after its appearance, within a few days of its publication, most of the leaders of the province were in agreement. Penn's agent and secretary of the council, Richard Peters, declared his satisfaction with the association and advised Thomas Penn that arms for the new military force could be obtained "for a Trifle."[23] The city government requested that the proprietor provide cannon for a battery; the council told Penn of its agreement that the guns were needed. Merchants in Philadelphia put up their own money for sixteen 28-pounders and several smaller guns and appealed to the admiralty to provide an armed ship to defend Delaware Bay. Perhaps more important, a thousand men signed the association, which was a document as well as an organization, and began to ready themselves for service as a militia.[24]

All this happened in November. Franklin was pleased but saw at once that money was needed if a real defense was to be sustained. To raise it, he proposed that a lottery be established and set about to put one in place. Money and men impressed everyone, but Franklin, leaving nothing to chance, early in December persuaded the council to proclaim a Fast Day, the observance to be held on January 7 of the new year. Since no one on the council knew how to write such a proclamation, he did it himself, invoking divine assistance and protection for Pennsylvania. There was more to be done in the following weeks: military organizations took form, the men elected their officers, batteries were emplaced along the river, and drills were conducted. Franklin himself took his turn as a common soldier manning the batteries.[25]

To lead to war a province whose leaders had long espoused pacifism was an extraordinary achievement. To do so through private means, without coercing anyone, was even more remarkable. Franklin accomplished these aims, moreover, without alienating any save a few members of the Society of Friends.

But he did not avoid alienating Thomas Penn, whose distrust for him seems to have proceeded from this episode. Penn heard of Franklin's achievements from Richard Peters—and perhaps from others as well. Penn was not pleased, even though Franklin's actions cost him nothing and, in fact, protected his property along with that of others.

Penn's fears poured out almost as soon as he heard of the association, and he found no comfort in his friend Richard Peters's reassurance that the action in the colony held no threat to proprietary control. To Lynford Lardner, a councillor and the local official who received rents paid on his lands in the province, he wrote that he was "sure the people of America are too often ready to act in defiance of the Government they live in, without associating themselves for that purpose."[26] That he was deeply offended by the local action came out even more directly in his letters to Peters, in which he also revealed his fear of Franklin. The association, he wrote Peters, "is founded on a Contempt to Government." He said he could see no other end for it than "Anarchy and Confusion." But in fact he could, for in the same letter he predicted that the people who "in general are so fond of what they call liberty as to fall into Licentiousness" would soon learn that they could act in "a Military manner, . . . independent of this Government" and establish "a Military Common Wealth." Such action Penn described as "acting a part little less than Treason."[27]

There was more than a little hysteria in Penn's reactions and a flood of venom in his blaming Franklin for what he took to be a disorder "in the heads of the Wild unthinking Multitude." Franklin was "a dangerous Man," and Penn told Peters that "I should be very Glad he inhabited any other Country, as I believe him of a very uneasy Spirit."[28]

Peters soon yielded before this onslaught of complaints and dread, agreeing with Penn that the association was not what it claimed to be, that it was in fact an illegal combination, and that it posed a threat to the interests of the proprietor. Hardly had Peters told Penn of his change of heart when the war ended, and Penn stopped shouting his fears.[29]

But he did not retract his statements about Franklin. In the long crisis of the 1750s, his hatred of Franklin grew, and before the end of the decade Franklin returned it in full measure.

The crisis of the 1750s assumed several forms and seemed to involve several discrete issues. But in fact whether it revolved around Indian relations, land, taxes, money, or war, it really came down to a question of who would govern Pennsylvania. Constitutional issues often seem abstract, seem in fact to be above the ordinary affairs of human beings, because they can be stated in theoretical terms. Their human faces have a way of appearing, however; and in the case of Pennsylvania the tangible—the appearance of things—may have deprived the actors in provincial politics of any sense that they were engaged in a constitutional drama.

Money entered into every aspect of the political fray. Who would issue currency and collect the interest on it, for example, was a persistent problem. By the 1750s, when disagreements showed their sharpest edges before the Revolution, the Assembly was accustomed to order the issue of paper currency through the loan office, which it controlled, and then to collect an excise tax in excess of the sum required to retire it. The Assembly put the surplus to good use, according to its lights, but not those of the proprietor and the governor. For in the process, the Assembly had come close to taking over the powers of the executive: it not only raised the money and determined how it would be used but also usually bypassed the governor in spending what it raised. Had the proprietor (who of course appointed the governor) had his wits about him, he might have persuaded the Assembly that the governor properly should have a larger voice in the disbursement of public money. But Thomas Penn was too stiff and too convinced of his own rectitude to lower himself to the arts of changing the legislative mind. He preferred the bludgeon to persuasion. He also knew of his father's sufferings at the hands of the Assembly, and when he seemed about to forget, there were friends to remind him.[30]

Thomas Penn would also surely have strengthened his own hand, and his governor's, had he allowed his lands in the province to be taxed. But he consistently refused until late in the 1750s, when he gave way only after receiving ruthless criticism in Pennsylvania that began to echo in Britain. He offered murky explanations for his refusal. At times he seemed to say, through the governor, that since the proprietary lands had not been taxed before, they never should be. This was as close as he ever came to admitting that no man liked to pay taxes, and since he was a man, he disliked paying taxes—and indeed would not pay them in Pennsylvania. There was a principle of some kind hidden in these arguments, not a worthy one, but simply the assertion that the proprietor of the colony deserved exemption from taxes. When the issue reached white heat in the weeks immediately following the disaster to British arms and provincial defense that occurred in Braddock's defeat in July 1755, Penn's governor, Robert Hunter Morris, assured the Assembly of the proprietor's eagerness to pay his share of the expense of defending the colony. But when the Assembly produced a tax bill that placed a levy on Thomas Penn's lands, the governor, well aware that his instructions were to do nothing that encumbered the proprietary estates, discovered much that was objectionable in the legislation proposed. There were ways other than a tax on land to raise the money, Penn had insisted, and in any case he had his doubts about taxing land itself, preferring a tax on the income from land.[31]

Penn doubted, it seemed, the fairness of assessments made by officials appointed by the people. He clearly thought that assessors named by himself would have a better sense of what was fair and what was not. The implication barely concealed in all this rhetoric was simply that he smelled the popular plot to shift taxation from the people to himself. The governor was not to approve the bill: like governors before him he had posted a "performance" bond before leaving England; a good performance was one that satisfied Penn, and satisfying Penn required the governor to reject any measure that taxed proprietary lands.[32]

Money also entered into the disputes between Penn and the Assembly over Indian affairs. Negotiations with the Indians entailed certain expenses, especially for gifts to the Indians to seal treaties, one of the means used to bribe them. It was in the province's interest to persuade the Indians to give up their lands to white settlement, which encroached upon tribal holdings, treaties or no treaties. Long before the war began in 1754, the Assembly sought to enlist Thomas Penn's purse in the service of Indian relations. He refused, however, contending that the cost of diplomacy was a local responsibility. His own vast holdings in central Pennsylvania increased in value of course as negotiations with the tribes brought security. And when war occurred and the Indians devastated frontier farms and settlements, his lands lost value. But Penn knew his own mind and thought he knew his own interest, and he repeatedly turned down efforts the Assembly made to extract his share of Indian expenses. To be sure, in 1754 he offered to construct a fort on the Ohio and to pay for its yearly maintenance. These charges would not have been light—£400 for the fort and £1,000 for its upkeep every year. The Assembly, dominated by the Quaker Party with pacifist impulses, turned him down. And when war began, the Assembly proved no more eager to raise troops and maintain them.[33]

In Pennsylvania William Smith, the first rector of the Philadelphia Academy, proved more energetic than the governor in expressing Penn's dismay at the obstinacy of the Assembly. And Smith, initially the friend and protégé of Franklin, soon became his enemy and Thomas Penn's friend. Smith chose his enemy and his friend out of a sense of where his self-interest lay. There is no evidence that he ever regretted his choice.

Smith was born in 1727 in Aberdeen, at that time an increasingly lively town, in part at least because it increasingly took Enlightenment ideas seriously. The son of a modest landowner, he attended first the local parish school and then, a few years later, one run by the Society for the Education of Parochial Schoolmasters. When he was sixteen, he entered the University of Aberdeen, leaving four years later, in 1747. There is no evidence that he took a degree, and in fact not much evidence about anything in his life in these years. He seems to have served in London in 1750 as a clerk for the Society for the Propagation of the Gospel. The next year he took a job in New York tutoring the two sons of a Colonel Josiah Martin.[34]

Teaching these boys must have seemed pretty tame stuff to Smith, and by his actions he showed that he craved a larger arena. He soon found it in local newspapers, to which he contributed essays and poetry. His work as a tutor may have set him to thinking about education and schooling; in any case he announced in 1753 that he had something to say in *A General Idea of the College of Mirania.* Immediately after this tract appeared, Smith sent copies to important men—one of them Benjamin Franklin. It is not difficult to see why Smith's tract appealed to Franklin, for Smith proposed that the college he designed have under its general aegis a mechanics' school "much like" the English school "first sketched out by the very ingenious and worthy *Mr. Franklin.*"[35] Flattery would not have been enough to win Franklin's interest—he was used to it by this time—but in Smith's work he found concerns similar to his own. What appealed was Smith's insistence that educational principles have an application in practical life and that any educational scheme ignoring virtue and morals was inadequate, along with his apparently nondoctrinal Christianity and his loving treatment of natural religion.

Franklin read Smith's tract with admiration and decided that Smith would serve well as the head of the Philadelphia Academy, an institution all its supporters in Philadelphia believed would develop into a college. Smith was intrigued by the suggestion and, after visiting Franklin and others in Philadelphia, was persuaded that the appointment would suit him just fine. The board of the academy liked him, but despite everyone's approval of Smith, the post went unfilled until money could be found. Franklin, always careful about such matters, let Smith know that as the professor of the place, as well as its head, he could expect to raise his salary from the tuition paid by students. Smith accepted the post, but not before returning to England to take holy orders in the established church.[36]

Thomas Penn, soon to be Smith's patron, did not approve of Smith's becoming a priest. He feared that the Quakers in Pennsylvania would shun Smith, or at least that Smith's action in going into the clergy would make his road rougher. But Smith persisted—there is no evidence that Penn offered serious resistance—and made the most of his opportunities. He was an ambitious young man and later an ambitious older man. His ambition impressed many. Peter Collinson knew him when he was in London and wrote Franklin about him soon after Smith began to make a name for himself. Collinson, reporting that Smith was an "ingenious man," reflected in some disappointment, "Its a Pitty but He was more Solid, and Less flighty." Collinson also praised Smith's abilities while disparaging his judgment and understanding. In the end he seemed to believe that much in Smith's behavior could be explained by the "warmth and fire of youth."[37] Richard Jackson, a London barrister, who probably did not know him as well as Collinson did, simply found him to be "a very ingenious and modest man."[38]

The word "ingenious" was applied to Smith far more often than "modest." "Ambitious" was the other word, or some form of it, that appeared in characterizations of Smith throughout his life. In 1774, twenty years after Smith took up his appointment at the academy, John Adams remarked on this quality in him. By that time the common impression was that Smith's ambition was to become the first bishop of the Church of England in America. Adams disliked slick, smooth people and there was something slick about Smith. Adams thought he was artful, another way of saying clever, and wondered about his clerical ambitions.[39]

Franklin, in contrast, liked him at first. He also talked with him about provincial affairs, and in so doing played into Smith's and Thomas Penn's hands. For Smith soon became Penn's agent in America. Penn paid him for his services, especially for information about the political opposition in the province.[40]

Franklin, in happy ignorance of the double-handed game Smith played, put his trust in him with the hope that he would make the academy flourish. There was something about Smith that pleased Franklin, who was well disposed toward Englishmen and Scotsmen anyway. Smith rolled a concern for virtue off his tongue with ease, just as Franklin did, and he had the style of the moral man so admired by Franklin. Smith conceived of education as satisfying social and moral needs. So did Franklin. Smith professed to be interested in public affairs far more than his own. So did Franklin, and in his case at least reality matched profession.[41]

For a short period Smith was Franklin's protégé. Franklin took the lead in getting him appointed to the academy; he confided at least some of his political opinions to him and, by all the evidence, liked him. Protégés sometimes resent their patrons, find their attentions cloying, even smothering, and look for a way to get free of their claims, well-meaning or not. Something like this may have marked the relations of Smith and Franklin. The younger man was clever and ambitious, and in Philadelphia he surely felt himself to be deep in Franklin's shadow. But Franklin, if he was a patron at all, did not dominate the young men who came to him for help. He customarily simply tried to clear the way for them—he lent them money, gave them advice, wrote them letters of introduction, and sent them away with his encouragement ringing in their ears. He was always too busy and too divided to focus on anyone too long. And as far as he could see, William Smith deserved interest and assistance in getting the academy started. That was the source of his interest in Smith and probably would not have changed had Smith's ambition not driven him into politics.[42]

But drive him it did. Smith not only served as Thomas Penn's unofficial agent but also began to take part in local affairs. He saw his opportunity in the war that broke out along the Pennsylvania frontier in 1754 between the French, their Indian allies, and colonial settlers.

The war revived the old tensions between the proprietor and the Quaker-led Assembly. Penn had appointed Robert Hunter Morris governor in 1754, and Morris, no shrinking violet, stepped into the fray with a willingness that pleased his master. Morris's immediate problem was the one that his predecessor had faced—how to get money out of an Assembly determined to run the affairs of the colony and, if many of its members had their way, determined to uphold the pacifist principles of the Society of Friends.

Both sides soon resumed their old dance, the governor stepping forward with requests for money and the Assembly first sidestepping, and then stepping forward with appropriations on the old familiar terms. The music played by each side included harsh lyrics. Franklin hid his displeasure for a while, but by June 1755 he confessed that his patience was at an end, saying that he was "heartily sick of our present Situation: I like neither the Governor's conduct nor the Assembly's." He had tried to "reconcile" the two sides, but "in vain."[43]

Franklin's disgust with the governor was probably always greater than his disappointment in the Assembly. The Assembly after all acted—or refused to act—out of principle. Franklin did not share the members' pacifism and at times thought it near suicidal, but he recognized principled behavior when he saw it. Governor Morris he knew was Penn's creature—bought and beholden to him. And early in 1755 Morris took action that violated principles of honesty and common decency. Franklin met with General Edward Braddock in April and discovered that Morris had been telling the general lies about the Quakers and the Assembly. Braddock had requested wagons and teams to pull them; he wanted a road cut so as to move his troops and supplies. He needed help, and he received little from the Assembly. Morris told him the reasons: the Quaker-dominated Assembly was more interested in helping the French than the British Army. It had sold out. Morris also seems to have praised himself in these months, apparently letting it be known that he had spent his own money for the defense of the West. (There is no evidence that he had.)[44]

When Franklin learned what Braddock had been hearing, he made certain that the general learned the truth. And Franklin himself—without help from the Assembly—took to organizing wagons and horses for the army. Braddock may not have come to admire the Assembly in these last months of his life—he was killed with many of his soldiers in the disaster on the Monongahela, July 9, 1755—but at least he had been disabused of the fantastic stories told by Morris.[45]

By late 1755 Franklin considered Morris "half a madman."[46] About this time or perhaps a little before, he began to wonder about William Smith's intentions and his character. For in April, as Franklin was conferring with Braddock, Smith published *A Brief State of the Province of Pennsylvania*, a full-throated attack on the Assembly and the Quakers. Clergymen did not ordinarily write pieces marked by the harshness displayed in *A Brief State*, but Smith was no ordinary priest. He followed the usual practice of concealing his authorship of the pamphlet, and for a few months local gossip had it that Governor Morris had written it. There was not a trace of Christian charity in *A Brief State*, and its rough tone seemed to match the governor's style. That Smith was the author, however, was known almost immediately in London, where the pamphlet was published, and before long the word was out in Philadelphia, either from abroad or from local detective work.[47]

Franklin escaped mention in *A Brief State*—he and Smith were on good terms when it appeared—and he did not suspect Smith at first. But like most Quaker Party leaders, Franklin was angered by Smith's attack. The principal targets were so savagely handled that Smith's underlying animus against popular authority could hardly be missed.

Smith proposed in *A Brief State* to explain why Pennsylvania, one of the richest colonies in North America, was "the most backward in contributing to the Defence of the British Dominions in these parts." His answer to his question held that the constitution of the colony was flawed because it provided extravagant powers to the people. Popular power was acceptable when a colony was in its infancy; in fact it was necessary, for there was no other way to tie a people to a government. But when the people added to their property and with it their economic power, it was time to take away some of their political power. Their government should take on "mixt" forms. What should be mixed with popular power, it was clear, was a strong proprietary power exercised in the name of the Penns by their local agent, the governor. In Pennsylvania, this had not been done, and the government had become increasingly democratic. The people felt their strength and under the leadership of the Assembly they pushed for greater authority; indeed Smith thought they meant to push the proprietor out altogether.[48]

What drove the Assembly was the Quaker Party, a rump group, Smith said, which represented its own immediate interests. He was willing to concede that Quakers outside the Assembly were principled and opposed war out of genuine commitment. But in Smith's version of things, the Assembly wanted nothing so much as to draw all power into its hands. How did it hold power? How could a Quaker Party dominate an Assembly, an elected body, when the Quakers made up no more than a fifth of the population?

Smith answered that the Quakers could count on the Germans, many of whose sects were similar in doctrine and belief to the Quakers. And the Germans, "a Body of ignorant, proud, stubborn Clowns," voted "in Shoals" for Quaker Party candidates.[49] The Quakers had told them there was a sinister plot afoot to enslave them, to return them to their old conditions in Europe. Fear of such a plot kept them in line, and there seemed no way to persuade them to vote for the proprietor's interest.

Smith was prepared to abandon persuasion rather easily. An appeal to the Crown and Parliament offered the only solution, an appeal to bar the Quakers from the Assembly and to bar the Germans from politics (including voting) altogether until they had learned to read and write English. Smith urged that Protestant ministers be sent to wean Catholics among them from the Church and from France and to convert them to the Protestant religion as practiced in the Church of England. Smith would also have shut down German-language newspapers, or at the least required them to publish parallel columns of German and English. Nor should contracts, legal documents, or bonds be accepted as "legal" unless they were written in English.[50]

Smith's taste for controversy increased as the year went on, and his sense of restraint disappeared. By December, he was calling the Quakers "Enemies to their Country."[51] In his review of the year 1755 he reprinted a letter purportedly from someone in the backcountry, which had been ravaged by Indians, calling for the "extirpation" of the Quakers' religion "from the face of the whole Earth."[52] He was still reluctant to attack Franklin openly, but he did not hesitate to hit him privately in letters to Thomas Penn. In one such effort, probably written in September 1755, Smith said that a little more attention from Penn might have "so far fixed [Franklin] that he never would have prostituted his Pen to help the Assembly out in their present Embarrassment," but "he never would have warmly been your friend." Smith believed that Franklin—"now gone with a witness"—was permanently lost to the Proprietary Party. Smith made clear his intention to stay on Franklin's good side, "for he always did and still does treat me as his Bosomfriend."[53] In public pronouncements, however, Smith sang a sweeter song, praising Franklin as "this ingenious and valuable citizen" for supplying General Braddock with wagons.[54]

Smith was right about one thing: Benjamin Franklin either wrote all of the principal messages of the Assembly to the governor in these critical months in 1755, or he had an important role in their composition. And with the defeat of Braddock, he led the attempt to tax the proprietor's estates along with all others in the province. As he saw things in August and the months immediately following, the province's very existence was imperiled by the French and Indians. Defense had to be installed, and defense required money. Every owner of real property ought to pay, and the old exemption of the Penns' lands had to be discarded.

Governor Morris knew that Thomas Penn did not agree, and a few days after receiving an Assembly bill proposing to raise £50,000 by a tax on everyone's holdings, sent it back with the answer that Penn's lands were to be exempted. The Assembly found this stance intolerable and reminded the governor—and Thomas Penn—that his action was susceptible only to the interpretation that he had made "himself the hateful Instrument of reducing a free people to the abject state of vassalage."[55] For Thomas Penn a similar judgment:

How odious must it be to a sensible manly People, to find *him* who ought to be their Father and Protector, taking advantage of public calamity and distress, and their Tenderness for their bleeding Country, to force down their Throats

Laws of Imposition, abhorrent to common Justice and common reason.[56]

Neither the governor nor Thomas Penn was moved by such assaults. Nor was William Smith, who continued his own rhetorical forays even after the temporary resolution of the crisis in late November 1755. At that time a crowd of frontiersmen appeared in Philadelphia demanding protection from Indian raids that were devastating farms and villages. Exactly what brought about the compromise that was reached is not clear—the danger and the destruction played a part, as did the physical presence of angry men who marched into Philadelphia from the western parts of the province. Whatever the cause, the governor announced that Thomas Penn had offered a gift of £5,000 but would not pay taxes. The Assembly restrained its enthusiasm for this munificence but yielded and passed a tax bill for £55,000, exempting the proprietary estates. Under Franklin's careful leadership it also approved a militia law at the time it voted the new money for defense. The governor disliked the law for its provisions making service voluntary and for the egalitarian methods it established for choosing officers but signed it anyway.[57]

Smith, however, found little satisfaction in these measures and stepped up his attack on the Quakers in and out of the Assembly. By the spring of 1756, his authorship of *A Brief State* was known to everyone; and his *Brief View*,[58] written along similar lines, though with greater anger, confirmed a growing impression that he was a creature of the proprietor and a dishonest man. That Smith was pleased with his own judgment was clear in his insistence that all he had predicted had come true with the frontier sacked by the Indians and the Quakers revealing that they were enemies of their own country.

If there was an enemy of the province in the province, in popular estimation William Smith was the man. In March a series of
attacks in the newspapers fell on him, evoking his protest that his
pen was not for sale and that he wrote only in the public interest.
His critics clearly found all that he said unconvincing, and during
the spring of 1756 he was subjected to "Mild Advice" from
"Humphry Scourge" and then "More Mild Advice." None of it
was mild, for Humphry Scourge accused him of conniving to become "Bishop of America," a charge he was to hear off and on for
years. In these pieces Smith was teased for trying his hand at "Pastoral Letters" in advance of his elevation to a bishop's mitre, a
reference to his published reviews of Pennsylvania's affairs.[59]

The worst of it came after an encounter on a Philadelphia street
with Daniel Roberdeau, an Anglican merchant soon to be elected
to the Assembly, in which Roberdeau reproached Smith for entering politics and dishonoring the cloth.[60] Roberdeau reported that
Smith had replied that far from being committed to a political
faction, he would be willing to write for the Assembly side of the
party dispute if it were not already represented by men of ability.
Smith denied making the statement in a sworn deposition published in early June in the *Pennsylvania Journal*. Roberdeau swore
that he had made it, whereupon others published statements at-
testing to Roberdeau's truthfulness and by implication doubting
Smith's. The dust raised in this matter had not settled when Smith
found himself accused of attempting "to excite an Insurrection in
the Province,"[61] a reference apparently to the appearance in Philadelphia of the frontiersmen determined to obtain military protection for the frontier. According to this critic Smith's action
"showed the *Badness* of your *Heart*; as much as your Presumption
of Success and confident, premature, joyful writing abroad, *that it
actually* took *place*, showed the *Weakness* of your *Head*."

There is no evidence that Smith conspired to produce an insurrection, though his two pamphlets on the problems of defending a society pledged to pacifism invited action against the Quakers and the Assembly they dominated. And Smith in March offended Franklin and his friends by the vigor of his advocacy of the association, a military body, intended to push to the side the militia regiments called into being under the law of 1755. Here Smith's rhetorical thrusts missed their mark in their mean-spirited ridicule of Franklin and the militia law:

> Would it not be better [Smith asked] for a Philosopher to make a Law to try whether Foxes and Wolves will stand till Salt is laid on their Tales, than to make a Law to try whether a People will sign Articles to enslave themselves. To be convinced whether a Shock of the Electric Fluid will kill Rats or Turkeys, must the Experiment be made general on all the Rats and Turkeys on the Face of the earth?[62]

Franklin did not reply publicly to these attacks, but his friends did. One called Smith "a Frantick Incindiary" and "a Minister of the infernal Prince of Darkness, the Father of Lies."[63] Franklin, this writer pointed out, had been largely responsible for Smith's appointment at the academy. Now he found himself the object of Smith's "Slander and Abuse." A month after this piece appeared, another followed, adding to the charges of duplicity that filled so many articles about Smith and accusing him of trying to stop financial aid from coming to "the Jersey College." All this was in keeping with Smith's earlier behavior in New York, where he had attempted to exclude Presbyterians from any control of the college there.

These attacks on Smith pleased Franklin, and he remarked on

them in letters to Peter Collinson. In June Franklin wrote that Smith "is becoming universally odious, and almost infamous"; in November he reported that he and Smith no longer spoke to one another—"He has scribbled himself into universal Dislike here: The Proprietary Faction alone countenance him a little, but the Academy dwindles, and will come to nothing if he is continued."[64]

Smith continued as head of the academy, though for a short period he withdrew from controversy in the newspapers. Soon he was back in print and, in 1758, in jail. The Assembly by this time had had enough and ordered his arrest on the charge of libel. Smith had become a figure of sensationalism, an important leader in education and in the Anglican Church in Philadelphia, a journalist skilled in more than invective, though that was his specialty, and the proprietor's agent. This last assignment made him dangerous.[65]

In the struggles of these years, Smith had identified himself unwittingly as the enemy of popular government in Pennsylvania. This role suited him, for he was self-made, and sneering at the people, whether they were newly arrived Germans or well-established Quakers of genuine principle, strengthened his self-esteem.

Behind him stood Thomas Penn, who seemed unyielding on virtually all the issues important to the Assembly and Franklin. Changing Penn's mind, persuading him to loosen his grip on power, seemed unlikely, but the Assembly believed an attempt had to be made. And therefore early in 1757 it decided to send Franklin to England to look into Penn's mind. Speaker Isaac Norris thought of going with him, but in April Franklin departed Philadelphia accompanied only by his son, William.[66]

CHAPTER 3

The Irrational Mr. Franklin

Franklin crossed to England on the Atlantic Ocean, which for him was not exactly a sea of hope. Thomas Penn awaited him. Franklin did not like Penn and knew that Penn felt no affection for him. But the assignment had to be carried out: to persuade Penn to give up his power to instruct the governor and agree to the taxing of his estates in Pennsylvania. There was never any chance that Penn would give over his power to instruct his deputy in the colony; doing so would amount to renouncing his power to govern. Prospects for taxing proprietary lands were better, but they were not good.

If Franklin failed with Penn, he was next to try Parliament. For reasons not entirely clear, the Quaker Assembly and Franklin himself believed that Parliament might prove receptive to their pleas. They were to discover that Parliament felt no sympathy at all for colonials seeking to increase local power. In a way Franklin, for all his experience, brought a touching innocence to his mission. Innocence so pure, when dispelled, was bound to yield disappointment. In Franklin's case, anger and a loss of political, even personal, balance were to be even more severe consequences.

The long buildup to his English agency had been marked by events that in their own way recapitulated the political experience of other colonies, in which the central element was a fierce struggle for local autonomy. The Assembly, in the course of its conflict with Thomas Penn, had come close to an existence untrammeled by an effective English power. But it had failed—Penn was tough-minded and knew where his own interests lay, and he would not yield.

Franklin, a rational man determined to see things honestly and clearly, now entered upon a course that led to unusual irrationality and passion. But he was blind to the consequences of his course of action. Even after the beginning of the crisis that led to the American Revolution, he may not have recognized the implications of his reactions to disappointment and the political action he had taken. From a world of interest politics, ordinarily quite rational, he now entered a world of hatred and utopian schemes. On the eve of a revolution that he no more than anyone else could anticipate, Franklin cast his lot in favor of royal government for Pennsylvania, a decision shaped by delusions and anger.

Franklin once said that it was "convenient" to be "a *reasonable* creature, since it enables one to find or make a Reason for every thing one has a mind to do."[1] He was sixty-five years of age when he made this statement and growing a little cynical. He was in fact a rational man, as the eighteenth-century styled those who put their stock in reason and evidence. But by the time he reached middle age, he was used to getting his own way, and he rarely experienced disappointment. He often saw far into the motives of others, and acted accordingly, a talent that earned him, at least in part, his reputation as a wise man.

All the achievements in the public's interest—getting a fire department organized, the streets paved, a library established, schools for the poor supported, and much more—attest to his skill in reading others and persuading them to do what he wanted them to do. He calculated well; he recognized the terms and the interests that figured in decisions taken in the affairs of the world. This indeed describes what was most rational about Franklin's mind. He calculated and measured; he weighed and he assessed. There was a kind of quantification embedded in the process of his thought. This characteristic is visible in numerous incidents. For example, in November 1763 he learned from Richard Jackson, his friend in England, that Parliament planned to raise a large sum by taxing imports into the colonies. Franklin responded early the next year, saying, "I am not much alarmed about your schemes of raising Money on us." Why was he not alarmed? His answer was that Britain would see that its interests ("your own sakes") lay in not taking too much from America because to do so would hurt Britain—"for you cannot hurt us without hurting yourselves."[2]

The logic in this line of reasoning is not hard to fathom; in fact, logic dictated the reasons Franklin gave for his faith that the taxman would not shove his hand deep into American pockets. Principle does not raise its head here; nor in this case does power enter the calculation of behavior. The rationale consists of the simple tallying up of the weights of interests. The assumption underlying the logic is that Britain understands its interests and acts on them and nothing else.

In England in 1757 calculation of this sort, combined with ignorance of English politics, led him to his first mistake. Shortly after his arrival he attempted to see William Pitt, one of the great men of the realm, on the eve of his greatest triumph in the war. Franklin believed that Pitt might help in the struggle with the proprietors, but Pitt refused to see him. Pitt was in fact too high for a provincial agent to begin negotiations with, even one with Franklin's reputation. The unwritten protocol governing the working of the British government called for starting farther down the ladder of power. The middle echelons, the servants of the aristocracy, an administrative class, had to break the way and serve as messengers and advocates. They knew the paths to power, and they blocked them unless they were properly catered to.[3]

Franklin learned the lesson and soon was working with Pitt's secretaries. This technique mastered, he turned to similar officials at the Board of Trade, which gave the ministry advice on matters affecting America. Not long afterward he had won their confidence so far as to be allowed to inspect documents in the board's possession vital to the Pennsylvania cause.

Gaining access to Thomas Penn proved easier than seeing Pitt. There was a meeting in mid-August, but nothing substantial was accomplished, or even discussed, because Richard Penn, the brother of Thomas, was traveling outside the city. He soon returned, and the three men met on August 20. Richard Penn was of no real consequence at this meeting or afterward. Franklin had long since recognized that Thomas Penn stood as his major antagonist, but he was unaware of the animus Penn brought to the meeting. Penn was suspicious by nature, and his American informants had for years nourished his distrust of Franklin.[4]

Not that Penn's suspicions required sustenance. He had decided ten years before that Franklin was dangerous, a tribune of the people who shamelessly played to popular desires when he was not inciting them by some action smacking of republican leveling. Now all Penn had to do was review the anguished reports from his deputies in Pennsylvania to have these opinions confirmed.

His most eager informant was Richard Peters, a High Churchman who had come to America in 1734, when he was thirty years old. He had been ordained in the Church of England three years before, but after a short period of service in Christ Church, Philadelphia, in 1736 as assistant rector, he accepted a post as secretary in the provincial land office. This assignment made him the key official representing the proprietor's interests in immense land holdings. Peters did his job with care, efficiency, and a rare devotion to his master's concerns. Penn craved information on all sorts of subjects; Peters supplied it, though not always with accuracy. He was given to exaggeration, perhaps fed by an obsessive concern for his own health. He became hypochondriacal and for reasons not clear came to feel the same anxiety for public matters as for his own physical well-being.[5]

After Penn in 1748 had disabused him of the notion that Franklin could be relied upon to serve the public interest, Peters transformed himself into a reporter of the evil he observed in Franklin. The reports took on a heat that approached hysteria during the two years following Braddock's defeat. This period, especially from the autumn of 1755 through 1756, saw terrible suffering in the frontier counties of Pennsylvania as the Indians raided farms and villages. The call went out for money for troops and arms but, according to Peters, Franklin, as the leader of the Assembly, thwarted "an easy and expeditious mode of raising supplies" by blocking the extension of an excise tax. Most members favored this tax when it was proposed, Peters wrote Penn. But then Franklin stepped in and, with the assistance of Speaker Isaac Norris, introduced a tax on real property, including that owned by the proprietors. And after several days of "idle debates" the Assembly approved the tax, which the governor, bound by instructions, felt compelled to veto.[6]

As Peters told of this fiasco, his propensity to fret gave way to real fear. The situation he described seemed hopeless. The governor, Robert Hunter Morris, faced problems impossible to solve. He could depend on no one—not the receiver general of the quitrents, not neighboring colonies whose governments refused assistance, and not the Assembly, which seemed determined only to tax proprietary estates. Meanwhile the governor faced a "mutiny" in the frontier counties, where women and children fled slaughter by Indians and "the Roads are full of starved, naked, indigent multitudes."[7]

Peters wrote this dismal report on November 8, 1755. Four days later he described the public's mood and offered another prediction. Penn may have thought that Franklin, by frustrating attempts to extend the excise tax, would earn the people's disapproval, but Peters disabused him of this notion with the news that "you universally bear the blame here." Blame was one thing, but there was worse to come: Peters predicted an end to "all government" if the governor failed to control the use of public money and if a law creating a militia was not passed.[8]

The next day he delivered to Penn a similar, perhaps more frightening, message: "The Body of the People are against you." What seemed afoot in Pennsylvania was a massive effort at transforming the government. Peters suspected that Penn might be dissatisfied with the government in the colony, but it struggled with uncontrollable forces and under present circumstances—by implication, a conspiracy hatched by Franklin—"there is no stemming a torrent."[9]

Franklin indeed figured prominently in virtually all these reports. Penn read in one November letter of the possibility that Franklin would be coming to England to press a complaint against the proprietor. Peters had no doubt about Franklin's abilities as an advocate for the Quaker Party and against Penn, "for he has an excellent Understanding, and can think well under the Force of very violent Passions."[10] The violence of these passions seemed obvious to Peters, who in the spring of 1756 was describing them at work in Philadelphia, a city in "Infinite Distraction" owing to militia officers all "puffed up" by Franklin, who now enjoyed the rank of colonel in a military force he had created. But it was not simply the militia that had been corrupted. Franklin had succeeded in drawing the Church of England to his side and the "people in general," both "so poisoned by Franklin that they may prove even worse Enemys to the Proprietors than the Quakers."[11]

This sort of comment flowed from Peters's pen for the rest of the year, indeed almost until Franklin left the colony for England. Apparently Franklin's influence was everywhere: he drafted the Assembly's messages expressing the popular bile against the Penns; he even frightened the Quakers at times; he placed his minions on the board of the Philadelphia Academy; his control in public life extended to the city and county elections, which he controlled. He intimidated Governor William Denny, the agent of the proprietor, and before Penn could replace him had Denny in the Assembly's pocket. All this was evidence of Franklin's "implacable Enmity" against the proprietors and of his skill in provincial politics.[12]

Penn heard of Franklin's plots and his actions from others besides Peters. Governor Morris also detected a conspiracy in Pennsylvania against proprietary interests, with Franklin lurking at its center and at the head of the Assembly. Morris did not always seem certain what Franklin's schemes were and suggested (unwittingly, perhaps) that their very obscurity made them more sinister. Certain he was that Franklin's "designs are deeply layed and very Extensive."[13] At times, to be sure, Penn must have been confused by his American sources, for in October Morris wrote that Franklin had managed a plot which "embody'd" the German settlers against the government; shortly afterward William Smith reported that the Germans were on Penn's side.[14]

Morris, Peters, and William Smith all described a province always tending toward the instability of republicanism. The people were "a giddy and feeble mob," and what Penn faced was a "lev-

elling and licentious Race of Republicans."[15] The fear of republicanism sounds throughout Penn's correspondence from this time
to the American Revolution. What was meant by those who wrote
Penn using the word "republicanism" and what he meant can be
determined from the adjectives attached to it and from the context
of its use. "Levelling" and "licentiousness," both words used by
Smith, Peters, and Morris, suggest a concern to maintain a social
order that was hierarchical and stable. To refine the definition still
further, these men meant that the control of government by the
right sort of people was threatened by the politics of Franklin and
the Assembly.

William Smith published an analysis of recent Pennsylvania history in 1755 explaining how the rule of the proprietors had been
undermined. Privately, in his letters to Penn, he placed Franklin
in a prominent place in this history. His public effort in 1755, *A
Brief State*, argued that in the early years of the province, the proprietor had found it necessary to admit the people to a large share
of power. To survive, a weak colony needed all the support it
could muster. In Smith's judgment (and, we may infer, also in
Penn's) it was unfortunate that popular power remained in place
long after its value had disappeared; in fact, Smith wrote, once the
economy grew and society began to mature, checks should have
been imposed, and a mixed form of government should have succeeded popular government. But this line of development did not
appear. Rather the Quaker Party, contemptuous of established society and regular order, tightened its hold.[16]

By 1757, when Franklin traveled to England with a very different conception of provincial history and government, Penn was
convinced that the structure of power in Pennsylvania desperately
needed a transformation. And who was coming to see him on
behalf of that government? Benjamin Franklin!—steeped in the
stench of republicanism, by all accounts engaged in a popular plot

to erode proprietary authority further, and perhaps intending to obliterate it altogether.

The meeting on August 20 was friendly enough—on the surface. Franklin seems to have been better able to conceal his feelings than Penn, but all the evidence we have suggests that Penn recognized his dislike, and recognized that he faced a formidable enemy. Letters about Franklin from the likes of Richard Peters, Robert Hunter Morris, and William Smith had reinforced suspicions and dislike of some ten years' standing.

In their meeting earlier in August Penn had told Franklin that he needed something in writing, a statement explaining what the Assembly wanted. Now on August 20 Franklin handed him a document called "Heads of Complaint." As Penn complained later, this document was addressed to no one and loosely constructed. But though the "Heads" lacked a form that might satisfy a royal official, it did manage to convey its message in four short paragraphs whose meaning could not be missed. Its central contention was that the proprietors had violated the royal charter originally given to William Penn establishing the colony and its government. Franklin asserted in the "Heads" that the charter provided that laws were to be made for the colony by the proprietor's deputy, the governor, and the people or their representatives in the Assembly. By insisting on instructing the governor and requiring that he post a penal bond to ensure compliance, the proprietors intruded into a process of lawmaking and governance that properly belonged to the province. The consequences had recently proved disastrous: because the instructions held the governor to a policy of disapproving tax bills that included the proprietary estates, money for defense could not be raised except in a manner that was manifestly unfair. The "Heads" concluded that "this, to the Assembly and People of Pennsylvania, appears both unjust and cruel." [17]

Asking Penn to give up instructing his governors was tantamount to suggesting that he yield up the heart of his authority as proprietor. To be sure, no one proposed that he should not appoint his deputies in the colony, and no one imagined that the drawing of broad lines of policy would be given over to the Assembly. But eliminating instructions to governors tied down by penal bonds would deprive him of his part in the day-to-day decisions regarding provincial matters.

There was never any chance that Penn would give up his power—or his understanding of its constitutional basis in the charter. Franklin must have known this, but he knew also that to do the Assembly's bidding he would have to start with the proprietor. A fine historian of this episode has suggested that Franklin played into Penn's hands by stating in writing the Assembly's grievances, the "Heads of Complaint," and thereby became his "dupe."[18] Penn outwitted Franklin, this historian argues, for in obtaining the "Heads," he gained evidence that he used to secure an opinion from the solicitor general and the attorney general favorable to the proprietary cause. The weakness in this interpretation arises from the assumption that a fresh written version of the Assembly's discontents was needed. But in fact Penn and his own solicitor, Ferdinando John Paris, had ample evidence of Assembly demands in a stream of its messages from 1755 onward that denounced the proprietor, his agents in the province, and the use of instructions and penal bonds. The Assembly did not come out directly and say it wished for nothing so much as the power to run provincial affairs, but its intentions were clear. Penn needed only to use a fraction of its fulminations to respond to a summary of provincial grievances, and, more important, to secure a ruling from the British government that the Assembly demanded too much and that proprietary authority should continue to be exercised in time-honored ways. The "Heads of Complaint" pulled old frustrations together and gave them a voice, which could be answered. But they were not essential to Penn's purposes.[19]

The wheels of English politics turned slowly in the months following the August meetings. To Franklin they seemed not to turn at all. While he waited for a reply, with the Penns' excuses echoing vacantly in the rooms they used to see him, he kept busy. But he knew that he had not accomplished much. Some of his efforts had broken new ground, but some of his interviews with Thomas Penn had simply rehearsed familiar discussions.

In one of these interviews, on Indian affairs, Penn revealed a spirit so mean as to provoke Franklin to a reaction that led eventually to an open break. The meeting occurred near the middle of January 1758. The issue provoking the argument concerned the Assembly's claim to the power to appoint commissioners who would supervise Indian trade. Franklin insisted that because of the Assembly's character as an American House of Commons, established under the royal charter of 1682, it possessed the authority to name commissioners in all sorts of legislative acts. Penn disagreed, saying that the Assembly was only a kind of corporation acting by a charter from the Crown and could have "no such Privileges or Rights but what was granted by that Charter, in which no such Privilege as we now claim was any where mentioned."[20] Franklin refused to accept this interpretation: "But *says I* your Father's charter expressly says that the Assembly of Pennsylvania shall have all the Power and Privileges of an Assembly according to the Rights of the Freeborn Subjects of England, and as is usual in any of the British Plantations in America."[21]

The argument then took an ugly turn, with Thomas Penn in effect repudiating the actions of his father. Penn told Franklin flatly that if his father had granted the powers claimed by the Assembly, he had done so without any authority—and therefore "nothing can be claimed by such a grant."[22] To this shot Franklin, now obviously angry, retorted that if William Penn had made such a grant without authority, the immigrants from Europe had been deceived, cheated, and betrayed. Penn then delivered himself of a judgment that broke the argument open. It was simply that the people who came to the province had only themselves to blame if things were not as expected. What has survived of Penn's argument is undoubtedly a paraphrase, though in certain passages Franklin may have remembered his words exactly: "That the Royal Charter was no secret; they who came into the Province on my Father's offer of Privileges; if, they were deceived, it was their own Fault."[23]

The manner of Penn's delivery of this judgment shocked Franklin almost as much as the words themselves—"a kind of triumphing laughing Insolence, such as a low Jockey might do when a Purchaser complained that He had cheated him in a Horse." Franklin reacted with horror and fury, recalling that "I was astonished to see him thus meanly give up his Father's Character and conceived that moment a more cordial and thorough Contempt for him than I ever before felt for any Man living—a Contempt that I cannot express in Words." Franklin remembered later that his face probably expressed the disdain he felt for Penn, but "finding myself grow warm I made no other Answer to this than that the poor People were no Lawyers themselves and confiding in his father did not think it necessary to consult any."[24]

Franklin might have used other terms to describe Penn's manner—and his character. But he made his meaning clear by the reference to the complaints of a buyer of a horse who thought he had been cheated. "Jockey" meant a fraudulent bargainer, a cheat, a trickster. Adding the adjective "low" pushed such a man as far down the moral ladder as Franklin could imagine. Indeed, as he confessed, the contempt he felt—the moral and physical revulsion—robbed him of his capacity for full expression.[25]

Somehow, Franklin's ability to find words returned as events unfolded. In February, a little more than a month after the angry encounter with Penn, he wrote his friend Joseph Galloway that his patience with the proprietors was almost at its end, "though not quite spent." The delay in obtaining a response to the "Heads of Complaint" irritated him, but fearful of appearing rash, he could not push further until the Penns gave him an answer. He clearly felt that relations with the Penns were about to be transformed into open conflict. But he feared that if he initiated it, he would then be charged with throwing away the chances "for very reasonable Terms" that "an agent of more Temper" (that is, patience) might have secured.[26]

Franklin phrased his dilemma and the prospects of the Assembly in the language of warfare. His words betray the violence he felt—he expected "war" soon, and thought that perhaps the *Historical Review*, written by a friend on behalf of Pennsylvania and published the next year, would "be one of the first Acts of Hostility," preparing the people for what would come soon enough, a conflict "in which the Proprietors will be gibbeted up as they deserve, to rot and stink in the Nostrils of Posterity."[27]

The language also reveals Franklin's determination to rid the province of proprietary control. His plans were not yet fully formed, but the bent of his mind was. And his actions over the next few months while awaiting the proprietor's response showed how determined he was. For just as his revulsion against Penn gathered force, an opportunity to wound him by striking one of his creatures in the province presented itself. The target was Provost William Smith, in the Philadelphia jail at this time, imprisoned by order of the Assembly.

Smith had plunged into trouble a few months before by arranging the publication in a German newspaper of a piece by William Moore, a justice of the peace in Chester County, that had first appeared in English. Moore attacked what he considered the Assembly's failure to provide for the defense of the frontier. The Assembly took offense, had him jailed for libel, and not too long afterward added Provost Smith to the list of inmates in jail.[28]

Smith defended himself in a manner that surprised no one who knew of his propensity to celebrate himself in public. He delivered a flamboyant speech to the Assembly when called before it, denied the charges, and took his place in jail. The sheriff did not lodge him with common criminals but set aside rooms where Smith lived in relative comfort, taught his classes from the academy, and apparently courted Moore's daughter, who visited him there. He also petitioned the king-in-council for his release.

Thomas Penn took up Smith's cause in England, arranged for his defense, and found himself confronting Benjamin Franklin, who hired solicitors to present the Assembly's case. In Philadelphia the charges against Smith attracted much attention, and Smith took a beating in the legislative chambers and the newspapers; in England, of course, the affair was beneath the public's notice. But it did provide one more avenue of attack on the proprietor along which Franklin, in notes prepared for Joshua Sharpe, the solicitor representing the Assembly, confidently marched. Among other things, he chose to emphasize the contributions the Quakers had made to the defense of Pennsylvania, and he scourged the proprietor for failing to pay taxes.

Whatever the pleasures of bashing Provost Smith and annoying Thomas Penn, this particular dispute was a sideshow. The main event came in November, when Penn's lawyer, Ferdinando John Paris, informed Franklin that the proprietors found no merit in any of the charges in the "Heads of Complaint." In fact they considered several "injurious" and "unjust." There would be no yielding of the power to instruct the governor; nor would they agree that the charter gave the Assembly an equal part in the making of

laws. They were especially offended by the charge that they had
not paid their share of the costs of defense, and Paris reminded
Franklin and the Assembly that the Penns had contributed £5,000
in 1755 (but failed to note that three years later some £600 of it
had not been paid). To remove any discontent on this score, however, Paris wrote, the proprietors were willing to reopen the question of taxation and to pay their share on what "is in its Nature
taxable," a seeming concession but not necessarily one that would
result in any payment.[29]

The day after Paris wrote, Penn seized the occasion to snub
Franklin. Although the "Heads of Complaint" had come from
Franklin, Penn chose not to respond to him as agent for the Assembly but directly to the Assembly itself. His letter rejected the
request for elimination of instructions, offered vaguely to discuss
taxation of proprietary estates, and made it plain that he would
not deal further with Franklin, who was not a "Person of Candour." To illustrate the good faith of his efforts to treat with
Franklin in the past, Penn told of Franklin's confession that he
lacked power to agree to a supply bill. As Franklin observed later,
no one outside the Assembly could enter into such an agreement;
only that body itself could pass legislation. But Penn, like Franklin, was more interested in winning a political fight than in hon-
oring constitutional niceties.[30]

Whatever Penn thought about the constitution, Franklin still
carried the responsibilities of an agent, and in this role he wrote
immediately, asking for an explanation of Penn's apparent offer to
pay taxes. Penn refused to reply directly but had Paris tell Franklin
in conversation "that we shall always be willing to receive any representation from the House of Representatives, but that we do not
think it necessary to keep up a Correspondence with a Gentleman
who acknowledges he is not impowered to conclude proper measures." That was a pretext. The real reason lay in his long-standing

dislike of Franklin, which had turned into rage when, several months earlier, he read Franklin's characterization of him as a low jockey.[31]

Penn's hostility was assured, and he would do everything possible to retain power and property. What course remained for Franklin? As agent of the Assembly he now had to consider an appeal to the ministry or to Parliament. He could appeal to one or both, but he could not be certain of the results. What he really wanted was to take Pennsylvania away from Thomas Penn. The illusion that he could do it began now to obsess him, with consequences for the clarity of his vision and the sureness of his judgment.

For the remainder of his stay in England, until he sailed for home in August 1762, his agency business revolved around three matters: Indian affairs, statutes passed by the Assembly under review of the Privy Council, and Pennsylvania's share of £200,000 voted by Parliament to compensate the American colonies for expenses of war. The first two items brought him into conflict with Thomas Penn, and the third attracted Penn's interest. Eventually it provided Penn with one more opening for an attack on Franklin.[32]

The Indians of the middle colonies interested Franklin all his life. He recognized more clearly perhaps than most Americans that the Indians had their own culture, which, if it were to be judged fairly, required the exercise of empathy and imagination. He also recognized, as most whites along the frontier did not, that the Indians had sometimes been treated barbarously. He sympathized with them as they faced the steady encroachments on their lands by a white population increasing in numbers and aggressiveness.

These attitudes made it easier for Franklin to act as the advocate of the Delawares in opposition to the interests of Thomas Penn.

But his chief impulse was to strike Penn in almost any way available, and in 1756, the opportunity came when Teedyuscung, the chief of the Delawares, accused the proprietor of defrauding the Delawares of lands in northeastern Pennsylvania. Teedyuscung made this charge in November, and in March 1757 the Board of Trade, on the urging of Thomas Penn, decided to ask William Johnson, the superintendent of Indian affairs in the northern colonies, to investigate. Teedyuscung opposed Johnson's assignment to this task and, probably under coaching, suggested that the king do it. About this time Franklin went to work preparing a petition on the Delawares' behalf. The first version was completed in the late summer and stated more clearly than the one that followed just what Franklin believed. There had been two purchases of lands from the Delawares in recent years and both aroused their dismay. The first was the "walking purchase" of 1737, so named because it provided that the lands ceded to Pennsylvania include all those across which a man could walk in a day. The more recent one, of 1754, also rankled. The Delawares believed they had been cheated and, encouraged by the Quakers, said so.[33]

Franklin felt disposed to believe them, and his petition put the Indians' case in bald terms. Generally, he said, more lands were taken from them than were purchased. He left no doubt that truth and decency had been flouted in the treaties of purchase. And in the case of the walking purchase, "the Proprietaries Extending that Trace of Land agreed for in Terms so vague by such Arts of Jockeyship gave the Indians the worst of Opinions of the English."[34] Franklin's use of the word "Jockeyship" was a nasty touch, calculated to annoy Thomas Penn, who had been furious at being likened to a low jockey in the letter to Norris in January 1758. Penn had read the letter—the theft of letters in Pennsylvania political circles seems not to have been uncommon—and pronounced it "most infamous." He probably never saw this version of Franklin's petition because by the following February Franklin had softened its edges and removed such touches as "jockeyship." But what remained had a bite to it that Penn felt.[35]

If presenting a petition on Teedyuscung's behalf and repeating the Indians' complaints before the agencies of the British government offered a way of showing the mismanagement of the proprietors, the review of legislation passed by the Assembly opened up vital issues of public policy and political power. Under review, in these last years of Franklin's mission, were nineteen statutes passed by the Assembly; Governor Denny had approved them in September and October of 1759, after being paid off by the Assembly. The Penns objected to eleven of these acts and asked the Privy Council to disallow them. Franklin, and his colleague the agent Robert Charles, engaged solicitors to represent the Assembly, and the arguments were begun.[36]

The hearings before the Board of Trade the next year were not entirely satisfactory to either side. Seven of the acts objectionable to the Penns were recommended for disallowance; that left four the board said ought to be approved. These four were not a source of unhappiness for the Penns, but the board's comment that the proprietors had not defended adequately the prerogatives they exercised in the name of the Crown was. Franklin had even more reason for concern—several of the seven acts recommended against were of critical importance for the Assembly's power, and so was the board's rebuke to the effect that the Assembly's claims were "dangerous." Moreover, the board added that there was "not a single Act," even among those it felt obliged to recommend for approval, "that does not contain either some Encroachment on the Prerogative of the Proprietaries, as they are Trustees for the Crown, or on their Property as Land holders in the Province."[37]

These judgments and the recommendations made their way to the Privy Council's Committee for Plantation Affairs and eventually to the council itself. Something of a compromise was then reached in September on the key matter at issue—the Supply Act of 1759, which taxed Penn's lands as well as everyone else's in the province. Penn agreed that his lands might be taxed at the lowest rate paid "on any located uncultivated lands" by inhabitants in the province, and Franklin promised that the Assembly would amend the statute so as to allow the proprietors a voice in the assessment of their estates and the use of money raised.[38]

One of the statutes over which these struggles occurred was the Agency Act of 1759 which, among other things, allowed Franklin to collect the province's share of reimbursement for expenditures incurred in the campaign of 1758. The governor had refused his assent to the statute on the grounds that it was simply one more case of the Assembly's monopolizing public funds. Thomas Penn agreed, but he had a further interest in the matter: the naming of Franklin as the agent authorized to accept the province's portion of the money voted by Parliament.

Franklin received the money in November 1760. The next month he began to invest it in stock on behalf of Pennsylvania. Because of demands for payment of bills of exchange drawn by the Loan Office, an agency of the Assembly, he was soon selling stock. Unfortunately for provincial interest, he sold it at a loss—the market had turned down and he had no choice but to sell. Penn heard of the losses and chortled. The last of the stock was sold early in 1762, but Penn did not stop his carping. Franklin had speculated with the money of the province; he had lost money. There was something wrong, and he should make good the losses himself. Penn's animus is clear, and he exercised it with pleasure. But money for the use of the Assembly exclusively eroded his control, and it rankled that Franklin should deliver still another blow.[39]

The next blows were struck at a distance, for in the remaining years of Franklin's mission he and Thomas Penn did not see much of one another. Penn hoped not to see Franklin at all: when it became necessary to communicate with him, he attempted whenever possible to use his attorney to do it. But he watched Franklin obsessively and speculated on when he would present a petition to Parliament for a change in the government of Pennsylvania. When early in 1759 Franklin had not acted, Penn reported to Peters that Parliament had adjourned, and therefore under its rules no petition could be submitted that session. A few months later Penn wrote another correspondent that though Franklin had submitted a petition on Teedyuscung's behalf, he had failed to follow up so that the petition might be considered by the Privy Council. This prompted a reflection filled with satisfaction and, perhaps, a little foreboding—"Mr. Franklin, though a very crafty subtle Man, I think errs in this, that when he is provoked will go too far, and advance things without proper foundation."[40]

When he did encounter Franklin, his face betrayed the passion he felt. Franklin thought that Penn's feeling was especially strong after the long book *An Historical Review of the Constitution and Government of Pennsylvania* was published.[41] Penn attributed the work, with its attack on his government, to Franklin, unaware that Richard Jackson had written it. After running into Penn shortly after Jackson's work appeared, Franklin reported that "the Proprietor is enrag'd. When I meet him any where there appears in his wretched Countenance a strange Mixture of Hatred, Anger, Fear, and Vexation." There was no regret in this statement and none felt about the comparison of Penn to a low jockey—"I cannot say that I much repent of it," Franklin said about this time. He had been justified, and he was pleased to have injured Penn's self-esteem—"It sticks in his Liver" sums up the pleasure he took in looking into that "wretched Countenance."[42]

Puncturing Penn's liver may have had its joys, but its sources in Franklin's own mixture of anger and hatred did not make for realistic political judgment. What was extraordinary in Franklin's assessment of the political atmosphere was his inclination to draw absolutely wrong conclusions from reading the attitudes of powerful men in Britain toward the colony of Pennsylvania. He knew that the "great men" of the ministry felt no sympathy for American claims of rights. Shortly after arriving in 1757 Franklin had had the doubtful pleasure of listening to Lord Granville tell him that the instructions of the Privy Council in England had the force of legislation in America. In Granville's oral disquisition, royal instructions were the "LAW OF THE LAND" and the king-in-council was "THE LEGISLATOR."[43] Granville was hardly the only one who believed that the Americans demanded too much control for themselves—most men of consequence believed that the colonies had too many privileges. The president of the Board of Trade, Lord Halifax, was one. His attitudes could be grasped easily when one remembered that he had tried to impose a "military government" on Nova Scotia. To be sure, the Americans did have friends in England who counted for something. But they did not control colonial policy, and it seemed clear that they would not gain control.[44]

Even appealing to Parliament constituted "something hazardous," Franklin said, for "a good deal of prejudice" against the colonies prevailed there despite the friends of liberty; "the Courtiers think us not sufficiently obedient; the illicit Trade from Holland etc greatly offends the Trading and Manufactoring Interest; and the Landed Interest begins to be jealous of us as a Corn Country that may interfere with them in the Markets to which they export that Commodity."[45]

This analysis of English attitudes leads to an unavoidable conclusion: a change to royal government would have brought a heavy hand down on Pennsylvania. In any case, no one of importance or sufficient power was disposed to act to strengthen provincial autonomy—far from it. The weight of opinion and policy rested on a conviction that the colonies should be brought to heel.

Franklin did not draw these conclusions. He surely would have recognized what English attitudes meant for political action had he not been blinded by passion. But in defiance of all the evidence he, a man usually extraordinarily responsive to empirical realities, now concluded that the Crown would not be "displeased" with an application by the province "to be taken under its immediate Government" and, as far as Franklin could see, "our circumstances would be mended by it." Virtually all that he had been told suggested otherwise. Neither the Crown nor Parliament would welcome proposals from America that would relax control from England. And should the Crown take over a colony, it would look to tighten the reins, not loosen them.[46]

But Franklin could not see these consequences; he could not reason to a conclusion that reckoned with the facts of British policy and disposition. The truth was that he wanted to hurt Penn more than anything else. He said—and believed—that he wanted a royal government for his province. More than that, however, he wanted to take the province away from Thomas Penn. Thus far had this reasonable creature come.

Benjamin Franklin, 1778,
by Joseph Siffred Duplessis.

Metropolitan Museum of Art, the Friedsam Collection,
bequest of Michael Friedsam, 1931.

Thomas Penn,
mezzotint engrav-
ing by D. Martin,
from a painting
by Davis.

Yale University Art
Gallery, the Mabel Brady
Garvan Collection.

William Smith,
D.D., engraved
by John Sartain,
after the oil portrait
by Benjamin West.

Historical Society of
Pennsylvania.

*Franklin before the Privy
Council in the Cockpit,* 1774,
by Christian Schussele.

Henry E. Huntington Library
and Art Gallery.

Arthur Lee,
by Charles Willson Peale, 1785.

Independence National Historical Park
Collection, Philadelphia.

Ralph and Alice
Delancey Izard, 1775,
by John Singleton
Copley.

Courtesy, Museum of Fine
Arts, Boston, Edward
Ingersoll Browne Fund.

John Adams in 1766,
by Benjamin Blyth.

Massachusetts Historical
Society.

Abigail Adams
in 1766,
by Benjamin Blyth.

Massachusetts Historical
Society.

John Adams,
by Charles Willson
Peale, 1785.

Independence National
Historical Park Collection,
Philadelphia.

John Jay,
by Gilbert Stuart, 1783.

John Jay Iselin and the Frick
Art Reference Library.

William Franklin,
by Mather Brown.

Frick Art Reference Library.

BENJAMIN FRANKLIN.

Né à Boston, dans la nouvelle Angleterre le 17 Janvier 1706

Benjamin Franklin, engraved by Augustin de Saint-Aubin from a
drawing made in 1777 by Charles-Nicholas Cochin.

The Papers of Benjamin Franklin, Yale University.

CHAPTER 4

The Triumph of the Enemies

Franklin, his mission a failure, returned to America on November 1, 1762. He felt some uneasiness about his reception in Philadelphia, for several months earlier he had heard stories William Smith told in England to the effect that his friends at home were abandoning him. They were not, and when they visited him to renew old ties, he discovered that they held him in high regard. His political friends had also made it their business to see that Franklin was reelected to the Assembly every year that he was absent. Thus once again he had been returned to his old seat in the election held just a month before his arrival.[1]

The conflict with Thomas Penn simmered rather than boiled well into the new year. Franklin had not forgotten his enemy in England, nor had he forgiven him for slights and snubs—and for what he regarded as selfish and tyrannical actions at the expense of the province. At the end of 1763 events occurred that led him back into the struggle with Penn.

The events were the brutal slaughter of Indians living peacefully in Lancaster County by whites, apparently Scotch-Irish Presbyterians, who entertained a relentless hatred of all Indians but preferred killing those close at hand, and helpless, to fighting armed bands along the frontier. The first group attacked was mostly old men, women, and children living in the small community of Conestoga Manor. On December 14, 1763, a large group of frontiersmen broke into the Indians' home quarters there and murdered six. About two weeks later they repeated their attack on a similar group at Lancaster, killing fourteen. They made it plain that they did not intend to stop until the toll went much higher.[2]

The governor at this time was John Penn, nephew of Thomas and son of Richard Penn. He had been in the colony since October 1763 and was still feeling his way in the strange practices of Pennsylvania politics. Never a strong leader, or even a well-organized one, he reacted swiftly in this case and issued proclamations calling for the arrest and "condign Punishment" of those responsible. The second proclamation, in early January, offered a reward to anyone who apprehended or helped to arrest the ringleaders of the mob.[3]

Franklin also acted rapidly. He could not issue proclamations, of course, but he could write a denunciation of the killers, now usually called the Paxton Boys after the village that produced many of them. Franklin's attack on them, *A Narrative of the Late Massacres*, was published in Philadelphia at the end of January 1764. It is one of his most passionate expressions, devoid of both the irony and the sarcasm that he frequently resorted to in his writings for the public. It did not make him popular with the people along the frontier, nor did his actions in the days immediately following.[4]

For a brief period in early February he found himself in league with John Penn. The frontier settlers had not been cowed by the governor's proclamations, and Franklin's *Narrative*, if it was widely read in Lancaster and adjacent counties, left them cold. But they were hot for Indian blood and, upon learning that the authorities had moved peaceful Indians to Philadelphia, prepared to march to the city. Word of their intentions reached the governor, who proposed that the Assembly enact a Riot Act, similar to one passed in England earlier in the century, to give the government the power to deal with lawless, indeed murderous, mobs. On February 3, the Riot Act was passed and signed by the governor. The next day a group of citizens, with Franklin taking part, formed a rough militia to defend the city and the Indians.[5]

The governor learned at this time from sources in the frontier counties that men full of anger were gathering for a march on Philadelphia and an attack on the Indians sheltered there. Estimates of the size of the frontier groups were undoubtedly inflated, but they shook everyone's nerves. An especially frightening alarm came to Governor Penn the next day, the Sabbath, and late that night, clearly undone, he fled to Franklin's house for aid and advice. Franklin took an understandable satisfaction in having the proprietor's chief representative, a Penn to boot, come begging to his door. But Franklin proved his public spirit once again and took the governor in—and probably did not gloat outwardly. What went on inside his head was another matter. Remembrance of the scene that night gave him pleasure more than a month later. He recalled the affair in March for Dr. John Fothergill, the leader of the Quakers in London: "More wonders! You know I don't love the Proprietary, and that he does not love me. Our totally different Tempers forbid it." Then follows a short account of how, when Governor Penn arrived the previous October, he, Franklin, had treated him with civility, given advice on request, promoted a cooperative spirit in the Assembly, and generally behaved with respect. And when "the daring Rioters" attacked the Indians and ignored with "Contempt" the Governor's proclamations, he, Franklin, had written *A Narrative of the Late Massacres*

> to render the Rioters unpopular; promoted an Association to support the Authority of the Government and defend the Governor by taking Arms, sign'd it first myself, and was followed by several Hundreds who took Arms accordingly; the Governor offer'd me the Command of them, but I chose to carry a Musket, and strengthen his Authority by setting an Example of Obedience to his Orders.

The implication of all this sterling conduct was plain in Franklin's judgment that virtue was rewarded in a most pleasant way: "And would you think it, this Proprietary Governor did me the Honour, on an Alarm, to run to my House at Midnight, with his Counsellors at his Heels, for advice, and made it his Head Quarters for some time." Two days later, February 7, Franklin joined six others appointed by the governor to meet with the rioters at Germantown, where they had gathered apparently in preparation for a march on Philadelphia. This delegation persuaded the frontiersmen to return home after agreement was reached that two would come to the city and present their grievances.[6]

Having the governor as his suppliant was delicious—so indeed was the entire spectacle of governor and advisers running to him in the middle of the night—but that Franklin's amusement over the affair extended to himself is clear in his comment that "within four and twenty hours" he had been "a common Soldier, a Counsellor, a kind of Dictator, an Ambassador to the Country Mob, and on their Returning home, *Nobody*, again."[7]

The crisis could have ended in more bloodshed; as it was the rioters were unhappy but they dispersed; and for the moment tranquillity reigned in the relations between Governor Penn and the Assembly. Franklin was slightly bemused by this conclusion, but he did not expect the calm to last.

The governor and the Assembly soon proved him right. The men designated by the rioters to lay out their grievances—James Gibson and Matthew Smith—soon appeared. The Assembly listened and then proposed to the governor that he should join them in formulating a response. This tactic smacked of Franklin's influence, for it would have confronted the frontiersmen with the united force of the city. Governor Penn, however, unable to rid himself of the old proprietary suspicions of a body that seemed determined to encroach upon his authority, turned down the offer. The governor's rejection included a statement that his agreeing to the Assembly's plan would be "unbecoming the Honour and Dignity of the Government." The Assembly, affronted by this expression of proprietary power and the way the governor phrased his rebuff, proceeded to other business in no very happy frame of mind. In Pennsylvania's politics things usually got worse, and in the following weeks Governor Penn and the Assembly struggled over a simple bill authorizing the construction of a lighthouse at the mouth of the Delaware and a bill to raise money by taxing lands. The Assembly proposed to tax the proprietor's lands at the rate imposed on every other landowner.[8] Governor Penn held out for more favorable terms.

Within a few weeks, according to Franklin, Governor Penn's arbitrary actions had brought him and the proprietary government into "sudden contempt" and destroyed all regard for him in the Assembly. As far as Franklin was concerned, "All Hopes of Happiness under a Proprietary Government are at an End." Indeed regard for Governor Penn sank so low that "were another Mob to

come against him," he probably could not find a dozen men "willing to rescue him."[9]

Franklin provided this assessment for his old friend John Fothergill. It undoubtedly exaggerated the importance of recent events
in the animosities felt in and out of the Assembly toward the governor and proprietary government. Those feelings were old and
would not disappear easily, though they did need nourishing occasionally. In writing Fothergill, Franklin intended to prepare the
London Quakers for an attempt in America to replace the proprietor with the Crown. He had also to exercise care in dealing with
Quakers in Pennsylvania who, though they detested the proprietor, were not as determined as Franklin was, primarily because
they were not altogether convinced that the civil and religious
liberties of the province would survive intact a change from proprietary to royal government.[10]

And how to persuade the Crown to step in and take over the
government? The appropriate tactic, Franklin evidently believed,
was to persuade the king's ministers that the Penns could no
longer govern, that their American colony existed in conditions
of anarchy, with mobs threatening not only the Indians but Philadelphia itself. Franklin knew that the Crown and the men who
served it hated disorder, and so did those in Parliament for
that matter. They were suspicious of democratic tendencies in
America, of leveling, and of anarchy, which they believed inevitably followed in the train of popular or republican government.
But because the ministry did not wish to incite rebellion, it must
also be persuaded that the people of Pennsylvania had lost faith
in the Penns and their government. The Crown must conclude,

if it was to take over Penn's government, that doing so would preserve order and traditional social arrangements with the best men on top. A change acceptable to them, in other words, should not really change anything at all—except who held ultimate power.

The province itself presented no easy problem. To be sure, little love for the Penns existed outside the council and the men who served in proprietary offices. There was also William Smith, still feeding at Thomas Penn's trough, and a handful of others similarly beholden or perhaps still respectful of the Penn name out of a lingering affection for the memory of William Penn. But the fear of change lurked among the Quakers and the Quaker Party, in particular change that might reduce their political and religious freedoms.

Confronting the people of Pennsylvania and the English ministry, both skeptical of a shift to royal government, a reasonable man would have given up the game as lost before it began. Franklin and the Assembly he now led in all but name were not reasonable, and not in a mood to equivocate. They wanted a change, wanted nothing more to do with Thomas Penn.

The strategy Franklin and his colleagues devised to get their way seems curiously askew. They began by concentrating on the colony. The Assembly passed in late March twenty-six resolves condemning the proprietors and all their works. Given Franklin's and the Assembly's purposes—to replace Penn's government with the Crown's—their best chance of success lay, not in seeming to claim power for provincial institutions such as the Assembly, but in emphasizing the need for control from outside the province. After all, they were asking for a new government, presumably because they desired someone to govern. Their resolves told another story, however. The first resolve seemed to say that the proprietor—in England—had no right to exercise power in America. For it argued that in appointing a deputy who served as governor in the province, the proprietors in effect gave up all their power to participate in lawmaking. They had reduced themselves to private landowners in the colony, nothing more and nothing less. This argument, intended for local consumption, was certain to be noticed in England, where the Board of Trade four years earlier had repudiated it. In 1760 the board had specifically criticized Thomas Penn for acting as this resolution insisted he should—as a private landowner with no rights to governing power. The board had suggested that Penn had improperly vacated his authority to run the colony, and it pointedly directed him to attend to the business of government. Of course that was just what the Assembly did not want him to do.[11]

The remainder of the Assembly's resolutions covered familiar ground. The proprietor had done everything from issuing too many licenses for public houses and dram shops, thereby corrupting the morals of the people, to claiming the best lands for the Penn family and then attempting to sell them off at exorbitant prices. But the Penns, it seems, were not even very good at extortion, for the prices they demanded for lands they should not have owned were too high for immigrants to the province, who soon commenced their travels again to nearby colonies where they could afford to buy lands. Pennsylvania thereby lost people who might have made the economy bloom. If this were not bad enough, the Assembly pointed to the proprietor's reluctance to help defend the province from Indian attacks, his refusal to pay taxes, and his propensity to drive hard bargains at times when the people of the province had "the Knife of Savages at their Throat." Indeed the proprietor did not permit the people "to raise Money for their Defense" unless they complied with Penn's "arbitrary Will and Pleasure," "a Practice" the resolutions held to be "dishonourable, unjust, tyrannical and inhuman."[12]

These resolutions, which Franklin called the "Necklace of Resolves," closed by declaring that the Assembly would adjourn to consult the people of the province whether to request the king to replace the proprietor with royal government. The resolves were to be made public, and within a week the *Pennsylvania Gazette* printed them. The *Journal*, a paper that ordinarily defended the proprietary interest, did not.[13]

The next step—consulting the people—actually involved persuading them to sign petitions asking for a dissolution of proprietary government and the introduction of royal control. Franklin printed around a hundred copies of the petitions from a text he wrote himself.

On the face of it, demonstrating the existence of local support for a change in government made sense. But there was danger too. More might be demonstrated than was intended, and petitions themselves, though a revered part of the mixed government of England, were not revered by everyone—especially when they came from a province that had been founded by dissenters who at times seemed willing only to listen to themselves. What Franklin and the Assembly had to avoid was the appearance of claiming too much, indeed of seeming to claim virtual independence. They might easily affront the king's ministers by sending over petitions that cashiered a man of the ruling classes, a man much like the king's ministers.

The difficulty in the resolutions was that they addressed two audiences—each with its own interests. The first was the Crown. The Crown wanted its colonies to contribute to the welfare of the empire. In these years of war with the French, the Crown expected support of its military forces in the New World, and it did not want to be told that provincial assemblies, considering themselves parliaments, meant to raise money on their own terms and to control expenditures. Yet that message seemed to come from Pennsylvania.

The people of Pennsylvania composed the second audience—and what a fragmented and contentious audience they were. Geography, religion, and nationality all played a role in separating these people and in setting them against one another. The frontier counties distrusted Philadelphia and the eastern counties; "distrust" is too mild a word, for there was nothing subtle in the hatred and scorn the frontier felt for the old established areas. Religion and nationality had a part in these feelings. The frontier was Scotch-Irish and German, with the Presbyterians, Lutherans, and sects none too comfortable with one another but united in their anger at the city of Philadelphia and its Quaker leaders. There was another reason for frontier disaffection—its five counties sent ten representatives to the Assembly, whereas the three old counties of the east held twenty-six seats. In the city itself and the three eastern counties, the Church of England regarded the Quakers with suspicion and did not admire the local Presbyterians. It reserved its deepest disdain for the Quakers, an attitude returned in full measure.

The Assembly's approval of the Necklace of Resolves was a triumph for Franklin, the last he would enjoy before he left for England later in the year. Controversy frequently raised his spirits, and when the Assembly adjourned to collect signatures on a petition calling for the removal of the proprietors, he clearly felt invigorated. The hard work of agitation did not daunt him, and in the attempts that now began to persuade the people of the province to sign the petitions, he showed his organizational genius as well as his strong spirit. His newspaper, the *Pennsylvania Gazette*, almost immediately printed in its columns the messages that passed between Governor Penn and the Assembly concerning the supply bill that had foundered. The resolves and these messages were also put together and published as a broadside at this time, the end of March. Franklin's press ran off some three thousand copies and added the same number of his little tract *Explanatory Remarks*, amplifying and defending the Assembly's action.

Getting the petitions out for signing proved simple. Franklin's shop printed at least three hundred copies before the effort ended in May. Quaker interests printed others, and several (the number is not known) were distributed in German. A great meeting was held in front of the State House in Philadelphia, and Joseph Galloway, Franklin's henchman, excoriated the proprietors and praised the king. This was not Galloway's first appearance on behalf of the Assembly's and Franklin's cause, nor would it be the last.[14]

Joseph Galloway, the son of a rich Maryland landowner, was almost a quarter century younger than Benjamin Franklin. Like Franklin he came to Philadelphia as a youth, and as a mature man served in the Assembly for more than twenty years before the Revolution. In these years he became as committed as Franklin to a change in the government in Pennsylvania. There, perhaps, the resemblance of the two men ends. Political allies, and friends of a sort, they actually had little in common apart from their disaffection from proprietary government. Galloway had none of Franklin's scientific interests, little of Franklin's capacity for friendship, none of his geniality, and little of his style or common touch. Galloway was a lawyer by training, and he was successful in his profession. Franklin's son William studied with him, and that relationship undoubtedly brought his father and Galloway together. Socially, even in the 1750s, they were worlds apart. Galloway had been born to a very good Maryland family that was related to the Shippens and Pembertons of Philadelphia. He married well—his wife was Grace Growdon, the daughter of a wealthy Philadelphian who had served in both the Assembly and the council. Galloway was proud of his connections—some thought him arrogant—and he made his way in political life in part because of his social position. There was more to him, however, than good breeding. He was smart, he had a nose for political power, and he was very fast on his feet. The ability to speak with force and clarity was not prominent in Franklin; it was in Galloway, and it made him especially useful in the rough-and-tumble of Assembly debates and the extraordinary circumstances of 1764.[15]

Galloway wrote on behalf of royal government as well as speaking for it. His first effort was made in answer to Hugh Williamson's *Plain Dealer No. 1*, the first serious blow struck in defense of the proprietors and in opposition to the petitions. The struggle now assumed the form common to factional conflicts in the American colonies, with the contending sides issuing increasingly extravagant attacks. Williamson, a professor of mathematics in the College of Philadelphia, began fairly moderately but also oversimplified the issues. "The foundation of all our trouble," he insisted, arose from inequitable representation, which had its "origin from Quakers."[16] That Galloway's answer failed to match Williamson's in moderation was not a surprise—he had a fondness for strong words and lacked a sense of restraint when engaged in political combat.

The petitions had come back by early May, and soon after, the Assembly resumed its meetings. The astute among its members must have known that they had failed: the petitions carried 3,500 signatures, from a population of around 250,000. Franklin scrambled around for reassurance in this fiasco, but about the best he could say was that the colony's population numbered only 110,000. Inspection of the petitions revealed that support for a switch to royal government was confined to Philadelphia. The petitions had met a cold refusal everywhere else. And the backing for the petitions was hardly overwhelming in Philadelphia.[17]

The first step in Franklin's strategy had led to a fall. But undaunted, he pulled himself and the Quaker Party upright and resolved to appeal to the British government. On May 24 the Assembly took up a proposal that the Assembly petition the king to take over Pennsylvania's government. Isaac Norris, the Speaker, presided over the beginning of these deliberations, but though he was a power in the Quaker Party, he did not agree that an appeal to the Crown for royal government should be made. His younger colleague John Dickinson strengthened his resolve to oppose such an appeal by giving an extraordinarily able speech soon after the session began. Dickinson was thirty-one years of age, born in Maryland, and trained in the law at the Middle Temple, London. He did not attack Franklin, nor did he suggest that there was a malevolent conspiracy to replace the Penns with the Crown. Rather, he suggested that the change would put in jeopardy the old religious and political freedoms of the king's subjects in the colony. The Quakers, after all, were in bad repute in English governing circles. They opposed war; they prevented an effective defense being mounted against the Indians and the French. In Pennsylvania they ran the government—holding office, sitting on juries, voting—and in fact they pretty much had things their own way. But, Dickinson asked, was it realistic to expect that with their refusal to fight and pay taxes to support war they would retain these old privileges? Their religious freedom, which Dickinson characterized as "perfect," would also give way to a dominance by the Church of England. Nor would the Presbyterians enjoy safety, for their reputation in the ministry, which blamed them for the recent riots, was almost as bad as the Quakers'. As for the expectation that the Crown, once it had taken over, would allow the Assembly to tax the proprietor's lands—that too seemed doubtful.

The king will not have the time to weigh the matter, Dickinson said, and his ministers will follow the rule that men in authority always invoke—"never to deviate from a precedent of power." Dickinson felt the unease common to radical Whigs, who feared executive power, that it would inevitably seek to destroy liberty. This urge was in the nature of things as far as these eighteenth-century liberals were concerned. Dickinson likened power to "the Ocean; not easily admitting limits to be fixed upon it."[18]

Joseph Galloway delivered the answer of the Quaker Party to these assertions. Exactly what he said on the twenty-fourth of May is not known. He apparently spoke without notes, rising to his feet immediately after Dickinson sat down. He published on August 11 what he claimed to have said in the Assembly that day some six weeks earlier. Dickinson replied to this reply in September and insisted that Galloway's published version bore no relation to what he had actually said in May. Galloway's printed version was, Dickinson stated, "a *pretended speech*." Whatever the truth about the relationship of the extemporaneous speech to the one in print, Galloway's remarks reflected the judgment of Franklin and his followers.[19]

Dickinson had invoked the specter of power encroaching on liberty. Galloway agreed on the dangers of power, but it was power in private hands, the power of the Penns—"a great private interest"—that concerned him. The Crown, he insisted, knows its limits, but proprietary power did not—"where its Limits will be fixt, and its Encroachments end is uncertain." By implication the recent history of Pennsylvania was the history of the "illegal Usurpations of Proprietary Tyranny."[20]

But Galloway did not intend to allow Dickinson to set the terms of the argument. Power and ancient privileges (by Pennsylvania standards) were at issue, and so was the entire governing process. Dickinson had insisted that there was more to fear from royal authority than from the proprietor's. Galloway was having none of that, pointing out that the proprietor had violated the charter given by William Penn, which had established the rights of the subject in the colony. Under the charter the legislature worked with the governor to pass the laws governing Pennsylvania, a well-practiced system that worked, at least until the proprietor corrupted it by giving the governor instructions that prevented any modification of them. This undercutting of the basic process of legislation was, according to Galloway, the essential cause of strain. The proprietor's refusal to allow his lands in the colony to be taxed at the rate paid by everyone else was unfair, but beside the issue of instructions it seemed secondary, at least as Galloway presented the colony's grievances in this speech.

Galloway's speech made it plain that for the Quaker Party the self-serving character of the proprietor's interest threatened the public welfare. It was self-serving because it was private. The Penns owned immense amounts of land from which they expected to make a profit, and their powers of government, as proprietors, served this private interest. The Crown, in contrast, would have "no sinister motive"—royal government sought only the public good. Proprietary government could not be more different; proprietary government was private government, "a private Interest, like some restless Fiend, . . . always alive, . . . ever active."[21]

Speaker Norris listened to the argument and found he could not advocate the substitution of royal government for the proprietary form. He asked permission to speak, a departure from the neutrality and official silence of the Speaker, and expressed his opposition to the petition. The next day, pleading ill-health, he resigned. Franklin was elected in his stead and signed the petition, which the House had approved by a near-unanimous vote.[22]

The Assembly's action hardly stopped the debate, and over the course of the following summer the struggles over proprietary government remained before the public. Elections of the Assembly were to be held in October, and both sides saw an opportunity to drive the other from power. Something resembling a debate over the colony's constitution had defined the arguments of May, when the petition for royal government was discussed. Now the tone and substance of the discussion in public assumed a different form, familiar to anyone who had watched colonial factions at work.

Franklin had played a quiet role in the drive to gain approval for the petition for royal government. But from June until the elections to the Assembly in October he would not be able to remain quiet, working behind the scenes with his legislative colleagues. He would have to take the lead in public, as he had in April when he attempted to rally the people behind the petitions to the Assembly. That attempt had ended in disaster, an outcome soon recounted to Thomas Penn by his friends in Pennsylvania. Franklin knew that Penn would tell the British government that despite all the hubbub in the colony there was little support for a change in government. Yet he was determined to seek the change and in his willingness to ignore all the evidence to the contrary he revealed an obsessive conviction that he would succeed. Yet even he recognized that for the petition on behalf of royal government to prosper, it would have to come from a legislature whose action in sending it had a loud echo of approval in the autumn elections.

John Dickinson, the new recruit to the Proprietary Party, gave Franklin little opportunity to act on his own, to take the initiative and carry the argument against the Penns. To be sure, Franklin used his influence to fill the *Pennsylvania Gazette* with articles and notes attacking the tyranny of proprietary government. Philadelphia printers were soon busy turning out broadsides, squibs, and tracts against the Penns and for the royal government. But much of their effort and Franklin's took the form of counterattacks and replies to blows struck by their enemies, now full of zeal and energy thanks to Dickinson and, from mid-June on, to William Smith, just returned from England.[23]

Dickinson in June decided to use a tactic Franklin had tried. With the help of proprietary supporters, he began circulating petitions in opposition to royal government. In Franklin's and the Quaker Party's hands the results had been embarrassingly sparse. Franklin reported on Dickinson's effort in early July, remarking that he had no idea what it would produce. The yield turned out to be better than four times his own, with some 15,000 signatures put down by September.[24]

Before the extent of the opposition could be known, Franklin found himself engaged in a major struggle with William Smith, who wrote a long preface to John Dickinson's speech in the Assembly on May 24. Dickinson's speech appeared in print on June 24 with Smith's anonymous introduction included. Franklin recognized that both Smith and Dickinson were dangerous adversaries. Galloway's response, which had been made in the legislature immediately after Dickinson's attack, would be the Quaker Party's answer. Franklin would have to deal with Smith, a task he took on with zest in his own preface, which proved to be longer than the speech by Galloway that it introduced.[25]

Smith had begun his preface by accusing the Assembly of corruption. It had bribed Governor William Denny during the French and Indian War to give his assent to a supply bill, as an appropriations bill was called, providing money for the war. Denny had withheld his assent, just as his successors had, until certain "considerations" were paid him, "considerations" being the polite word for bribes. Governors ordinarily referred to these payments as "their arrears," Franklin reported; to him it seemed obvious that the appropriate word was "extortion," as in his phrase "an Extortion of more Money from the People." The governors, encouraged by the proprietor, established this process of passing legislation, demanding to be paid before they gave the approval that transformed bills into laws. Franklin styled this practice "the Bargain and Sale Proceedings in Legislation."[26]

Behind the problem with the governor stood the proprietor, Thomas Penn. Franklin's preface took aim at the proprietor even when it seemed to be shooting at a governor. The issues of land and taxation appeared complicated, but Franklin's explanation of them stripped away inessentials to demonstrate that what remained was a flawed constitutional structure allowing manipulation by the proprietor for his own interest. The province had not tried to put the Penn family estates at a disadvantage in taxing them. It had always acted so as to put the family's lands on the same plane as everyone else's. But Penn resisted paying any taxes, or at his most generous seemed to agree that his most valuable lands, surveyed and located, should pay taxes at the rate of unlocated and uncultivated lands—waste lands, in other words. And as Franklin pointed out, in 1761 an assembly committee, of which William Allen, the chief justice and a supporter of Thomas Penn, was a member, found that Penn's estates had been rated no higher than those of inhabitants of the colony, and "in *many* instances *below others*."[27]

Franklin delivered part of what he had to say in this preface in a matter-of-fact style, with the issues of the constitution laid out and the proprietor's conduct explained. What was at stake regarding the Penns' lands, the process of legislation and governance, and the interests of the colony appears clearly in his simple prose. Yet there is an edge to his words. He is, after all, giving an answer to an attack on the Assembly and himself. But frustration and anger contribute even more to the tautness of his writing. Both frustration and anger break through his survey of the constitutional history of the province as he denounces the opposition with the sarcasm that seemed at times natural to him:

Pleasant, surely it is, to hear the Proprietary Partizans, of all Men, bawling for the Constitution, and affecting a terrible concern for our Liberties and Privileges. They who have been, these twenty Years, cursing our Constitution, declaring that it was no Constitution, or worse than none, and that Things could never be well with us, 'till it was new-modell'd, and made exactly conformable to the British Constitution. They who have treated our distinguishing Privileges as so many Illegalities and Absurdities; who have solemnly declared in Print, that though such Privileges might be proper in the Infancy of a Colony, to encourage its Settlement, they become *unfit for it* in its grown State, and *ought to be taken away*: They, who by numberless Falshoods, propagated with infinite Industry, in the Mother Country, attempted to procure an Act of Parliament for the actual depriving a very great Part of the People of their Privileges: . . . [and] of some of their most important Rights, and are daily endeavouring to deprive them of the rest![28]

In cashiering the proprietor and his party in Pennsylvania, Franklin pretended to believe that no honest observer of the political scene could doubt the accuracy of his argument. And thus it followed that no one in his right mind would trust the Penns or their provincial agents to defend the rights of the people. Have

these agents, he asked, "become patriots and Advocates of our
Constitution? Wonderful Change! Astonishing Conversion! Will
the Wolves then protect the Sheep, if they can but persuade 'em
to give up their Dogs?" Franklin rarely quoted the Bible in his
writings but now resorted to St. Paul's Epistle to the Hebrews,
saying that only one with "faith" could believe that the proprietary
interest would, if given unchecked power, protect liberty. For, he
asserted, if faith is "rightly defin'd" as "*the Evidence of Things not
seen*, certainly never was there more occasion for such Evidence,
the Case being totally destitute of all other."

Given Franklin's anger, it was inevitable that he should refer
directly to the Penns. Smith had attempted to demonstrate that
the Assembly was so inconsistent as to be out of control by quoting
its praise of William Penn in several formal addresses to Richard
and Thomas Penn, his sons. Franklin dismissed this effort with
contempt by observing that the Assembly genuinely admired William Penn and really had no choice in bestowing compliments, for
"in attempting to compliment the Sons on their own merits, there
was always found an extreme Scarcity of Matter." As for John
Penn, Thomas Penn's nephew and Richard's son, he had earned
the scorn of the Assembly, which had rallied to him at the time of
the Paxton riots only to receive "affronting" messages from him
once the danger had passed. Franklin did not refer to his own
conduct during the riots, though he clearly felt badly used afterward. John Penn's conduct reflected, he insisted, a "fixt deep-
rooted Family Malice."[29]

Franklin himself felt the family's malice and that of their agents
as the election campaign gathered its fury. He was a big man with
a big record and therefore provided a big target. William Smith
and Governor John Penn undoubtedly organized some of the attacks, and they and their henchmen seem not to have missed much
as they tore and twisted at Franklin's character.

There are levels of invective. Distinguishing the lowest in what fell on Franklin is not easy, and his correspondence of this time gives no clues to his reactions. What was written about his sex life will serve, however. While still a young man Franklin fathered a son out of wedlock. Rumors about the mother apparently began circulating early on, perhaps even before Franklin made his reputation. Deborah Franklin, whom he married in 1730, was not the mother of this child, William Franklin (who became a figure of weight in his own right). In the election of 1764, Franklin's enemies inserted into print stories about the mother and Franklin's libidinous urges. The mother, they wrote, was Barbara, a maid who worked in his house, worked apparently so hard that she was his "slave," a "Kitchen Wench" and "Gold Finder." This last term referred to a servant who cleaned privies. According to the story told in Philadelphia, Franklin denied Barbara her wages, "the *pitaful* Stipend of *Ten Pounds per Annum*," and allowed her to "*STARVE*" and then "stole her to the Grave, in Silence," without indeed a "pall" and certainly without "a *Groan*, a *Sigh* or a Tear." Other accounts, which had nothing to do with Barbara, simply presented him as a lecher:

> Franklin, though plagued with fumbling age,
> Needs nothing to excite him,
> But is too ready to engage,
> When younger arms invite him.[30]

Just as he had robbed Barbara of her virtue, so also had he stolen the discoveries of others in electricity. William Smith had first charged him with this theft in 1758, attributing the invention of the equipment used in his experiments to Ebenezer Kinnersley, another "electrician" in Philadelphia. But Kinnersley denied that Franklin had taken anything from him—far from it; he said that he had learned much from Franklin. The memory faded of that incident, which saw Franklin's name cleared almost immediately, but in 1764 Smith was at it again. This time others repeated the old story and at least one insisted that Franklin was not only a thief of ideas but also a beggar, when not actually a buyer, of honorary degrees. He had recently received a degree from Oxford, at about the time one was bestowed on Smith. Smith had tried to persuade the Oxford faculty that Franklin lacked merit and should be denied the degree. Here then was another case of a failure being transformed by Smith into a charge against Franklin.[31]

According to an unfriendly newspaper, Franklin was greedy for political offices as well as degrees and honors and fame that he had not earned. The real reason he wanted royal government was to make himself the royal governor of Pennsylvania. He was a political climber, surrounded by men of similar tastes: Galloway; Joseph Fox, the barracks master; and John Hughes, all of whom wanted land as well as royal appointments.[32]

That Franklin as agent had bilked the province out of money seems a mild charge compared with several of the others brought against him. Still, the accusation was made, and with it the charge that he had wasted £6,000 of the public's money when he was last in England. There was real basis for this accusation, though the "waste," which came from Franklin's investing the reimbursement paid in England for expenditures made during the French and Indian War, was closer to £2,000.[33]

One of the blows against Franklin concerned his reference in 1755 to the Germans as "Palatine Boors," a term he used in a tract on population growth. His enemies accused him of blatant prejudice. By boors, they said, he meant "hogs," a designation not likely to endear him or the cause of royal government to the immigrants from German provinces. What Franklin intended is not clear, though the word "boor" was often construed in the eighteenth century as referring to peasants, not hogs, and to German peasants in particular. But the usage was not helpful to the campaign, and it was featured in newspapers in English and German.[34]

The most interesting charge against Franklin had a long history. It was that he was a leveler, contemptuous of a proper hierarchy in society, a leader of a movement of the socially unqualified. William Smith insisted that the signers of the petition for royal government were "very generally of a low rank, many of whom could neither read nor write." The "wiser and better part of the Province," a group that did not include the likes of Benjamin Franklin, opposed the petition, convinced that should the proprietary government be lost, so also would their "birthright," their claim to religious and political liberties.[35]

Tying the opposition to royal government to the defense of the traditional liberties of Pennsylvania was a shrewd tactic—and probably one founded on fact. The Quaker minority and religious dissenters of all sorts probably would have faced disabilities imposed by a royal government buttressed by the Church of England. How serious for their actual right to worship these disabilities would have been cannot of course be known.

But Smith implied in his preface to Dickinson's speech of May 24 that he knew and that behind the movement for royal government lay a plot to fasten a leveling government on the province. A small group of plotters would seize the advantage that dispossessing the proprietor would give them to impose their own control. Only a "patriot Minority" opposed their schemes.[36]

Thomas Penn had entertained such fears of Franklin for almost twenty years. He had often used the word "republican" to describe Franklin and his ideas. The word had a certain plasticity; its uses revealed some deep-seated fear about American society. There apparently was something unhealthy in America, some design to overturn social arrangements. And Franklin represented this dark design. He was, as Penn had written in 1748, the "tribune" of the people.[37]

Someone failed to let the people in on this secret in 1764, and in the election they turned Franklin out and with him Galloway as well. Franklin stood for election from both Philadelphia County and the city of Philadelphia, an unusual arrangement on first sight, but customary in Pennsylvania. He lost in both races, finishing second from the bottom on a ballot that included fourteen candidates for county seats. Eight openings were to be filled; Franklin finished fourteenth. Isaac Norris finished at the top with 3,874 votes; Franklin received 1,906; Galloway had twelve votes more than Franklin. His chief critic in the election, John Dickinson, was third among the winners.[38]

This outcome surprised Franklin, although it did not surprise his enemies. He had been elected every year since 1751, and he expected his tenure in the Assembly to continue. His enemies read the political portents better than he, with no illusions about the way the public regarded the proposal to discard the proprietor in favor of the king. By September, ten days before the election, John Penn wrote home to Thomas Penn that the whole province seemed determined to turn Franklin and Galloway out. The governor and his friends took heart from more than the local signs. Thomas Penn had sent word that he had approached Halifax, the secretary of state, and Hyde, the postmaster general, about Franklin's threat to the proprietor. He told these two officials that Franklin, the deputy postmaster in America, was in violation of his oath to uphold the government. Penn wanted Franklin warned against persisting in his opposition. The likelihood of losing his appointment, a lucrative post, should not escape him. Thomas Penn assumed that the British officials wrote letters of warning. If they did, they do not survive, though Governor Penn reported home that when the subject of the letters was mentioned to Franklin, "he attempted to be witty upon it, and said that whatever the other party might think, he was not to be *Hyde Bound.*" The quotation, with its play on Hyde's name, has the feel of Franklin about it. The governor and Chief Justice William Allen, who despised Franklin, thought Franklin's quip was simply whistling in the dark. Allen noted that Franklin was "gloomy" and "silent" about the time the letters were thought to arrive.[39]

Soon, however, the enemies felt gloom. For as the governor reported to his uncle in mid-October, some two weeks after the election, Franklin might be out of the Assembly, but he still ran it. And Benjamin Chew, another proprietary partisan, remarked in early November that Franklin and Galloway met every night before each sitting of the Assembly to lay their plans for what should happen there.[40]

What happened next displeased the Proprietary Party. Three weeks after the election, the Assembly refused to recall the petition for royal government and then decided to send Franklin to England as an agent to join Richard Jackson, already its representative there, to present the petition at an appropriate time. The Proprietary Party fought hard in the Assembly, but it was outnumbered and lost every vote, including one on a proposal to enter in the minutes their resolutions against Franklin's appointment.[41]

Franklin sailed for England on November 7, sent off with what seems to have been a carefully plotted celebration of his merits. Besides praise there were cheers, the salutes of cannon, and this song sung to the music of "God Save the King":

O Lord our GOD arise,
Scatter our Enemies
  And make them fall.
Confound their politics,
Frustrate such Hypocrites
Franklin, on Thee we fix,
GOD save us all.[42]

Scattering his enemies surely appealed to Franklin. He left
America having delivered a volley at those who had opposed his
appointment as agent. "I forgive my Enemies," he wrote in the
last line of his *Remarks on a Late Protest Against the Appointment of
Mr. Franklin an Agent for this Province,*[43] apparently published the
day he left Philadelphia. He may have forgiven them, but he gave
them a good drubbing while extending forgiveness. They had mis-
construed much that he had done in the service of the province.
They distorted his motives in opposing the proprietor; they mis-
stated the reasons for his investment of public money in the London stocks; they exaggerated the extent of his defeat at the polls.

Franklin's concern for his reputation is very much in evidence
in this tract. His skin, usually so thick, never felt thinner and never
sweated the smell of disappointment so powerfully. His dislike of
William Allen, referred to here indirectly as the "Informer" or
directly as the chief justice, was clear. Allen had come back from
England in August saying that several powerful men in the government had little use for Franklin. An Anglophile most of his life
and an especially strong one in these years just before the Revolution, Benjamin Franklin felt the sting of these reports. They were
false, he asserted, given by a man practiced in lying about others.
Indeed Allen's "long Success in maiming or murdering all the
Reputations that stand in his Way, which has been the dear De-

light and constant Employment of his Life, may likewise have given him some just Ground for Confidence that he has, as they call it, *done for me*, among the rest."[44]

Almost inevitably someone responded in print to Franklin's defense of himself. The "someone" was almost certainly Provost William Smith. Franklin was still on the Atlantic Ocean when Smith's *Answer to Mr. Franklin's Remarks* appeared. Calling this screed an answer did not do it justice, although Smith attempted to reply to all of Franklin's argument. Perhaps knowledge that Franklin was on board a ship carrying him thousands of miles away stripped away Smith's inhibitions. Whatever the reason, his hatred of Franklin now found unrestrained expression. Franklin's *Remarks* were "artfully" but not "honestly" presented. They exposed the "wicked and virulent spirit" of an "inflammatory and virulent man." His mouth was "foul"; he was "crafty" and "ambitious"; "slander and scurrility" came naturally to him. He was an "ungrateful incendiary" whose "delight" was in "contention." His conduct had earned the dislike of all religious groups save one in the province, and that group (unnamed by Smith, who obviously had the Quakers in mind) contained many "serious men" who "detested" him. Franklin was, in short, "a very bad man, or one delirious with rage, disappointment and malice"—bearing "the most unpopular and odious name in the province."[45]

Thus Franklin left for England with cheers, songs, and doubtful verse sounding in his ears and jeers and sneers echoing not far behind. No one seemed indifferent to his virtues and flaws, both of which excited much discussion in Pennsylvania. The Quakers with stern consciences—the sort he referred to at other times as the "stiff-rumps"—may have regarded him with the least passion of all, but even they felt uneasy about his mission. Israel Pemberton, one of the greatest and most powerful of this group, suspected him of political ambition and speculated that Franklin had the governorship of the province in mind. He did not believe that Franklin would simply follow the Assembly's instructions to protect the constitutional and religious liberties of Pennsylvania above all else if a bold gamble would give him power. Pemberton told David Barclay, one of the London Quakers, that whatever happened, the "aversion" with which Franklin and Thomas Penn regarded one another would make any political accommodation difficult. In any case, Pemberton implied, Franklin's chief interest was in himself, and he would conduct himself accordingly.[46]

Franklin's friends in Pennsylvania would not have found Pemberton's opinions shocking, though of course they thought them mistaken. They expected much from this mission—he had left them with the belief that the proprietor would be displaced, and nothing in the first months of his absence discouraged them. In March of the new year—1765—word came from England of Franklin's safe arrival. His supporters in Philadelphia immediately set off a loud celebration with bells ringing half the night, bonfires, and much parading about. John Penn listened in misery, but there was nothing he or anyone else could do.[47]

London provided no similar greeting, and Franklin quietly settled again on Craven Street with Mrs. Stevenson. But if there were no celebrations of his arrival, there were those who watched his every move. Thomas Penn was the most observant—and the most interested.

Penn professed not to fear Franklin. He refused to have anything to do with him, but he tracked his steps obsessively. What most interested Penn was the timing of submitting the petition. Franklin had scarcely arrived when Penn reported to correspondents in America that he had not put the petition before the Privy Council. But, he, Penn, had no fear of Franklin and his schemes for royal government. The ministers of the king did not want to hear such a request according to Penn. They had other things on their minds. In any case, Penn insisted that he was unconcerned; Franklin would fail.[48]

In these ruminations and in these professions of bravery the truth stood out: Penn feared Franklin, despised him, and in his heart of hearts recognized that there was something deeply personal in Franklin's actions, for he recognized Franklin's hatred and commented on it. In July, as he reported Franklin's inaction, he also perversely noted Franklin's "dishonourable" way of acting. Franklin, he wrote in July, was "doing me all the mischief" he could. Franklin, he told John Penn, was "our plague," and acted out of "private pique and resentment."[49]

For a moment in November 1765, the fear seemed to vanish. Franklin presented the petition to the Lords of Trade, who immediately postponed considering it. One of them told Penn that it would never be considered, and the postponement could be taken as rejection. Penn wrote of his pleasure to the governor in Pennsylvania. The move for royal government had been stopped; the danger had passed.[50]

But if this were so, Penn's reactions to Franklin thereafter are incomprehensible. For the familiar pattern of reports soon appeared again. What was Franklin doing, he asked? A leading minister told Penn that Franklin had nothing to do in England; yet there he remained. Would he try again? Penn claimed not to be concerned—he did not fear Franklin even though he was evil and scheming.[51]

Franklin through all these months, which stretched into years, waited for an opening. Meanwhile he said little about Thomas Penn. The first failure did not discourage him, and he found encouragement where in fact none existed. For a while he thought that Shelburne favored his cause, though in fact, as far as one can tell, Shelburne cared little for it. And Shelburne in 1765 married the niece of Lady Juliana Fermor Penn, wife of Thomas Penn. During these years Franklin wrote Galloway several times that the prospects for a change were good. All his letters home carried a similar message: the petition would be submitted again, and it would succeed. To be sure, from spring 1765 on, the growing crisis over taxation (which raised constitutional issues) preoccupied him. He tried to stop passage of the Stamp Act, and when it was passed, he appeared before Commons to testify against it. Thereafter he threw himself into the struggle against parliamentary control.[52]

These years in the late 1760s saw frequent changes in the English government as one coalition after another attempted to establish its control. Early in 1768 one of these changes brought a new organization to handle colonial affairs and put a new man, Lord Hillsborough, in charge. Franklin at first did not sense that this change promised trouble for the movement for royal government. He met with Hillsborough, told him of his mission, and was told that Hillsborough would think of it. In August Hillsborough let him know that he and the king's government did not favor the petition. Franklin thereupon wrote Galloway that he would do nothing more: the struggle for royal government was over. He, and the Assembly, he might have added, were beaten.[53]

The news of failure hit Galloway hard. The Quaker Party, which included several important merchants who heard from Franklin fairly regularly and wrote him even more often, never recovered from the blow. Its disintegration began when its principal reason for being disappeared. Galloway became sick shortly after Franklin's letter reached him, but had he remained healthy there was nothing he could do. After almost a year's silence he wrote Franklin again, but the friendship had changed and their old confidences disappeared from their letters. Almost as a reflex, one suspects, the Assembly Committee of Correspondence repeated the old formula about the petition the next year. Franklin ignored this message. He had given up, he seemed to say, and so should the Assembly.[54]

Why had he persisted so long in any case, especially since all the evidence—on both sides of the Atlantic—forecast failure? The immediate reason was his hatred of Thomas Penn, a hatred so powerful as to overcome his reason. The hatred of Penn was obsessive, uncontrollable, and almost without limits.

Franklin's obsession can be explained, though it remains surprising even after it is considered. For his passion led Franklin into conduct that defied his most profound impulses. Franklin's social being nourished itself after all in tolerance of aberrant behavior; it resisted—ordinarily—extravagant action. Franklin respected evidence and generally seemed willing to assume the best about others. At least he acted this way, whatever he actually felt about those around him. His was a generous and calm spirit. But in this case his feeling about Penn overcame all of his usual standards of conduct, skewed his vision, and set him on a course that he abandoned only after years of reckless behavior.

In any undertaking Franklin expected to get what he wanted; he regarded success almost as his due. He was a dominating man, often without seeming to be. Indeed, one of his skills was the ability to get his way, even in difficult circumstances, usually without crushing others. His skill in disguising his purposes led others to regard him as bland. And in fact his surface was ordinarily smooth;

his temper modest or even nonexistent; his manner kind and generous. But at his core a powerful will throbbed, and its desires were almost always satisfied. It was this will to overcome all obstacles that kept him in this struggle. Too simply put, there was in Franklin a deep impulse to succeed, to win, even to dominate while appearing not to.

Occasionally the mask of blandness slipped and Franklin showed his teeth. Such an event had occurred in late 1756 shortly after the arrival in August of the new governor, Captain William Denny. Franklin and several other members of the Assembly confronted Denny and the council over the old question of taxes. Franklin, according to Richard Peters, secretary of the province and a member of the council, "behaved with great rudeness and insolence" to the governor. At the height of anger Franklin told Denny that because he did not "protect the People" he was "no Governor," but a "meer Bashaw." Likening Denny to a Turkish leader while suggesting with the adjective "meer" that all in all he was not much could only be taken as a major insult. For Turkey was synonymous with despotism in eighteenth-century America and Britain. Denny submitted to this sneer "tamely," according to Peters; and Franklin, who had evidently read his man correctly, demonstrated that his repertoire included abusive, near-violent behavior.[55]

Franklin believed that the movement for royal government would succeed. He did not enter the fray with a faint heart, and he did not shrink when he and his colleagues in the Quaker Party encountered strong and ruthless resistance. That he would fail did not occur to him.

Long before he decided to try to drive Thomas Penn from control of Pennsylvania, he had worked out his methods of getting what he wanted. They had become as natural to him as breathing. They depended upon reading men; some tactics worked with one sort; others had to be tried when the first failed. Most often Franklin relied on rational persuasion. His own good will was obvious in most of his projects—getting the streets paved or a fire company, a lending library, a hospital, an academy organized. His spirit and his interest in the public and his ability to persuade others that what he wanted was in the public's interest were usually enough. Evidence, reason, persuasion, and honesty came into play in much of his success.

But reading men taught Franklin early in his life that the acts of rational persuasion were not always sufficient to the task at hand. He resorted to manipulation just as often as he did to persuasion. And no doubt nothing he tried—no tactic, no device—was ever free of cleverness, of some manipulation in leading men to work on causes they really did not wish to undertake. He was not a trickster but an adroit man who did not always proceed along a straight line to what he wanted. For that reason he rarely revealed all of himself, or the hand he held, while seeming to be perfectly open. He offered in *Poor Richard's Almanac* advice to be open to others but also to conceal oneself: "Let all Men know thee, but no man know thee thoroughly; Men freely ford that see the shallows."[56] He also played several roles when they suited his purposes. The public-spirited benefactor was a favorite, and most of the time it actually reflected what he was. There was no falseness in his efforts to improve life in Philadelphia.

These methods of dealing with the world served him well in Philadelphia—and for a time in Pennsylvania's politics. But they were not enough in dealing with Thomas Penn, a mean and unbending man with a well-developed sense of his own interest. Penn's character was only one part of the problem he posed. He was, after all, the proprietor and armed with a charter that the Crown had issued to his father. He was also a part of the English establishment, a gentleman who knew the hidden rocks and shoals of English politics and the safe passages through them to political power.

In dealing with Penn, Franklin first tried the techniques that had served so well in provincial politics. His first mission in the years 1757–62 was to persuade the proprietor to pay his share of taxes and to allow his local representative, the governor, to act as an executive free of crippling instructions. Franklin attempted in this effort to appeal to Penn's pride in William Penn, his father, only to discover that Penn felt little or none. Certainly he felt no obligation to follow his father's example—at least as Franklin and the Assembly understood it. Franklin also appealed to Penn's sense of fairness, an effort that brought him nothing. Invoking an interest that he argued the province and the proprietor had in common produced no results. Thus persuasion—appeals to an enlightened past as well as a common interest—fell flat. The rebuff Penn delivered sent Franklin home frustrated and angered.

For the first time in his life he met failure. This sent him off in quest of royal government. But the people of Pennsylvania told him plainly in 1764 that they wanted nothing of royal government. So it was back to England, where he persisted in the face of evidence obvious to everyone else in the country that in England the opposition was even more inflexible than in Pennsylvania. In 1768 he gave it up—a failed mission, a lost cause.

A powerful man, a man accustomed to dominating in any situation in which he found himself, at the peak of his powers, and recognized for his genius in science, was frustrated by the conservatism of the people he served in Pennsylvania and defeated by an English gentleman apparently inferior in morals and intellect. Thomas Penn's character made defeat hard to take, and Penn's sneers, snubs, and aloofness made it worse. Franklin was one of those winners who learned only belatedly when to cut his losses. The anger that arose in this situation is surely understandable, and it helps us comprehend—at least in part—his dogged, some said mad, persistence in the movement for royal government.

There may have been one other source of his anger and stubborn refusal to give up. Franklin at times felt unsure of his place in the society that set the standards of gentility in England and America. He was not by most criteria a gentleman and did not really feel himself to be one even after he retired from business. Nor did the knowledge that he had attained a fame few men ever secure relieve the uncertainty about his place on the social ladder. In a peculiar yet forceful way, this uncertainty may have sharpened the edge of his hatred of Thomas Penn.

But it did not ordinarily trouble him, and he was never pretentious enough to suffer anything so grand as "status anxiety." His social origins were in the lower or middle classes, a fact that interested him greatly, and of which he made skillful use in demonstrating that he had risen far above his beginnings. He described the English branch of the family from which his father sprang as "obscure." His father, a dyer in England and a tallow chandler in Boston, was one in a long line of freemen, virtually all craftsmen generation after generation. His grandfather had been a scrivener, a writer of contracts and other legal documents. The uncle after whom he was named was a silk dyer who served his apprenticeship in London.[57]

Franklin's father was an emigrant, born in 1658 in England, coming to America in 1683. His mother, Abiah Folger, born in Nantucket, came from equally undistinguished stock—her father earned his living as a weaver, miller, and surveyor and also taught school while he served as clerk of the town court. Her mother had been an indentured servant before marrying Peter Folger, who first bought her and then married her. Franklin described her as a woman with "an excellent Constitution; she suckled all her ten Children." She was, he reported, "a discreet and excellent woman." The American branch of the Franklins, like the English, remained in the ranks of craftsmen, skilled and solid in reputation but in no way of the gentry.[58]

The use Franklin made of his "low" beginnings and his simple family is clear in his *Autobiography* as well as in a variety of occasional writings. That he offered himself as a model of what a man devoted to work and virtue might do with his life has been remarked upon for many years. He describes his arrival as a boy in Philadelphia, with all he owned on his back and with the rolls of bread he purchased bulging out of his pockets, "that you may in your Mind compare such unlikely Beginnings with the Figure I have since made there." He also reports on his public recognition in his election to offices of government, saying that his "Ambition" was "flatter'd" by these "Promotions." And he cannot resist concluding that considering "my low Beginning they were great Things to me." His pride stands out in these accounts—my beginnings were not much, he seems to say, but look at me now.

By the time Franklin began his effort to replace the proprietor with the Crown, he had earned a modest fortune and a reputation as a great scientist. He was also a writer, a printer of a newspaper, a faithful servant of his country—Pennsylvania—and by most lights a worthy man. He was also well known and admired in England and France. But not by Thomas Penn and apparently not by the men who ran the British government. Franklin had in a sense transcended his class. He had not repudiated it, nor was he ashamed of his origins, but he was still not a gentleman. He had neither the land nor the family that would have given him gentle status.

Thomas Penn had a way of getting under his skin that owed something to Penn's crabbed spirit and his selfishness but also to the impression that Penn conveyed that Benjamin Franklin was beneath him. When Penn first heard that Franklin was coming to

England, he said that Franklin's reputation as a scientist would not carry him far with those who counted—those of social standing—in England. Those who made decisions on political questions, Penn implied, either did not know of Franklin's electrical experiments or were not impressed by such achievements in science. Penn often remarked on Franklin as a leader of the people, a crafty and adroit man, but of republican principles. Popular leaders did not stand high in Penn's estimation, and he did not trust "the people." Nor did the gentry and aristocratic classes in England. Franklin was of the people and, according to Penn, despite all his talents, a leveler. He was also a colonial, another classification that put him on the outside—and down the social scale.

The social scale provided an important measure in Penn's estimation. He once upbraided his nephew John, then governor of Pennsylvania, when in a letter that worthy addressed the Privy Council as gentlemen. Nephew John should know, his uncle wrote, that the council was not composed of mere gentlemen—its members were peers, men of noble blood, and should be addressed with appropriate deference as "Lords."[59]

There were echoes of these attitudes in Pennsylvania among the proprietor's supporters. Some of these men in the election of 1764 took to referring to Franklin as the "Philosopher," a scientist, in other words, who worked with his hands using Leyden jars and other electrical apparatus. One of them, most likely William Smith, implied that Franklin ought to confine himself to such work, the implication being that in the political world his gifts were insufficient or irrelevant.

Undoubtedly, such scorn wounded Franklin and made giving up the fight for royal government harder. Especially wounding was the assumption at the root of Penn's disdain—Franklin was an outsider, a leveler and a republican, and therefore inferior. In this political struggle he was, at least in Penn's eyes, socially unworthy. Franklin had never faced such attitudes before and would not encounter them again until the early phases of the crisis leading to the American Revolution. He knew he was not a marginal man, but in Thomas Penn and the British officials behind Penn, he ran up against political power greater than any he could command. The disparity in power provided the context for his struggles, a context he attempted to change by going over Penn's head with the petition for royal government. But Penn's power was too much for him, despite all his efforts to overcome it. Through all his failures, he saw Penn's smugness and felt his force. His own anger grew as he failed and soon turned into hatred. This hatred trapped him just as effectively as Penn ever did, long after it should have been clear that he could not replace proprietary with royal government.

What made giving up finally possible for Franklin was another struggle, much larger and, in the end, of momentous consequences. For in the three years preceding his admission of defeat in 1768, the king's government, the government for which he had expressed over many years immense trust and faith, took actions against American liberties. And in the seven years following 1768, before Americans declared their independence, it revealed its contempt for American claims to self-government in the empire. Franklin saw the threat and threw himself into the defense of America. In the process he acquired another enemy—Britain and her ministers. Perhaps Britain was an essential enemy, essential to his discovery that he was an American.

CHAPTER 5

An Old Friend Becomes an Enemy

Celebrated in American popular culture today as a skirt-chaser, or among more informed and genteel circles as a suitor of the ladies of Paris, Benjamin Franklin was derided in his own day as the lover of low women. He was responsible for both reputations. When he was old, he confessed that as a young man he had consorted with women of the streets, and he explained his marriage to Deborah Read as a means of satisfying those physical urges that had carried him to the whores of Philadelphia. As for the ladies of Paris, his papers are full of letters and bagatelles revealing his fascination with those glittering creatures. Others in Paris found watching the old man in action interesting and often shocking, and they reported to friends in America their prurient observations. But not content with mere reporting, they often added their own scandalized comments.

Most of the gossip about Franklin's sexual exploits in Paris can be safely discounted. He was seventy years of age when he arrived in France in 1776. During his long stay there he often suffered from gout and sometimes could hardly walk. He had other ailments during this period. But his mind remained active in his afflicted body, and perhaps it led him to expectations and even hopes impossible of fulfillment. Indeed, reading his correspondence of this period and remembering what we know of his physical condition, we might conclude that Franklin's sex life was very much like Jane Austen's novels—all talk and no action.

Yet thinking of Franklin as a lover is not an absurdity. He was a man who needed affection and who gave it. And he did like women. Well into his mature years he conducted a flirtation— usually at long distance—with Catherine Ray Greene of Rhode Island. She was much younger than he, and if he actually tried to seduce her, he seems to have been turned down. How serious he was about Madame Brillon remains hidden. But he was fond of her. Margaret Stevenson, his landlady in London for many years, was also the subject of speculation. She too drew his affection, but we do not know how far their relationship went. We do know that he loved her, and loved her daughter, Polly, as well.[1]

But the great love of his life was not a woman. He loved his work more, and his science, and his country. Before the American Revolution, he loved England and the British Empire more than anything else and probably more than anyone else. They were the great loves that stirred him most deeply.

Franklin's first visit to England, in 1724, did not create his affection for that nation, though he was happy there. He was young, and he stayed a little less than two years. His return to America was not accompanied by lamentations over opportunities left behind in England. He knew then that his future lay in America, and he plunged back eagerly into Philadelphia life.

The next visit, in 1757, stretched into a five-year immersion in London life and English politics. By this time he enjoyed a great reputation for his scientific achievements among English intellectuals, some of whom had read at least a part of his writings. He was a mature man, a delightful companion, sure of himself, and prepared for the give-and-take of any circle he joined. Although he had come to England on an assignment given him by the Pennsylvania legislature, and even though he had work to do, he had ample time to meet many luminaries and to make a big splash. And that he did, though it was not his purpose to do so.

The English took to him, all except Thomas Penn and his friends, and Franklin came to love his hosts. Almost everything about England pleased him, and when he left the country in 1762, he took his leave resolving to return. At this point he was probably as much an Englishman as an American. While he waited in Portsmouth in August 1762 for friendly winds and tide to carry him to America, he consoled himself and his friends with the thought that he would most likely soon come back. He had to go home to consult the Assembly about the next step in the struggle with Thomas Penn; he also knew that he must see Deborah, who missed him. He missed her too, but his feelings did not equal hers. While awaiting favorable weather in ugly and depressing Portsmouth, he wrote the following to Strahan, his dear old friend: "I cannot, I assure you, quit even this disagreeable Place without Regret, as it carried me still farther from those I love, and from the Opportunities of hearing of their Welfare. The Attraction of *Reason* is at present for the other Side of the Water, but that of *Inclination* will be for this side." Franklin, the rationalist, recognized that reason did not usually triumph over feeling, even in his own life, and he added these words about reason and inclination—"You know which usually prevails. I shall probably make but this one Vibration and settle here for ever."[2]

Once back home, he learned that Deborah did not wish to be taken to England, and in December Franklin admitted that he still had to persuade "the good Woman to cross the Seas."[3] While he was about it, he recalled the good times in England and ruminated on the qualities that made that nation great. To Mary Stevenson he declared in 1763 that "of all the enviable Things England has, I envy it most its People." And then he asked the question: "Why should that pretty Island, which compared to America is but like a stepping Stone in a Brook, scarce enough of it above Water to keep one's Shoes dry; why, I say, should that little Island, enjoy in almost every Neighbourhood, more sensible, virtuous and elegant Minds, than we can collect in ranging 100 Leagues of our vast Forests."[4]

Franklin never tried to answer this question. It was a rhetorical effusion in any case, an expression of the affection he felt for his friends in England and evidence of his romantic conception of their nation. In his more sober moments, which he experienced when he was not thinking of friends but rather of abstractions— or at least of the nation and the empire in general terms—a certain ambivalence found its way into his thought. England was great, but its power arose from an empire that included the American colonies. Franklin had believed for many years—at least since 1751—that the growth of the colonies' population and production forecast a transfer of the center of the empire to America. In 1763, on the eve of the crisis with Britain, with his patriotism near white heat, he suggested that the foundations of the future grandeur and stability of the empire lay in America; foundations were low to the ground and therefore not easily seen, but they were soon to be sufficient to support the greatest political structure human wisdom had yet erected. Pride in the colonies and the empire is obvious in these statements, but at this point it was England's greatness—and the beauty and wisdom of its people and institutions—that Franklin most insisted on.[5]

Cracks appeared in his certainty in 1765 with the passage of the Stamp Act. With others, Franklin attempted to dissuade George Grenville, the English minister who proposed the act, from placing it before Parliament. The Stamp Act imposed taxes on Americans for the purpose of collecting a revenue, an innovation in their governance, Franklin and most Americans believed. But shortly after the passage of the statute he arranged for the appointment of John Hughes as the stamp distributor in Pennsylvania. People will be unhappy with you for this appointment, he wrote Hughes, but they will recover. Three thousand miles away in America such cheer was poor solace. Hughes faced an angry mob when the news of his appointment got out, and he soon resigned his new post. Franklin was shocked by this outcome. He had never liked riots and tumults, and the reaction to the Stamp Act surprised him. In fact, even before Hughes had felt the wrath of the people, Franklin had learned of the Virginia Resolves, which delivered a direct challenge to Parliament's authority to levy taxes in America. Taxation by a body in which they were not represented constituted tyranny, the Virginians insisted. Franklin may not have liked what the Virginians said, and he had even less use for the mobbing of stamp distributors up and down the colonies in late 1765 and early 1766, but he soon put himself with the opposition to parliamentary taxation.[6]

By the end of 1765, when the stamp tax was imposed, Franklin was referring to the "insolence" of British judgments of American resistance. It was a word he was to use often in the coming ten years in describing English attitudes toward America. These years in fact saw a transformation of almost all his convictions about England, and they also saw the affection he felt for the English converted into hatred. It was a process that picked up speed after 1768, when he gave up one of his prized illusions: the notion that substituting royal government for the Penn dynasty would win the approval of the Crown.[7]

The process of shedding his illusions lagged behind his thought about the empire and the rights of the colonies under the British Constitution. Once he made up his mind about what Parliament could and could not do under the Constitution, there was not much change in his political thought—not much change, that is, until he renounced all allegiance to the king. It was the monarchy that he clung to in these years before independence, a monarchy that served as a symbol of both power and virtue.

Franklin defined his constitutional theory during the crisis over the Stamp Act. Resistance at home had a marvelous effect on him, clarifying the issues and his mind. Parliament, he soon decided, had no authority in America, and the only connection between England and America was the king. The colonial legislatures were in fact parliaments and only they possessed the power to tax and legislate in America. Even the colonial allegiance to the king proved tenuous in this theory. Franklin asked in 1765 whether the children born in America of English parents were subjects of the king. The answer was, only if they gave their consent—an early version of volitional citizenship. Franklin pointed out, moreover, that if Parliament violated colonial charters—most of which had been issued in the seventeenth century by the Crown—it would destroy even this flimsy basis of loyalty.[8]

To persuade Parliament and the ministry to give up taxing America, Franklin performed all the conventional acts of imperial politicians: he wrote letters and essays for the newspapers in defense of the American position; he talked with English leaders, making the same arguments; he encouraged the colonial legislatures he represented to make evident their own displeasure at English measures. Besides Pennsylvania and Georgia, Franklin took on Massachusetts, accepting appointment as agent of the lower house late in 1770. He was now in direct communication with the most radical resistance in America.[9]

Franklin's own preferences for resistance were not radical. Nor did he really expect much to come from his letters to newspapers. Although from the very beginning of the crisis he felt affronted by what he called the "insolence, contempt, and abuse" of Americans for their rejection of Parliament's claims to unlimited sovereignty, a violent response seemed inappropriate. Anything that smacked of rebellion would simply bring greater oppression to the colonies. The most promising tactic for Americans, Franklin thought, was economic pressure. He had threatened the House of Commons with the prospect of a rise in American manufacturing when he testified before it against the Stamp Act, and during the Townshend crisis and in the years between 1773 and 1776, he returned to this theme. Stop importing British goods, he told his American clients; when that tactic failed, the message became stop imports and begin making goods yourselves.[10]

This strategy appealed to Franklin's deepest values. Work, productivity, industry, and frugality always struck him as proper aims of a good people. Resistance to Britain could be made to serve virtue, could indeed make the Americans a better people. This was an idea that made its way into much of his thought in these years before independence.

Beneath such recommendations to Americans, beneath all his ruminations on the scope of Parliament's power and colonial rights, beneath his search for means to change British policy, the transformation of his love of England occurred. The years between 1765 and 1775 were years in which affection died and anger was born. These years saw hatred replace love.

The process was not one he was conscious of, and in fact he struggled against his feelings. Surely as aware as anyone of how the conflict with Britain might end were Parliament not to give up its claims to the power "to bind the colonies in all cases whatsoever," he nevertheless fought against his own inclinations to repudiate his Englishness. At times others pointed out that he was more of an American than an Englishman, but he resisted the characterization until it could not be escaped.[11]

Initially the feeling he found hardest to admit to himself was that the king was an enemy. His reluctance might have had some basis in the old convention, weak as it was, that the monarch could do no wrong though his government could. In the crisis of the 1760s Franklin may at first have been inhibited by this old assumption; but more powerful in his feeling was an admiration for the young king, an admiration fathered by sentiment and ignorance of the man he admired.[12]

In the first years of the reign Franklin could see only the benign side of the king's government. Rid of that misconception in the mid-1760s, he discovered that royal government had another face. And the young king, he came to believe, was not quite as he had imagined.

But bringing himself to denounce George III was difficult even as the colonies approached and then plunged into war. Early in the king's reign Franklin had declared himself convinced that the monarch was a man of virtue. He wrote Strahan in 1763 forecasting a "happy and truly glorious" reign. Closer to the scene and unawed by the likes of kings, Strahan coolly offered a different assessment—that the king was virtuous but lacked any "striking talents."[13] This was not the only exchange between the two men on George III. Franklin expressed dismay that the treaty ending the Seven Years' War was a subject of dispute in England and worried about its effect on the king. In the end he declared himself convinced that George III would transcend factions by his firmness and virtue. Strahan did not share this simple faith, but he did not disabuse Franklin of his illusions.[14]

After the crisis of the Stamp Act, George III largely disappeared from Franklin's thought as a decisive figure. He saw almost nothing of the king in these years before independence, but much of the king's ministers. These men—Hillsborough, North, Dartmouth, and a scattering of others in the government—drew his attention and eventually produced his deepest disillusionment and then his anger and hatred.

As much as he came to dislike the king's ministers, especially

Hillsborough and North, Franklin shrank from the final rupture that brought independence. He cherished his affection for the empire—it was, after all, a center of power and strength. It was also a structure within which American liberties and rights had flourished. But the men who governed in the king's name seemed heedless of the dangers they ran in taxing the Americans and in sending troops to put down their resistance to taxes. They seemed indifferent to American interests and American opinion. And before too long they seemed to Franklin unyielding enemies of America.

It was easier to dislike and then hate them than it was to contemplate the smashup of the British Empire. But Franklin's encounters with the king's ministers completed the process of alienation from the empire and its leaders. First Lord of the Treasury George Grenville, who pushed the stamp tax into being, never really inspired Franklin's worst anger. Grenville had a simplicity about him that led men to dismiss him, but he never loomed large enough to draw Franklin's ire. He had a one-track mind and evidently a single purpose—reducing the Americans to due subordination while squeezing money out of them. Grenville did not last in power; by summer 1766, a few months after the Stamp Act's passage, he was gone from the king's government, never to return. He became quirky in his last years, a development Franklin remarked on in late 1767, when he reported that Grenville had stood up in Parliament in the debate on the king's address and insisted on talking about the colonies even though the king had not mentioned them. Franklin concluded that Grenville seemed "a little out of his Head on the Article of America." [15]

Others in the governments that followed impressed him as having all their senses, and an overdeveloped sense of their own importance. Lord Hillsborough was the worst. When in 1768 Hillsborough was appointed American secretary, with the colonies as his responsibility, Franklin may have hoped that he himself would join the new minister as Hillsborough's deputy. Franklin's friends in England suggested this possibility, but it never seemed likely to Franklin; he dismissed the rumors by saying that he was thought too much of an American to join the British government. Indeed he was too much of an American, though he did not know it yet. Hillsborough soon irked him anyway with his high-handed conduct toward the colonies. What made Hillsborough hard to take was his easy dismissal of the seriousness of American efforts to stop importing goods from England, which were undertaken to compel Parliament to repeal the Townshend taxes on imports into America. Hillsborough let it be known that he thought that American claims to virtue were a sham and that the Americans would soon get their fill of a life without British manufactures. According to Hillsborough they could not live without them, and any organization they formed to support a boycott could only be insubstantial—"a Rope of Sand."[16]

A few years later Franklin's annoyance at Hillsborough turned into disgust and anger. The occasion was Franklin's attempt in January 1771 to present to Hillsborough his credentials as the agent of the Massachusetts lower house. Hillsborough would have none of it, telling Franklin that an agent of a colony could be appointed only by a legislative act, a very remote possibility for the likes of a Franklin in Massachusetts, where Thomas Hutchinson, a strong supporter of the ministry's position and the governor, would have to assent to any bill before it became law. The discussion that day was altogether one-sided, with Hillsborough rejecting Franklin's arguments almost before they left his mouth. Franklin emerged with his feathers ruffled, his pride hurt, and an impression of Hillsborough as an inveterate enemy of America. "Conceit, wrongheadedness, Obstinacy and Passion" circumscribed Hillsborough's character, he said immediately after the argument.[17] He never changed his mind even though the next year

Hillsborough, learning of Franklin's journey to Ireland and Scotland, insisted that he include a visit to the Hillsborough estate in Ireland. Obviously wishing for tactical reasons to conciliate Franklin, Hillsborough turned on his charm—exuding kindness and indicating his need for American advice. The spigot was open, but the tank was low, and Franklin received the flow of goodwill with silent amusement and skepticism. He was anything but won over and likened Hillsborough's wooing to the "patting and stroking the Horse to make him more patient while the Reins are drawn tighter and the Spurs set deeper into his Sides."[18]

Hillsborough soon reverted to form, which included open dislike for opponents such as Franklin. He was present at the notorious scene of Franklin's humiliation before the Privy Council near the end of January 1774. But he did not play the role of chief antagonist that day. That part was left to Alexander Wedderburn, the solicitor general. The ostensible reason for calling Franklin before the council was to hold a final hearing on a petition from Massachusetts seeking the removal of Governor Thomas Hutchinson and Lieutenant Governor Andrew Oliver on the grounds that by their actions they had lost the confidence of the assembly and the people of Massachusetts. The hearing was held and the petition rejected, but that was only a part of the proceedings. The Privy Council, its meeting room packed with spectators including Edmund Burke and Joseph Priestley, before giving its decision listened to an attack of more than an hour on Franklin's political and personal conduct. The councillors present, some thirty-five, were apparently delighted as Wedderburn sank his barbs into Franklin. For they broke into laughter throughout the talk—only Lord North, the king's chief minister, remained quiet. Franklin later likened the mood of the hearing to that prevailing at a bull-baiting, a favorite English spectacle. In this instance he served as the bull, with Wedderburn his major tormentor.[19]

Wedderburn's attack had virtually nothing to do with the petition, but the presiding councillor gave him his head. The center of Wedderburn's assault on Franklin's political conduct was the contention that Franklin was part of a sinister plot in Massachusetts to destroy the king's government there and to lead the people into open opposition. The petition in this version of recent history was an aspect of a larger design, and Franklin acted as "the first mover and prime conductor" of what now stood revealed as a dangerous conspiracy.[20]

Wedderburn saved his deepest thrusts for Franklin's part in the scandal over the letters of Thomas Hutchinson and Andrew Oliver. These two officials had corresponded with friends in England about the American crisis. Among their correspondents was Thomas Whately, a subminister who had served George Grenville. In 1772 Franklin obtained a large number of these letters—exactly how is not known today, but someone must have stolen them and passed them to him. He read them avidly and, so he always claimed, with a feeling of relief, for the letters showed that some of the actions against America taken by Grenville's ministry and those that followed were suggested by Hutchinson and Oliver. Franklin professed to believe that this took away some of the sting of English policies—the policies were not strictly English after all, because these two Americans had proposed them. For that reason, Franklin contended, he sent them to Thomas Cushing, the Speaker of the lower house of the Massachusetts legislature and his master. Cushing, whom Franklin instructed not to make the letters public, was supposed to be as reassured as Franklin himself to find the real enemies of Massachusetts at home, not in England. Presumably, if Franklin's intentions were carried out, Cushing would share the letters in a confidential way with the legislature. Thus informed that the British government was not full of malevolent originality, the Massachusetts legislature might extend its patience, turn its cheek, and try to end disagreements in the confidence that the old benign policies of the British government might be recovered once everyone understood that English hearts were pure.[21]

Cushing published the letters in the *Boston Gazette* and thereby undercut Franklin's innocent scheme. We may doubt that Franklin was optimistic about reviving good relations by the expedient of sending the letters to America. We may also doubt that he expected Thomas Cushing and his colleagues to keep the letters within their tight little circle. Franklin, after all, once said—or at least printed in *Poor Richard's Almanac*—that "three may keep a secret if two of them are dead."[22] It is also difficult to think he really believed that the English governments of the 1760s and early 1770s were so pliant as to follow the lead of two American provincials. English ministers surely read the letters written to them in these years, and just as surely they did what they wanted to do.

Whatever Franklin's motives in sending the letters to America, he discovered standing before the committee of the Privy Council that he had aroused Wedderburn's fury. Nine days before this scene, news of the Boston Tea Party had arrived in England. Franklin later speculated that this example of Boston's spirit did not create sympathy for him. Wedderburn knew that his audience—the councillors and as many other leading lights of London life as could squeeze into the room—had evidently heard that the committee's session would not be the usual sleep-inducing performance of bureaucrats. Wedderburn kept them awake:

I hope, my Lords, you will mark [and brand] the man, for the honour of the country, of Europe, and of mankind. Private correspondence has hitherto been held sacred, in times of the

greatest party rage, not only in politics but religion. He has
forfeited all the respect of societies and of men. Into what
companies will he hereafter go with an unembarrassed face,
or the honest intrepidity of virtue. Men will watch him, and
lock up their escrutoires. He will henceforth esteem it a libel
to be called a *man of letters; homo trium literarum!*[23]

Franklin had to listen to much more; Wedderburn spoke for
almost an hour. He was lavish in his abuse, apparently encouraged
by the laughter of many in the audience whenever he landed what
was perceived as a telling blow. Most of his performance—for it
was political theater that he played in—ignored the issues that had
brought the council into session. But no one on the Privy Council
called him to order; the whole affair afforded too much pleasure
to men who had yearned to pull the colonials back into line.

As for Franklin, his self-control held. An observer standing
where he could look into Franklin's face reported that his expression, revealing nothing, remained the same throughout. Of course
he resented serving, as he said a few days later, as the "butt of his
[Wedderburn's] invective and ribaldry." The importance of his
humiliation was not lost on him. What the hearing revealed, he
thought, was more than coarseness in British governing circles; in
fact it provided an appalling example of the arrogance of a government so certain of its rectitude as to stoop to ridicule any who
questioned its conduct. When petitions expressing grievances became "so odious to government that even the mere pipe which
conveys them becomes obnoxious," Franklin wrote to Cushing, "I
am at a loss to know how peace and union is to be maintained or
restored between different parts of the empire."[24]

It was an understandable question even though it glided over
the extraordinary circumstances of the hearing. Had he not sent

the Hutchinson letters to Massachusetts, the mood of the Privy Council and of Wedderburn surely would have been different. The councillors would not have felt any sympathy for the request that Hutchinson and Oliver be removed, but their disposition would not have been so soured as to encourage a personal attack on Franklin.

Franklin's "anger," which he confessed to Cushing, and his humiliation led him to draw the implications out to an extreme. Or perhaps anger and humiliation helped him admit to himself that the possibilities of reconciliation were few. The British were as stiff-necked as any of the Quakers he had dealt with in the Pennsylvania Assembly years before. They were arrogant, and they looked down on colonials. As Franklin had noted a few years before, "Every Man in England seems to consider himself as a Piece of a Sovereign over America; seems to jostle himself into the Throne with the King, and talks of *OUR SUBJECTS in the Colonies.*"[25]

Franklin might have accepted the implications of these attitudes years before had he not been so romantic an imperialist. For all practical purposes, his estrangement from England was now complete, though he was not quite prepared to admit it. Still, his sad comment in the letter to Cushing that "when complaining is a crime, hope becomes despair" suggests that he had few illusions left.[26]

At the end of 1774 old friends in England, John Pringle and David Barclay, gave him some reason to moderate his despair. They told him that the ministry of Lord North wanted reconciliation. Franklin was skeptical, but he felt compelled to make one more effort. At almost the same time Mrs. Caroline Howe, sister of Rear Admiral Viscount Richard Howe, brought him together with her brother, who seemed to represent the government. Franklin and Mrs. Howe had begun their friendship a short time before by playing chess; he thought that chess was the reason for her interest in him. He now learned that the diplomatic game hovered over the chessboard. Throughout the next three months he talked with Admiral Howe—tantalizing talks, elusive, with Howe feeling him out, asking, for example, what would bring the Americans to settlement and at one point suggesting that if Franklin could present an acceptable plan of reconciliation, he could expect a reward within the power of the government to bestow. Franklin, who about twelve months before had felt wounded and angry, now experienced a sense of revulsion. To his son William he wrote that this offer of a bribe "to me was what the French call *Spitting in the Soup*."[27] Howe also proved expansive—would Franklin accompany him to America on a mission to restore the old good feeling? Franklin listened and told his friends and Admiral Howe that he was not authorized to enter into any agreement. By this time the First Continental Congress had met and adjourned, and if America had a voice, it was the Congress.[28]

While Howe made his moves and Franklin peered through the fog of British maneuvers, Lord Chatham, one of the great men in the nation and a hero to Franklin, sought him out to talk about American problems. Chatham charmed Franklin and impressed him, but his efforts, which were undoubtedly well intentioned and honest, failed in Parliament. Neither the House of Lords nor the Commons saw the danger, and neither house felt inclined to listen to Chatham, who had earned his reputation as a maverick and an eccentric.[29]

Franklin went home in 1775. The year was not quite three months old. His anger at Britain seems to have subsided, replaced by despair at imperial prospects. He probably still favored an America inside the empire—not outside it—but he had no hope, and his affection for England, if it existed at all, was covered by layers of dismay and suspicion.

These feelings overlay a profound sense of loss. The efforts of the past ten years had returned nothing except defeat in the political arena and disenchantment with almost everything he had admired in the English. The failure to persuade the British government to take over the proprietorship had been bad enough, but failure at least could be explained away as the product of recalcitrant ministries. At that time, 1768, he could still believe that governments do change. The political winds might yet blow from different directions, and in any case, his inability to expel Penn had not revealed flaws in the political system—as far as he was concerned.

All seemed different in 1775. The system of government stood exposed in its tawdry corruption. Where virtue had prevailed, bribery now served. Franklin reported to William in 1768 that "£4000 is now the market price for a borough." Equally shocking was how deep into society corruption had seeped—Franklin told William that "this whole venal nation is now at market, [and] will be sold for about Two Millions; and might be bought out of the hands of the present bidders (if he would offer half a million more) by the devil himself." There was bitterness in these remarks, a sense that virtue as well as elections had been put up for sale.[30]

As Franklin knew, the radical Whigs had insisted since the early part of the century that morality had departed public life and that the people themselves were not immune to the insidious effects of a general loss of standards in England. Franklin had read the radical Whig essays; he had heard the same sorts of assessments in the meetings of the Club of Honest Whigs. But it took his own experience in England to make him see and feel the loss. Almost all his old idols came tumbling down in these years. British ministers had never been his heroes, with the exception of Pitt, but he had a provincial's respect for powerful men, especially if they were in the imperial government. And what did these men look like close-up? George Grenville, the framer of the Stamp Act, had not proved to be as open to suggestions from colonials as he first professed, and then, out of office, he showed his talent for monomania. Hillsborough never offered much hope of reconciliation and then proved to be so sure of himself as to be incapable of listening to any questioning, let alone dissent. Franklin also soon recognized that Hillsborough was intellectually a very limited man. Though not the most powerful colonial official the Americans faced, he was in certain ways the worst—of limited ability, full of himself, and, to use Franklin's word for him, "insolent" in style. Dartmouth, Hillsborough's successor, also disappointed Franklin even though he had none of Hillsborough's snotty qualities. Franklin may have detected in Dartmouth a sympathy and a receptiveness he did not possess. Within a year of his appointment Dartmouth had shown an inability to aid the colonies, and Franklin had begun to question his influence in the ministry. North, whom he viewed for the most part from a distance, was polite and implacable.[31]

Perhaps the hardest disappointment came from the king. Franklin stopped praising him, indeed stopped mentioning him in his correspondence, about the time the crisis began in 1765. Disillusionment came soon enough, however. In 1773 Franklin told William that the king belonged to the party of "firmness," a quiet way of admitting that the king had become an enemy of America.[32]

By the time Franklin sailed for America, he had lost faith in almost everything English and everyone in England. There were exceptions, principally old friends in the Club of Honest Whigs such as Joseph Priestley and Richard Price. They and a handful of other friends of long standing constituted a remnant of what he had long regarded as virtuous in England. But not even they were a saving remnant.

Over the next few years—years of war—the sense of loss, the estrangement, and the disillusionment turned into hatred. War and its brutalities produced this effect in Franklin. The strain the war put upon his English friendships is clear in the letter he wrote—but never sent—to Strahan, one of his warmest friends of almost twenty years. He wrote about three weeks after the Battle of Bunker Hill, a bloody encounter that saw Charlestown, Massachusetts, burned and hundreds of New England militia engaged against over fifteen hundred British regulars. Following on the fierce encounter that began at Lexington in April, in which losses were heavy on both sides and part of Concord, Massachusetts, was consumed by fire, this battle offered evidence, if any were needed, that a revolutionary war had begun. The ferocity of these encounters and the aggressiveness of the British, who had attacked in both cases, convinced Franklin that America faced an unforgiving and relentless tyranny. To Strahan he wrote:

> You are a Member of Parliament, and one of that Majority which has doomed my Country to Destruction. You have begun to burn our Towns, and murder our People. Look upon your Hands! They are stained with the Blood of your Relations! You and I were long Friends: You are now my Enemy, and I am, Yours,
>
> *B. Franklin*[33]

Franklin did not retreat from this assessment in the years to come, though he relented in his condemnation of Strahan. But his indictment of England and all its works; its government, including its Parliament and king; its character and morals; and its people increased in bitterness as the war went on. Before the first year of the war drew to a close, the outlines of the grudge he bore the English was clear. He could not forgive them for attacking towns, and as the year wore on the evidence grew that other towns would be burned, that, as he wrote David Hartley, ships of war fired on American cities and villages "filled with Women and Children."[34] He felt revulsion at Lord Dunmore, the royal governor of Virginia, calling on slaves to "murder" their masters, and at the attempts of several British commanders to enlist the Indians to fall on settlers in the West. For Franklin all these actions marked out a different kind of war—one in which all the rules of civilized conduct had been suspended. They "are by no means Acts of a legitimate Government: they are of barbarous Tyranny and dissolve all allegiance."[35] Franklin wrote this letter in September. The next month he wrote Hartley again, breathing defiance of the force arrayed against America. He seems to have received the impression that the British government, despite its ferocity in the first months of the war, did not really take the Americans seriously, for as he wrote Hartley: "You despise us too much; and you are insensible of the Italian adage, that *there is no little enemy*," an adage Franklin had reprinted over sixty years before in *Poor Richard's Almanac.*[36]

Franklin never softened these charges but rather elaborated on them in the years of the war, and he—"no little enemy"—made them sting. His language indeed reflected a richer bitterness throughout the war. Experience and fatigue undoubtedly contributed to the way he framed his attacks on his enemy; and whatever disposition he felt to exempt the English people from his loathing soon disappeared, as did all the fine and bland discrimination that observers sometimes find in him. His feelings took their rawest expression in letters to friends. These letters were not written to affect behavior or conduct; they were simply the effusions of a wounded and bitter spirit determined to find satisfaction. To Joseph Priestley (1777): "Of all the Wars in my time, this on the part of England appears to me the wickedest"; [37] to James Hutton (1778): you are "the worst and wickedest Nation upon Earth"; [38] to Hartley (1778): "Your Nation is hiring all the Cut Throats it can collect of all Countries and Colours to destroy us," and you "thirst for our Blood and pursue us with Fire and Sword," and you are a "barbarous" enemy; [39] to Hutton again (1778): "The Slaughter of Men in Support of an unjust Cause is nothing less than Murder. I therefore never think of your present Ministers and their Abettors but with the Image strongly painted in my View of their Hands red, wet, and dropping with the Blood of my Countrymen, Friends and Relations"; [40] and to John Jay (1781): the English are like "pirates," the "Enemies to all Mankind." [41]

These thrusts struck new targets as Franklin learned early in the war how difficult it was to deal with his English enemies. Among the problems brought on by the war were the conditions of American prisoners held in English prisons. These men had served on American ships of war cruising in the Atlantic and sometimes off the English coast. As far as the American government was concerned, they were prisoners of war and in that status deserved humane treatment under conventions long observed by European states. British army commanders, for the most part, observed these unwritten rules in holding American soldiers they captured in battle. Sailors held in England received harsher treatment—they were officially considered rebels, nothing more and nothing less. Translated into practice, this position meant short rations, little clothing, and virtually no medical treatment; it also meant that the English used punishment and virtual starvation as means of enlisting Americans into the Royal Navy. [42]

At several times as naval action picked up, American sailors held
in English prisons—most at Mill Prison in Plymouth and Forton
Prison in Portsmouth—numbered as many as three thousand.
Many attempted escape, and those who succeeded in making their
way across the Channel wrote Franklin of the sufferings of those
left behind. He also received letters from those still imprisoned
and from sympathetic English civilians, some of whom sought to
relieve the misery of the prisons by providing food, clothing, and
small amounts of money.[43]

The distress of the prisoners moved Franklin deeply. Most of
those who wrote were barely literate, but their pain simply leaped
from their letters. Franklin tried various tacks to exchange captured British seamen for Americans but for the most part failed as
the British Admiralty turned back all his appeals. Before the
French entered the war, in June 1778, he was operating under
severe disabilities because he had no place to hold the British sailors captured by American vessels. The admiralty knew that he
would have to release sailors soon after they were captured, and it
therefore saw no reason for an exchange.[44]

Frustrated in this tactic, Franklin next concentrated on getting
better treatment for the captured Americans. At this time—April
1777—he seems to have believed that his British enemies might
be shamed into changing their conduct. Accordingly he and Silas
Deane, one of his colleagues in the American mission, wrote Lord
Stormont, the British ambassador to the French court, noting that
the British practice of threatening and starving prisoners until
they agreed to join the Royal Navy "is a new Mode of Barbarity,
which your Nation alone has the Honour of Inventing." The sarcasm did not ruffle Lord Stormont, who sent the letter back with
a crisp message: "The King's ambassador receives no applications
from rebels, unless they come to implore his Majesty's mercy." In
the next eighteen months Stormont relented slightly and a small

exchange began, but most American captives remained in prison until after the war ended, and British treatment of them did not improve. An early appraisal of British captors that Franklin received from an American who managed to escape Mill Prison as "the More Cruel than Turkish Ennemies" summed up his own attitude, which prevailed throughout the war.[45]

Indeed his bitterness at the British government for approving the mistreatment of prisoners soon extended to all of England. The English were a nation "too corrupt" for reform, he wrote in 1780, and the next year he insisted that there was "not a Spark of Honour left in that corrupted Nation."[46] Virtually everything the English did in these years confirmed that they were "barbarians," a word Franklin used over and over again to describe them. When he learned that the English had welcomed the traitor Benedict Arnold, he remarked, "There is no being in Nature too base for them to associate with, provided it may be thought capable of serving their Purposes." And when peace seemed to become a possibility, he insisted that the British could not be trusted in any fashion.[47]

Franklin's was a ripe hatred, nourished by events and by his failure to compel the British to yield on any point of substance—especially on the treatment of prisoners—until their will for war finally collapsed after Cornwallis's surrender at Yorktown. The war made it a hatred without reservations, a hatred that encompassed first a government and then an entire people.

The feeling liberated Franklin—freed him from his old romantic illusions about the English. It also nourished his strength of purpose—to see the war through to the establishment of the American republic. The war had, he thought, noble purposes. Their attainment forced a transformation of his old attitudes. Simply put, a friend was now a hated enemy.

When he went to France in 1776 to serve his country—and to

forestall the worst efforts of a people he had once loved—he thought that he would have at his side Americans who were friends. He soon discovered that he had American enemies, who wished to serve the American cause in their own ways—and had little use for his.

CHAPTER 6

"Wedderburnes in France"

Arthur Lee and Ralph Izard

The Paris Franklin entered in December 1776 no longer served as the unchallenged center of European diplomacy. Paris was a magnificent city and France a great power, but the European state system they had long dominated had been transformed by the Seven Years' War. For roughly the hundred years preceding that war three nations—France, Austria, and Britain—exercised most of the power on the Continent. During much of this period, say from the Treaty of Westphalia (1648) until the Seven Years' War, Britain and Austria had expended their energy and resources trying to restrain the French. For France wished to exert itself in much of this period. French policy was to attack Austrian power in an attempt to eliminate or reduce Hapsburg control. To maintain the balance of power—usually Britain's objective—some counter to the dominance of France had to be found in Europe. British policy often called for Britain to ally itself with a European state both interested in countering France and capable of doing so. In 1745 Britain went so far as to form the Quadruple Alliance with Austria, Savoy-Sardinia, and the Dutch Republic. This policy of finding an ally or allies against France, called "the Old System," did not command universal assent in Britain, where in the early part of the eighteenth century the Tories argued for maintaining some distance from the Continent and relying on the navy instead of entering into alliances with European powers. The navy could strike the French colonies, if force were necessary; otherwise peace, even friendly relations, with the French should be sustained. The Whigs in Britain saw things differently: France was always the enemy, and opposition to her designs on other European states should be sustained. To do this usually required finding an ally or allies in Europe and keeping up the pressure, sometimes to the point of committing British troops themselves to the Continent.

French defeat in 1763 brought new conditions to Europe. Instead of three great powers on the Continent there were now five, as Russia under Catherine and Prussia under Frederick II assumed increasingly important roles. France stood second to Britain in the eyes of European governments. The war had revealed the weakness of the French navy and the recognition that in the aftermath of defeat it was clearly inferior to Britain's. As for Britain, though the world seemed at her feet in 1763, in the next twelve years before war broke out in America, she found herself increasingly isolated from the European continent. For with the rebuff of the French, neither Prussia, Austria, nor Russia needed her friendship to hold the French at bay. In fact these three states began to act in ways that demonstrated their own sense of strength and independence. Prussia had emerged from the Seven Years' War on bad terms with Britain and in 1764 signed a defensive alliance with Russia. That country would have welcomed an alliance with Britain, but only if the British had been willing to pay a subsidy. Austria worried about Russia and Russia's conflict with Turkey and certainly dreaded any resurgence of French strength.

These three states had their own internal strains, but in the altered European system each felt a new confidence. The evidence of just how secure they felt came in 1772 when they partitioned Poland without so much as a diplomatic "by your leave" to either France or Britain. French ministers, kept in the dark during the maneuvers leading to the partition, recognized in the actions of the eastern powers that a new alignment of strength existed on the Continent. British officials seem to have been less affected. Lord North was always preoccupied with domestic concerns, and many of his colleagues in the government had by this time come to recognize that an ally on the European continent was unlikely to be found. British policy makers had always been more concerned about relations with France in any case. Isolated from the Continent and its centers of strength in eastern Europe, these men began thinking in the late 1760s and early 1770s that the security of their country rested more with the navy than any European ally, if one could be found. Thus on the eve of the American war in 1775 their interest lay in maintaining peace with France and building up their traditional source of strength—the Royal Navy.

The American war intensified British fears of the French. The British soon realized that the scale of the American revolt had no precedents, and the danger in America was matched by the threat at their backs in Europe. With France at peace and a continental war that would draw French interests away from Britain and America seeming remote, the French became an object of dread because they presumably could attack Britain with all their resources.

The French foreign minister, Vergennes, who had assumed office in 1774, shortly after the accession of Louis XVI, did not favor an immediate plunge into war with Britain. The depleted state of the French treasury, caution, and the dilapidated condition of the French navy provided additional reasons for inaction. There was also the Family Compact with Spain to consider. The Spanish had played second fiddle to France for many years as the weaker of the two nations. But Spain had recently shown signs of a more independent attitude. In part the independence was a necessity growing from problems that had no interest to France. One of the most pressing occurred in Brazil, where a confrontation with Portugal over boundaries seemed likely. The Spanish had received a bloody nose from the British navy in the Falklands three years earlier—and France had offered no assistance then. Thus the French had good reason to feel concerned about the reliability of the Spanish in a crisis, and a crisis over colonies brought on by an American revolt did not appear promising to the Spanish, who of course had large possessions of their own in the New World.

In fact Spain regarded the American revolt with mixed feelings: any blow against Britain was welcome, and any war that siphoned off British power could not be despised. Britain was perceived as a threat to the Spanish Empire, but then so was a revolution of the English colonies for independence. The Spanish were uncomfortably aware that settling old scores with a Britain under siege by her colonies might well cost them their own holdings in America.

In summer 1775 Britain needed troops. A force had to be maintained at home to counter any French assault, and in America the demand for soldiers increased as the pace of the war picked up. The army at home in peacetime was never very large, and it had shrunk since 1763. With this fact in mind, North's government decided to send at least twenty thousand men to America by spring 1776, a decision that led to the stripping of forces from Gibraltar, Minorca, and Ireland. But this brought the army only a few of the troops it needed. Most of the twenty thousand would have to be hired—mercenaries from the Continent. The British first approached Russia in an effort to obtain soldiers, but the approach was clumsy and evoked a cold refusal. The empress Catherine II did not look kindly on treatment that suggested she was worthy of respect only as a purveyor of soldiers. She knew that her nation was a great power now, and her response to the British suggested they recognize that they were dealing with a major continental state. The British never found all the troops they needed for America, though they sent more from home and hired mercenaries in several German provinces.

They soon faced an equally pressing problem in the possibility that European nations might trade with the rebellious colonies. Policy on this matter was easy to formulate but difficult to carry out. The British position was that the American war was a rebellion and, as such, a problem internal to the empire. If Britain could maintain this point, European powers would not trade with America. The English sought to persuade continental states to accept the assumption that the Declaration of Independence had no validity. The American colonies remained colonies on July 4, 1776, and thereafter, and as colonies their trade could be denied to European nations. Long-standing practice in Europe recognized that neutrals could trade with warring states, but the British government insisted that the American colonies, despite their July declaration, were not a warring state: they were British colonies, nothing more and nothing less.

European states at first seemed to accept the English version of the American war. Their reasons arose from their own immediate interests. Portugal, for example, refused to allow American ships to enter her ports, for Portugal feared to offend Britain because she wanted English assistance against Spain in the Brazilian conflict. Sweden also wished to keep Britain's friendship and denied permission to most American ships to enter her ports. Denmark, with similar concerns, forbade trade.

The Dutch took a different tack. They did not want war with Britain; they did want profits the American trade promised. Their islands in the Caribbean—St. Eustatius and Curaçao—were a little out of the way for much of the ordinary West India trade but not so remote as to make them inaccessible. Dutch merchants found it easy to ship munitions and other supplies there, and American skippers managed during the early months of the war to slip in, reload the guns and powder, and slip out under sail for mainland ports. The ease of this trade soon disappeared as British warships moved into adjoining waters, but the Dutch, all the while professing neutrality, attempted to sustain what was for them a lucrative exchange.

The French had to be more careful. Since the end of the Seven Years' War their government had recognized the nation's weakness. Some among a succession of ministers believed that national financial weakness was even more serious than the decline in naval strength. The national debt was enormous, and it inhibited the desires of some for a rapid buildup of military power. But a buildup began with the intention of making the nation a naval power once more. Vergennes approved a policy that was animated by a desire to keep relations with Britain on a peaceful course while rearming proceeded. But he also saw that the American revolt offered an opening for a war against Britain that the French could win. Louis XVI, the monarch who had acceded to the throne in 1774, did not share Vergennes's eagerness for another war with Britain. Nor did Turgot, the minister of finance, who knew better than anyone else the precariousness of French finances and who sensed that even a successful war could prove calamitous to the nation. In April 1776 the struggle between the two sides of the French ministry—one favoring preparing for war and providing aid to America until war began and the other opposed to these policies—came to a head. Vergennes won, and in the next month Turgot left the king's service. The reconstruction of the navy now picked up speed while official policy continued along the familiar lines of peace and neutrality. But a decision had been made for war with Britain. The only question that remained unanswered was when? The decision for war was made in secret, and the secret was kept from the British, though the building of warships could not be hidden. Uneasy as they were, the British resolved to give the French no reason to declare war while the effort to subdue America intensified.[1]

Franklin arrived in Paris without knowledge of these complexities, but he was not unprepared. He possessed an immense reputation as a scientist and as a man of virtue, a man who embodied the essential innocence of the New World. He sensed immediately that his fame could be made to serve the American policy, and he set about to use it for all it was worth. Wearing a fur cap was a happy accident as far as its meaning was concerned. Franklin seems first to have worn it to protect his bald head from the cold. The French saw it as an emblem of uncorrupted nature in America.

Simplicity in dress and style came naturally to Franklin, and he cultivated without strain the myths, indeed the fantasies, the French began to weave around his name. They wanted him to be a good man, a man close to the best in nature, a man without affectation and pretense. He answered this expectation by maintaining his lean and direct style. His French was never good, but he spoke it without self-consciousness. In his first few months in Paris he did not protect his time and privacy. Rather he went out into the world, simply dressed and eager to meet the people. When they came to him, he listened to them closely and left them with no doubts about his regard for them.

His face soon became familiar everywhere. Artists sketched him, and his portrait appeared in all the likely and unlikely places.

Some artisans made small figurines, others fashioned his face on miniatures. The king of France, both amused and annoyed by all the attention Franklin attracted, had Franklin's face painted on the bottom of a chamber pot—inside the pot.[2]

Franklin could and did use his fame, but he could not operate as a free agent, nor is there any evidence that he wished to. The Congress that sent him to Paris gave him detailed instructions on what he was to do. While in Congress earlier in the year, he had taken part in making explicit the principles that were to guide American foreign policy during the Revolution. These principles were embodied in a Plan of Treaties, largely drafted by John Adams and modified by the Congress itself. Adams had clear ideas about how the new nation should approach old European powers. In 1776 at least, and for several years afterward, Franklin did not disagree. And as far as we know, the Plan of Treaties met all the conditions he believed desirable in an American approach to Europe.[3]

The approach to Europe should be in fact primarily an approach to France. Neither Adams nor Franklin had any doubts about where power lay on the Continent, and both recognized that France's interests accorded with America's in regard to Britain. The English were the ancient enemies of the French, and they had defeated France in the Seven Years' War, stripping her of part of her empire, including Canada, in the process. The French court had no ambition to recover the nation's major holdings in the New World, but it did believe that the balance of power on the Continent had been seriously tilted in Britain's favor by the French defeat in the recent war. If national interest, expressed in concern for a redress in the balance of power, moved the French, so also did an old, still smoldering passion—a desire for revenge. The yearning to crush the English—regarded after all as the wild men, the barbarous nation, of Europe—festered in French hearts.

Adams and Franklin and the Congress may not have known just how powerful such feelings were, but they were aware of their existence. The main thing for them was to approach England's enemy in Europe and gain her support in the struggle for independence.[4]

The need of that support shaped in part, but only in part, the Plan of Treaties (sometimes called the Model Treaty) and the instructions Franklin took with him to Paris. The Americans' sense of their own difference was equally important. Adams knew more European history than Franklin did, knew more, perhaps, than anyone in Congress. He also harbored an eighteenth-century Puritan's suspicion of Catholic power, and France, indeed much of the Continent, was Catholic. The history of Europe, filled with bloody persecution, corruption, and dreadful wars seemed sordid to these Americans. And European states at peace presented a picture no more attractive. They plotted and schemed and connived at getting an unholy advantage in the relations they maintained among themselves.[5]

As far as Adams could see, and Franklin agreed, there was no reason for America to allow itself to be trapped into permanent connections. So no political alliance with France should be sought. Rather, American policy would be to enter into an exclusively commercial arrangement with France. This principle should define American policy, and therefore the Plan of Treaties offered reciprocal trade to France. American merchants trading to France would pay no duties not collected from French merchants. The same condition would prevail in American ports for French traders.

Congress understood that such a commercial treaty might lead France into war with Britain. If it did, the French were on their own. The Plan of Treaties and the instructions carried by Franklin stated explicitly that the United States would not join in such a war. It would, however, agree not to provide Britain with men, money, arms, or contraband, and it would not end the Revolution without six months notice to France, its commercial partner.

Obviously the Plan of Treaties did not make a handsome offer to France, but in Adams's eyes—and the Congress saw things as he did—inviting the French into a world of commerce long denied them served not only as a powerful inducement but as a grand prize.[6]

Persuading the French to provide money and military supplies lacking the cover of a treaty was one thing; persuading them to enter into a formal commercial arrangement with colonies engaged in making a revolution, another. The second, by anyone's reckoning, was harder. Silas Deane, who was named to the American mission to France along with Arthur Lee of Virginia and Franklin, had already made a start on this second task. Deane had preceded Franklin and Lee to Paris. He had been a member of the First Continental Congress, but his home state, Connecticut, refused to keep him in the Second, which opened its meetings in May 1775. Deane, a popular man in the Congress, was sent by that body to Paris in July of the next year with instructions to extract money and other forms of aid for Washington's army.[7]

The Congress chose in Deane a man of enterprise, an ambitious man, and in 1776, at least, a patriot who wished to serve his country. Deane was born in Groton, Connecticut, the son of a blacksmith. The sons of blacksmiths did not usually attend Yale College, but Deane did and was graduated in 1758. He taught school for a short period and then married. Marriage brought him property and, with a second marriage after the death of his first wife, status as well as more property. His second wife was Elizabeth Saltonstall of the distinguished Connecticut family.

While in Congress, Deane exercised his curiosity about his colleagues and his Philadelphia surroundings. Both pleased him immensely, and his diary and his letters to his wife, who had not come with him to Congress, contain shrewd observations on the delegates and their work. But the Deane who took the fancy of Congress proved a different man in Paris as an agent and then commissioner with Franklin and Lee.[8]

Foreign merchants and diplomats in Paris at the beginning of the war entered an environment hot with the desire to make money. The American nation and its new army needed everything and stood ready to buy goods of all kinds. Deane had in his pocket when he sailed to France an agreement with Robert Morris, the great Philadelphia merchant. As an agent of Willing and Morris, the commercial firm, and of the United States, Deane had an opportunity to enrich himself as he served his country. But serving two masters proved difficult, and in the months following his arrival, though he succeeded in getting money and military supplies, he did not always succeed in serving his country's best interests. Nor as far as Robert Morris was concerned did Deane always do what was required for the firm. What Deane did do well was to mix public and private money and accounts. At times under his direction United States ships were made to carry the cargoes of merchants, with the proceeds slated to go to the merchants. On at least one occasion a U.S. ship was turned over to private parties and the return from its sale went into their pockets. Deane, despite his willingness to use public funds for his own purposes, as well as for public ones, did not make a lot of money and had trouble hanging on to what his business brought him. He was more successful in speculating in the English market. Here he was aided by Edward Bancroft, his secretary in name, but in reality a classic operator for himself. Edward Bancroft was also an agent in the pay of the British government. Deane probably did not know at first of Bancroft's double face, but he did recognize Bancroft's usefulness as an agent who crossed the Channel to London on a variety of business. Selling the secrets of the American commission to its enemy was a principal activity on these journeys, but Bancroft also played the market for Deane and himself when the occasion offered.[9]

Deane was not a traitor in the first year of the American commission; Bancroft was. But Deane's financial affairs—useful as they were at times—were tawdry even under the slack rules supposedly governing trade in Paris and London. The longer he remained, the less scrupulous he was, and the more making a great fortune appeared just around the corner, the bolder he became.

Franklin did not mind that Deane mixed public and private business. That, he knew, was the way of the eighteenth-century world, and if Deane was sometimes more concerned about his own interest than the public's, Franklin seems not to have noticed. Perhaps he averted his gaze; perhaps he was so busy that he did not know what Deane was doing. He was concerned that money and supplies were carried out of France for America, and Deane was certainly engaged in supplying America. Franklin had another reason for not restraining Deane if he knew that Deane sometimes got out of line. The reason was Jonathan Williams, Franklin's grandnephew, who was also engaged in the trade as commercial agent in Nantes. Williams worked well with Deane, and Franklin wished not to disrupt their collaboration.[10]

The third member of the American commission, Arthur Lee, had no such interest; he did not care much for Silas Deane and soon came to disapprove of Jonathan Williams. Arthur Lee in fact soon felt an enormous revulsion against Silas Deane and all his works. And when Franklin proved indifferent to the charges Lee made against Deane, Lee became his enemy.

Arthur Lee proved a formidable enemy. The enemy's role was one that came easily to him, and he filled it with relentless conviction. He seems to have learned contrariness as a child, an understandable attainment when his early years are recalled. He had been born—the youngest of ten children—to a planting family in Virginia in 1740. His father was Thomas Lee; his mother, Hannah Harrison Ludwell. Both parents died when he was ten years old. Arthur was left in the control of Philip Ludwell Lee, his oldest brother, who also managed to retain control of most of his father's estate, some 30,000 acres. His father was by the time of his youngest son's birth a figure of eminence, and he remained one until his death. He had held great offices in Virginia, including, for a short time, the acting governorship. Hannah Lee, perhaps worn out by frequent pregnancies, had not paid much attention to Arthur, and his father was otherwise preoccupied during Arthur's early years. Two of his brothers and a sister, Alice, had looked after him, and one of the brothers, Richard Henry Lee, would remain an affectionate and thoughtful guide throughout his life.[11]

But in 1750 Philip Ludwell Lee became his surrogate father, and Philip Ludwell Lee was not the loving sort. Shortly after the death of his parents, he shipped young Arthur, not quite eleven years of age, off to England for education at Eton. Arthur Lee learned much at Eton, if we may trust the evidence of his later knowledge of Latin and Greek, but the experience did not contribute toward making him a healthy personality. Relations with Philip Ludwell Lee did not help either, though because of his youth and his stay in England Arthur did not have much to do with his oldest brother. He did not have much to do with him, that is, until he and several of his other brothers, most notably

Richard Henry, attempted to claim their share of the family inheritance. Eventually the fight—a strong word but suitably descriptive of the nasty business of suing your brother—brought defeat, for the court found in favor of Philip Ludwell Lee.

Arthur Lee spent many of his young years in Britain after he left Eton. Without the land and the money that made life as a tobacco planter possible, he had to find a profession. His first choice was medicine, and he therefore took up residence in the University of Edinburgh, where he received the M.D. But he never practiced medicine for any length of time, preferring instead the political world of London in the 1760s. There he soon found John Wilkes, an English radical practiced in looking out for himself but also an ardent defender of others' rights as well. Wilkes's cause was the reform of Parliament, a closed body he wished to open up to a broader English constituency. But his actions on behalf of reform—Wilkes wrote brilliantly and incautiously—saw him thrown out of Parliament and imprisoned, when he was not just one step ahead of the law. Lee admired Wilkes's political principles and in 1769 joined the Society of Supporters for the Bill of Rights, a group that organized to pay off Wilkes's debts and to advance the cause of reform. There were other reasons as well for acting with Wilkes—some clear and observable, others obscure and hidden. Wilkes professed to sympathize with the Americans as they struggled during these years to hold off official British encroachments on their liberties. That much was obvious. Probably not so clear to Lee was how much he was drawn to Wilkes out of an instinctive identification with Wilkes's style of defiance. For Wilkes in these years did not hesitate to confront authority from the king on down. Wilkes's interest in America and his equation of radical principles in England with those of America, engaged in the struggle to maintain its rights, sealed Lee's attachment to him.[12]

Lee in these years of American crisis proved to be an able advocate of his country's cause. He knew a number of important men in government and Parliament, and he attempted to use their influence for America. But his most important efforts appeared in his writing for the newspapers and in his longer pieces that found their way into print as pamphlets. As Junius Americanus, Lee was a spokesman with an edge who cut through the justifications of ministerial and parliamentary actions with a sharp eloquence. He also wrote under other names, or no name at all. What he said stayed close to the conventional arguments made by others in America. There was nothing original in his writings—nor should there have been. But he was effective in arguing the merits of the Americans' version of the British Constitution, and he took pleasure in this work.[13]

There seems not to have been much other pleasure in Lee's life, at least according to normal expectations. But Lee was not "normal," by eighteenth-century standards. For the troubled child had grown into a troubled man. Lee indeed was an unfinished personality, confused about himself and uncertain of just who he was. He had begun life marked by disabilities: indifferent parents and a greedy and domineering brother who packed him off to a school in England not known for its gentle treatment of its charges. He was the youngest son; the land and plantations amassed by his father were almost all denied to him when his father died. He faced the usual problem of younger sons—what to do with himself. He had difficulty deciding on a career, shifting from medicine to law when he was thirty years old. He lacked the usual comforts of family in these troubled years, though his brother Richard Henry Lee did his best to help. Cut off by the Atlantic Ocean from his family, Arthur Lee also missed the experience of managing land and slaves that gave so many Virginians their strength and adroitness in dealing with the larger world.

Lee's uncertainty and confusion about himself found expression in his abrasiveness, in his mistaking inoffensive behavior for slights, in his overdeveloped sense of reputation; and in his support of challengers to an establishment that refused to recognize him in the manner he craved. And he yearned for recognition, for proof that he was someone to be reckoned with. This yearning fed another desire—for moral certainty. The good was known, and Lee recognized virtue when he saw it. Men of such temper often have an exaggerated sense of their own honor, and they seek confirmation that their conduct is virtuous. John Adams remarked on this impulse in Lee, but he also noted that it was tied to Lee's taste for the good things of life. He said that Lee could not always "govern his Temper" and that Lee had "some Notions of Elegance[,] Rank and Dignity that may be carried rather too far."[14]

Adams's estimate captured much of Lee's character, especially his fancy that he was a gentleman of elegance, rank, and dignity. What he lacked was a full understanding of the way the world actually worked, and as a consequence he was often surprised, even shocked, when others' behavior did not conform to his expectations. When others failed him, he felt anger and disappointment. Sometimes he simply exploded. One such instance occurred in Virginia in the aftermath of the Stamp Act crisis when he challenged a local enemy, James Mercer, to a duel. Dueling was not unknown in Virginia, but it was not common. Mercer, misunderstanding the agreed-upon time of this encounter, arrived on the meeting ground after Lee had left and believed that his antagonist had decided not to appear. Lee had departed under the same illusion.[15]

Lee's early relations with Franklin never reached the explosive state, though from the beginning Lee seems not to have trusted Franklin. They first came together in 1770 when the Massachusetts House of Representatives appointed Franklin its agent and

Lee his deputy. Lee wanted the agency for himself—like so many insecure men he found service in a secondary role difficult to accept. In the years that followed the two men did not really work together, for Franklin did things his own way, leaving Arthur Lee to suffer pangs of neglect. He did not suffer quietly but criticized his colleague for a number of his flaws. Franklin, Lee said, could not really be trusted to represent America's interest; his judgment would always be swayed by his desire for a royal government for Pennsylvania. Besides, he enjoyed royal patronage as deputy postmaster for America, and his son William was the royal governor of New Jersey, an office Lee insisted the old man had obtained for his son through his influence with Lord Bute, a sinister character in Lee's eyes who was responsible for much of the oppressive policy of the 1760s.[16]

Franklin must have heard rumors of what Lee had to say about him—or perhaps he heard the stories themselves. In any case he soon recognized that Lee was unstable and surely lacking the qualities a colonial agent required. He revealed his opinion of Lee soon after his appointment in 1771 when he traveled to the Continent, by leaving his young grandnephew in charge rather than Lee. The snub must have hurt, and Lee did not forget such slights.[17]

Still the two men got off to a calm start in Paris, where Lee, appointed to serve as a commissioner with Franklin and Silas Deane, arrived soon after Franklin had set up shop in December 1776. A part of the credit for this quiet beginning belongs to Lee, for he brought his intense patriotism to their work and a determination to serve American interests in Europe. Lee's absence from

the commission during most of the first half of 1777 probably also
made things easier. Eager to do something for the mission, he
soon went off to Spain in search of a loan for America. Franklin
encouraged this venture and gave Lee advice on how to proceed.
And Lee welcomed advice from Franklin, writing to him often
while he traveled. The good feeling on Lee's side must have been
reinforced by Franklin's action in looking after Ludwell Lee, Arthur's sixteen-year-old nephew, who was in Paris to attend a military academy. Franklin offered the reassuring news that though
the young man was slightly discontented at first, his spirits seemed
on the rise. That Franklin—a great man—dined with the young
one must have also pleased Lee.[18]

Lee also discovered that Franklin agreed with him on several
matters of substance. Both men believed in the traditional doctrine
of the sea that free ships made free goods, a rule they sought to
follow in order to protect the interests of France and Spain, neutrals who stood to lose if maritime law were construed in another
way. Franklin and Lee saw that the French and the Spanish must
not be offended by the self-interested actions of American privateers. Later the two also resisted Silas Deane's suggestion that
France be threatened with an Anglo-American reconciliation if
she refused to tie herself to the American cause. Such agreement
and the good feeling dissipated soon enough. Matters of substance
separated the two men, but in the end temperament and character
proved even more important.[19]

Lee was always concerned about both temperament and character—especially, given the events that followed his arrival in Paris,
the character of Silas Deane and by extension that of Benjamin
Franklin. He suspected Deane at once. Moreover, it did not take
him long to discover that Deane mixed public money with his
own, and he soon concluded that Deane did not suffer losses in
such transactions. The public probably did lose, as far as Lee could

see, and he often demanded an accounting, right up to the time when Deane—recalled by Congress in September 1777—left Paris at the end of March of the next year. Lee also contended that an immense amount of money the French had provided in 1775 was a gift, not a loan as Deane and Beaumarchais, the French agent who handled the assistance provided the Americans in 1775, insisted. Lee was convinced that Deane would profit from any repayment that came back to France from America, and he did not wish to be a party to a scheme that would strain an already impoverished treasury in America. Nor did he wish to allow Silas Deane to cheat the United States.[20]

Before Deane's recall the arrangements for obtaining and shipping weapons and supplies from France to America were made more complicated—and sinister—by the introduction of subsidiary agents appointed by Congress and Franklin and Deane. Congress sent Thomas Morris, brother of Robert Morris, Deane's partner in Willing and Morris, to serve as its commercial agent in Nantes. Thomas Morris proved to be a disaster, for he took to the bottle and left commercial business to a group of French merchants not overconcerned with service to anyone but themselves. Some in fact seized the opportunity that Morris's drunkenness gave them to virtually plunder American trade.[21]

Lee was right to question the use of public money and the methods used to supply American resistance. The difficulty arose from his assumption that Franklin could be held accountable for Deane's actions. Lee sometimes seems even to have expected Franklin to straighten things out, to manage Deane. He entertained this expectation only briefly, however, giving it up almost immediately in favor of a conviction that Franklin was implicated in the corruption Lee saw everywhere in the business of obtaining assistance for America.

But it was not simple corruption Lee suspected; nor were

his suspicions alone in sending him spinning into eruptions of anger. Just about everything that Franklin or Deane did set him off.

For example, in December 1777, Deane moved from Passy to quarters in Paris, "without," Lee groused, "any notice to Mr. L."[22] Lee, it seems, expected Deane to consult him before he changed his lodgings. At about this time the commissioners decided to send dispatches to Congress about their affairs. To carry the dispatches they decided first on William Carmichael, a young Marylander who served as Deane's secretary and who had accompanied Lee to Berlin earlier in 1777. But then they replaced Carmichael with Deane's brother, Simeon. A few days later the commissioners decided that a duplicate set of the dispatches should also be carried to America in case the first set failed to make it through the British blockade. Lee wanted the commission to choose as messenger William Stevenson, a onetime Maryland merchant who had lived in recent years in England, but Franklin and Deane now turned to Carmichael once more. When Lee discovered what they had done, he exploded. The whole matter has a tinge of the absurd about it and may have involved nothing more than a failure to communicate clearly, a failure often seen in relations among men who do not like each other. But there was also pettiness. For Lee, who had no sense of the comic, there was only betrayal. All had agreed on Stevenson, he insisted, and Stevenson had been told that he would go to America for the commission. Franklin and Deane had chosen William Carmichael, an action that besmirched Arthur Lee's honor. Indeed, they were—he wrote them—guilty of inflicting on him "one of the deepest injuries that can be offerd to a gentleman, a direct and unjust impeachment of his veracity."[23]

Lee took little satisfaction in the recall of Silas Deane a few months later. He disliked Deane, even hated him, but he wanted the pleasure of seeing Deane, and with him Franklin, discredited by the exposure of his financial accounts. Franklin told Lee that all he had to do was come to the commission's headquarters at Passy, about ten minutes from Lee's lodgings, to look at the accounts. Nothing would be denied to him. Whether this was true or not is unclear. The date of Deane's departure with Conrad Gerard, the French envoy sent with Admiral d'Estaing to America in the spring of 1778, was withheld from Lee, and Franklin joined in keeping Lee in the dark until the two sailed. The secrecy surrounding their departure had been requested by the French court, which distrusted Lee and did not wish him to know of the departure of d'Estaing's fleet, apparently for fear that he would notify the English. Americans were not the only suspicious ones in France.[24]

When Lee learned of the sailing, he reacted in his characteristic manner, first professing surprise that he had not been told in advance and then arguing that keeping the date of the sailing from him had damaged American interests. Lee revealed further cause for anger in his summary of what had transpired between him and Franklin in recent meetings—with Lee pressing for information about ships sailing to America, demanding to see Deane's accounts, and Franklin pleading ignorance of the times of ship departures and then responding to Lee's insistence by saying Deane's accounts were not his business but that he would settle them with Lee "any day after tomorrow." As far as Lee was concerned, Franklin had tried to "mislead" him. Lee's final question about Franklin's conduct answered itself: "Is this the example you in your superior wisdom think proper to set of order, decorum, confidence, and justice?"[25]

The cutting references to Franklin's supposed wisdom and the lip-curling superiority evident in Lee's letters did not provoke an open break between the two men. They could not afford an open break; Congress, after all, had appointed them to its commission and those Congress had tied together only Congress could split asunder. Three thousand miles away it did not yet have any idea of the conflicts of its chosen two in Paris. When Deane reached America, he took pleasure in telling them of life among the commissioners.[26]

Though Franklin and Lee did not stop writing or seeing one another after Deane's removal, their effective work together had come to an end. They had managed to keep their stomachs down in the months just preceding when they were together during the drafting of the treaties of alliance and commerce with the French. Franklin conducted the negotiations and did the work for the commission, a solitary effort made necessary by Vergennes's distrust of Lee, who, he thought, still kept his lines open to the British government.

But whatever possibilities had existed for a united commission disappeared in Lee's bilious attacks. Lee had ended his letter of April 2 with the demand that Franklin "not treat this Letter as you have done many others with the indignity of not answering it." Franklin's silence he characterized as one of "the many affronts of this kind which you have thought proper to offer me."[27]

On this occasion Franklin did write a response, but he seems not to have sent his letter. Had he done so, the fiction that the American commission as a whole still existed, which the two professed to believe, could not have been sustained. For Franklin's response went to the heart of his convictions about Lee, and these convictions would not have been acceptable to anyone with Lee's overdeveloped sense of honor. Franklin began by admitting that it was true he had "omitted" answering some of Lee's letters. His explanation for his omission began in staccato sentences and clauses reeking with his own anger: "It is true I have omitted answering some of your Letters. I do not like to answer angry Letters. I hate Disputes. I am old, cannot have long to live, have much to do and no time for Altercation." He then rebuked Lee and predicted that Lee's conduct could only lead to disaster:

> If I have often receiv'd and borne your Magisterial Snubbings and Rebukes without Reply, ascribe it to the right Causes, my concern for the Honour and Success of our Mission, which would be hurt by our Quarelling, my Love of Peace, my Respect for your good Qualities, and my Pity of your Sick Mind, which is forever Tormenting itself, with its Jealousies, Suspicions and Fancies that others mean you ill, wrong you, or fail in Respect for you. If you do not cure your self of this Temper it will end in Insanity, of which it is the Symptomatick Forerunner, as I have seen in several instances. God preserve you from so terrible an Evil: and for his sake pray me to live in quiet.[28]

Lee felt about quiet the way nature feels about a vacuum, and the remainder of the year noise abounded between his lodgings in Paris and Franklin's in Passy. With Silas Deane off the commission, replaced early in 1778 by John Adams, Lee now chose to strike directly at Franklin and at his grandnephew Jonathan Williams, still serving in these months as a commercial agent of the commission at Nantes. Williams's accounts of ships, cargoes, and money involved in supplying America distressed Lee almost as much as Deane's had. But he had other scores to settle with Franklin, and he looked for help wherever he could find it.

He found it in Ralph Izard, a merchant from South Carolina who had been appointed commissioner to Tuscany and who had arrived in Paris in summer 1777. Izard was the son of an affluent rice planter, Henry Izard. His grandfather, after whom he was named, was one of South Carolina's founders. His mother was Margaret Johnson, whose father, Robert, had been a governor under the original proprietors of the colony. By South Carolina standards, Izard had been born to a very wealthy and distinguished family—a circumstance he never forgot or, to use less generous terms, never got over. An English education did not reduce his pride; nor did his marriage to Alice De Lancey of the great New York family. The Izards were in London when the Revolution began. Not long afterward, finding life as an American rebel in England unmanageable, he decided to move his family to Paris and then to return to America, presumably to serve his country. He was in Paris when Congress appointed him to Tuscany.

He needed no urging to oppose Franklin. Naturally sour, Izard was more impressed with himself than anyone else was, though he was highly intelligent and had great energy. Because he could not get to Tuscany—the United States was not recognized there—he waited in Paris, full of frustration at the inactivity and yearning to do something useful.[29]

The question that drew Izard into the conflict between Lee and Franklin concerned an article in the commercial treaty with France. Lee opposed a provision guaranteeing that American exports to the French West Indies would be duty-free in return for duty-free molasses imported into the United States from the French islands. Izard, in agreement with Lee, made this matter his own. As a commissioner appointed to Tuscany, he believed that he had a right to see and advise on the making of the treaty with France. When he first indicated his interest months before Deane's departure, that worthy informed him that negotiating treaties with France was none of his business but was the assignment of the commissioners to France—not the commissioner to Tuscany. Franklin initially shrank from such bluntness and in his compliant way gave Izard the impression that he might properly contribute to the discussion of the treaty and of its provision providing for a balance of duty-free exports. But in fact Franklin had no intention of yielding to Izard, whatever the impression he conveyed. Izard, sensing soon that Franklin was not as pliable as he had first seemed, wrote him of his dismay that Franklin had left the article in the treaty. "I feel myself hurt," summed up a part of his feelings, but in telling of them he insisted that Franklin had acted in *"direct violation"* of the principles of the Plan of Treaties he had brought from America.[30] Not surprisingly, Franklin was offended. He was so offended in fact that he allowed himself to write in a fashion both sarcastic and condescending, telling Izard that "I must submit to remain some days under the Opinion you appear to have form'd, not only of my poor Understanding in the general Interests of America, but of my Defects in Sincerity, Politeness, and Attentions to your Instructions."[31]

The exchanges between Izard and Franklin that followed until Izard's departure from Paris did not raise the tone of their relationship, with Izard insisting that "you have repeatedly given me the strongest assurances that you would justify your conduct to me in writing, but you have not kept your word." Izard also echoed Lee's complaint at being kept in the dark about the sailing of Gerard and Silas Deane to America. Congress, he wrote Franklin, "will form a proper judgment, both of the fact, and of your motives." The implication was clear—the judgment Congress would form of Franklin's conduct and motives would hardly be favorable to him. A few months later—June 1778—Izard wrote a long letter to Franklin, filled with thinly suppressed anger, reviewing his complaints about Franklin's failure to explain why he had allowed ships to sail to America without notifying Lee and himself. His complaints did not stop there. His favorites, to which he returned over and over, concerned the provisions in the commercial treaty on the French West Indies and Franklin's conduct in ignoring the advice Izard proffered. Trade seemed to be the issue, but in fact Izard's pride, his desire, like Lee's, to be noticed and heeded, drove his charges and his hatred.[32]

Franklin preferred to give Izard as little notice as possible, and he probably felt no need of his help. Nor had he kept his word to Izard that he would explain almost everything to him about the treaties of alliance and commerce. Izard probably suspected then that Franklin would never explain. Privately Izard said much worse. If we may trust John Adams's memory, Izard had said to him even before the attempt in June to compel Franklin to answer his charges that "Dr. Franklin was one of the most unprincipled Men upon Earth: that he was a Man of no Veracity, no honor, no Integrity, as great a Villain as ever breathed: as much worse than Mr. Deane as he had more experience, Art, cunning and Hypocricy."[33]

Izard did not sate his urge to blacken Franklin's reputation by simply boiling over about the old man in front of John Adams. He had friends in Congress, and he wrote them. His pen may have been a minor weapon at Franklin's back in the course of a war in which more blood than ink was spilled, but had Franklin seen the letters Izard wrote, he would have recognized a genuine talent and no doubt wished for other uses for its expression. He would not have liked Izard's remark to Henry Laurens, head of a powerful committee, and later president, of Congress, that in a discussion of an article in the treaty of commerce "Dr Franklin's usual consciousness of infallibility was apparent." There was much more, some much harder on Franklin than this dismissal of his judgment.[34]

Congress did not believe all it heard, and during these months it was hearing about Arthur Lee and soon about Izard as well from Silas Deane, recently returned, and from Luzerne, the French minister. Deane took to the *Philadelphia Packet* and other newspapers and soon earned the nickname "Mr. Innuendo," given to him for his hints in Congress that Arthur Lee was not the patriot he claimed to be. Outside of Congress he was even less restrained. Luzerne did not publish Vergennes's good opinion of Franklin and his bad opinion of Lee and Izard but simply passed along to members of Congress the news of the high regard Franklin enjoyed in the French foreign ministry.[35]

In September 1778 Congress, persuaded by a number of arguments that American interests in Europe were no longer well served by the commission in Paris, abolished it. It was drastic action, but it pleased Franklin, for Congress then appointed him its sole representative to France. He was now the minister plenipotentiary. The official notification arrived in February 1779. Franklin told Arthur Lee about a week later, asking him on the same day to turn over all his papers "belonging to this Department." Franklin could have predicted the response—it came three days later, a refusal, in a letter that first took the literal line "I have no Papers belonging to the department of Minister Plenipotentiary at the Court of Versailles." But if Franklin meant the papers of "our late joint Commission" he, Lee, had few originals, and there were copies of most of them in the files at Passy. He added that he could not comprehend how one commissioner could "claim or demand" papers that belonged to them all. Besides, Silas Deane had sailed with commission papers in his possession, which he would use to savage Lee. Those Lee kept "are necessary evidence to answer Mr. Deane's accusations, which you know to be the most base & false, that ever the Malice and wickedness of Man invented." Reading these lines, Franklin could not have expected anything but a struggle if the commission's papers were to be pulled together.[36]

But he persisted in the next month, first telling Lee that John

Adams, who had left for America in June of the previous year, had given up his papers without so much as a request from Franklin. That shot, an attempt to shame Lee, missed its target, for the unscathed Lee fired back that John Adams was not a "calumniated person"—in other words, no Silas Deane connived in America to ruin him.[37]

Franklin gave way soon after and agreed to accept authenticated copies, which Lee offered with the disavowal of any desire to occasion a "dispute," after having occasioned one.

It was a ridiculous dispute in any case, with both men playing parts that by this time seemed made for them. Lee may have provided the solution—a reasonable one—because he had another "dispute" going with Franklin over the accounts of Jonathan Williams in Nantes. This affair was never resolved to anyone's satisfaction and ended only when Lee left France, recalled by Congress, in June 1780. Franklin made several efforts to satisfy Lee that Williams had not stolen the public's money. First he attempted to get an audit of Williams's accounts from French merchants in Nantes. Then he pulled John Adams into the matter, hoping that Adams might reassure Lee. To Lee he offered a full accounting, but he also made accusations of his own regarding Lee's finances. Through it all Lee drew satisfaction from charges that Williams had joined corrupt French merchants to cheat his country. He never accused Franklin directly of being a profiteer or taking his cut of Williams's booty, but he left the impression that he did not find serious Franklin's efforts to get an honest accounting.[38]

Franklin did not gloat when Lee left France, but he must have felt lighter, as if a load had been lifted from his back; and the recall of Ralph Izard that occurred at the same time surely released the same feelings. Neither of these enemies had done serious damage to the American mission or, in the long run, to Benjamin Franklin.

But they had made his life miserable at times despite his denial that they made him uneasy.

In one sense Lee and Izard may have strengthened Franklin's hand. Their style of diplomacy, a style so personal that it seemed they were incapable of any other, so offended the French that they felt uncommonly grateful to Franklin for his tact and for his understanding of the circumstances affecting the diplomacy of France. Whether this made the French more accommodating seems doubtful—interests guided their policy and practice—but they might well have seen their own interests less clearly had Franklin not been a trusted and reassuring figure. And it is obvious from Vergennes's correspondence that he did not trust Lee and Izard.

When he first felt Lee's fury, Franklin seemed surprised. He had known Lee for years, but he probably did not realize how deep Lee's sense of honor, his pride, and his irrationality ran. In any case men did not usually dare to insult Benjamin Franklin. How did he explain Lee's behavior and later Izard's?

The explanation he offered in letters written over the course of a year was not unflattering to himself, for he admitted no responsibility. Rather, the reasons he was "cordially hated and detested" lay outside himself. The essence of the matter was that the French loved him. "I am too much respected, complimented and carressed by the People in general, and a Deference a little too particular paid me by some in Power" distressed his colleagues—"those unhappy gentlemen; unhappy indeed in their tempers, and in the dark uncomfortable passions of jealousy, anger, suspicion, envy, and malice." He professed to believe that he was favored far above his merits, but he did not go around Paris extolling the virtues of others representing America in Europe.[39]

Nor should he have. Perhaps he might have been a little more forthcoming in keeping Izard informed, but nothing he could have done would have been enough for Izard. The suspicions of some in Congress were that Izard wanted Franklin's place on the commission, and his letters to members of Congress, full of free advice on all sorts of public matters and especially the conduct of American affairs in Paris, provide support for these suspicions. As for Lee, he was simply far too obsessed with himself, too full of pride, and also too ambitious for recognition to be reached by the sort of reason Franklin commanded.[40]

So Franklin had few possibilities in dealing with Lee and Izard. He chose public silence and most of the time something akin to sweet reasonableness in private. Allowing the disputes within the commission to break into public noise would have hurt the American cause. Therefore, he kept within himself whatever explosive impulses he felt. In private, he met the two with the "same Civility" that he brought to all his encounters with others, as if the "long abusive letters" Lee and Izard sent him had never been received. In his honest moments he recognized—and admitted—that he was being "a little malicious" in this behavior. He knew that his politeness vexed them even more than a "tart Reply," and this knowledge made him happy.[41]

Malicious his silence and civility surely were, but this style came naturally to him. It was fortunate that it did, for it served his interests and, more important, the interests of his country. Nothing would have been gained by an open break, and much would have been lost.

The wisdom in his conduct in the midst of the grief and heartburn Lee and Izard gave him had still another source. He expected, indeed knew, that the two of them would inevitably become as unhappy with one another as they were with him. He put this recognition in a few lines he wrote in 1779 to William Carmichael, then in America. Such "malignant natures" cannot get along together for a lengthy period, Franklin wrote. Therefore "no revenge is necessary from me, I need only leave them to hiss, bite[,] sting and poison one another." Time proved him right. Izard in particular proved unable to tolerate Lee and in letters stung him with all the venomous joy he had brought to his attacks on Franklin.[42]

The knowledge of his enemies' instability comforted Franklin as his own sly restraint did when he encountered them. He also resorted to satire in dealing with Izard. Probably sometime before Izard's departure from France Franklin wrote the little piece he called "The Petition of the Letter Z." It was his own private comedy, and no one saw it for years. "Z" was Izard, as the subtitle revealed in the words "The Letter Z commonly called Ezzard, Zed, or Izard." The piece has the letter Z petitioning "Isaac Bickerstaff, Esq; Censor General." This was a nice touch because Bickerstaff was the pseudonym of Richard Steele's *Tatler*, which had appeared in the *Spectator* for the last time almost seventy years before, in 1711. Treating Izard as a thing of the past had its own rewarding ring. In the petition itself Z claims to be "of as high extraction" and of "as good an Estate as any other Letter of the Alphabet." Yet Z was treated with "Disrespect and Indignity" by being placed at "the Tail of the Alphabet." Not only was he unjustly placed at the tail, but he was also excluded from "the Word Wise," supplanted there "by a little, hissing, crooked, serpentine, venemous Letter called s" which makes the word sound like "Wice" not "Wize." Z therefore asked that he "in Consideration of his *Long-Suffering* & *Patience* be placed at the head of the alphabet and that S be "turned out of the Word Wise, and the Petitioner employed instead of him."[43]

In his marginal notes to the petition, Franklin explained that the petitioner, Izard, "was always talking of his Family and of his being a Man of Fortune." Izard also complained of his treatment, feeling particularly aggrieved that he was at the tail of American ministers and not even a member of the commission to France, Arthur Lee filling a place Izard considered better suited to himself. The characterization Z gave of S was what Izard said in anger about Lee. As for his long-suffering, he was in Franklin's opinion "the most impatient Man alive."[44]

Poking fun at Izard and Lee was a treat Franklin gave himself infrequently during their stay in Europe. But he survived them and got his way. During this period of trouble with these two John Adams appeared in Paris, sent by Congress as the replacement for Silas Deane. Lee and Izard, able as they were, could not match John Adams in intellect. Few men could. Adams gave much to the American cause, which he loved with a passion exceeded by no one in the Revolution. John Adams had a formidable mind and energy to burn. As Franklin soon discovered, he also had a formidable temperament, a powerful moral sense, and an endless vanity. The combination of these qualities with the peculiar strains of trying to serve a glorious cause were to make him a relentless enemy of Britain and, in a strange way, of his comrade Benjamin Franklin.

CHAPTER 7

John Adams

If Arthur Lee was cold, calculating, and secretive, John Adams was warm, impulsive, and open. He shared one quality with Lee—he was suspicious of much that he encountered in the world. In Lee suspiciousness bordered on paranoia and suffused his outlook. In John Adams suspiciousness was confined to sophisticated society. He envied—and suspected—people with no rough edges, people who moved easily in the finer circles, people who knew what to say and said it confidently and at the right time. This attitude did not make him sour or even cynical: he could not muster such comfortable defenses.[1]

Adams rarely felt comfortable under any circumstances. He was an awkward man, seemingly incapable of the easy gesture, and incapable too of the small hypocrisies that carry other men through life. He had a sense of humor but his timing was usually off, as it was in most things. When others laughed, he scowled; when others preferred obliqueness, he went right to the point. He lacked a sense of the appropriate—the appropriate in behavior, words, and responses.

The awkwardness sometimes approached the maladroit. Not surprisingly, the worst of it appeared when he was a young man, before he showed what he could do in the law and in public life. In these years of his youth, Adams regarded every mistake, every gaffe with a deadly seriousness. He observed himself in action and recorded the painful episodes in detail. He was twenty-three years old and newly admitted to the Suffolk County Bar when he wrote the following sentence in his *Diary* about himself: "I have not conversed enough with the World, to behave rightly." The reason for this abject judgment was his feeling that he could not really talk to others, not even to old friends of his age.

> I talk to Paine about Greek, that makes him laugh. I talk to Sam Quincy about Resolution, and being a great Man, and study and improving Time, which makes him laugh. I talk to Ned, about the Folly of affecting to be Heretick, which makes him mad. I talk to Hannah and Easther about the folly of Love, about despizing it, about being above it, pretend to be insensible of tender Passions, which makes them laugh.

Adams was also ashamed of his efforts to impress his elders:

> I talk to Mr. Wibirt about the Decline of Learning, tell him, I know no young fellow who promises to make a figure, cast sneers on Dr. Marsh for not knowing the Value of old Greek and Roman Authors, ask "when will a Genius rise, that will shave his Beard, or let it grow rather and sink himself in a Cell, in order to make a figure?" I talk to Parson Smith about despizing gay Dress, grand Buildings, great Estates, fame &c and being contented with what will satisfy the real Wants of Nature.[2]

What these disquisitions meant was clear: "All this is Affectation and Ostentation. 'Tis Affectation of Learning, and Virtue and

Wisdom, which I have not, and it is a weak fondness to shew all that I have, and to be thot to have more than I have." If all this were not bad enough, he confessed that "I have insensibly fallen into a Habit of affecting Wit and Humour, of Shrugging my Shoulders, and moving [and] distorting the Muscles of my face. My Motions are still and uneasy, ungraceful, and my attention is unsteady and irregular."[3]

These reflections in all their anguish expressed the anxiety of the young Adams. But the uneasiness he felt as a young man never really left him, though it assumed different forms in his years of maturity.

Adams seems to have been born uneasy. He was of old Puritan stock, but he was not a Puritan in the classic sense: he did not consider life a search for salvation. Yet he felt many of the Puritan compulsions and many of the Puritan drives. In particular he felt the urge to work and to accomplish something. He also craved fame and reputation, those idols of the eighteenth century. This second kind of craving operated within well-defined limits of a conscience that would have been considered demanding even in seventeenth-century New England. While Adams valued honor, wealth, and learning, he also believed that the "real and everlasting Excellences" were "Piety and Virtue." The real and everlasting "excellences" ran headlong against the desire for the good things offered by this world—fame, honor, and success. Adams may not have understood all he found within himself in those introspective exercises that gave him so much unhappiness, but he could distinguish between the unworthy motives that served the self and those of generosity that served others. To the detriment of his contentment and happiness he perceived the worst in himself with much greater clarity than the best. He was almost always honest about himself—painfully so especially in his youth—and his disposition not to spare himself the truth bred a tension that dogged him all his life.[4]

The tension in Adams is exposed most revealingly in his *Diary*. Adams was not an introvert—he loved company and talk—but he was introspective. His *Diary* served him in his early years more as a document of introspection than as a record of the events of his life. The *Diary* reveals young Adams to have been a driven, compulsive creature, full of ambition to make his name, nagged by doubts that he would fail and sometimes guilt that he would succeed. He constantly exhorted himself to work harder, to study more, to spend longer hours at his desk. When he was twenty-one, and a schoolmaster in Worcester, he wrote in a typical entry:

I am now entering on another Year, and I am resolved not to neglect my Time as I did last Year. I am resolved to rise with the Sun and to study the Scriptures, on Thurdsday, Fryday, Saturday, and Sunday mornings, and to study some Latin author the other 3 mornings. Noon and Nights I intend to read English Authors. This is my fixt Determination, and I will set down every neglect and every compliance with this Resolution. May I blush whenever I suffer one hour to pass unimproved. I will rouse up my mind, and fix my Attention. I will stand collected within my self and think upon what I read and what I see. I will stand with all my soul to be something more than Persons who have had less Advantages than myself.[5]

Along with this internal imperative to strive, to work, to learn, he felt cravings for recognition:

Reputation ought to be the perpetual subject of my Thoughts, and Aim of my Behaviour. How shall I gain a

Reputation! How shall I spread an Opinion of myself as a Lawyer of distinguished Genius, Learning, and Virtue. Shall I make frequent Visits in the Neighbourhood and converse familiarly with Men, Women and Children in their own Style, on the common Tittletattle of the Town, and the ordinary concerns of a family, and so take every fair opportunity of shewing my Knowledge in the Law? But this will require much Thought, and Time, and a very particular Knowledge of the Province Law, and common Matters, of which I know much less than I do of the Roman Law. This would take up too much Thought and Time. . . .

After more of this he concludes his questioning of himself in this way:

Shall I endeavour to renew my Acquaintance with those young Gentlemen in Boston who were at Colledge with me and to extend my Acquaintance among Merchants, Shop keepers, Tradesmen, &c. and mingle with the Crowd upon Change, and trapes the Town house floor, with one and another, in order to get a Character in Town. But this too will be a lingering method and will require more Art and Address, and Patience too than I am Master of.

   Shall I, by making Remarks, and proposing Questions [to] the Lawyers att the Bar, endeavour to get a great Character for Understanding and Learning with them. But this is slow and tedious. . . .

   Shall I look out for a Cause to Speak to, and exert all the Soul and all the Body I own, to cut a flash, strike amazement, to catch the Vulgar? In short shall I walk a lingering, heavy Pace or shall I take one bold determined Leap into the Midst

of some Cash and Business? That is the Question. A bold
Push, a resolute attempt, a determined Enterprize, or a slow,
silent imperceptible creeping. Shall I creep or fly?[6]

Adams did not fly, but neither did he creep. His rise was slow, but
his hard work and the relentless study paid off.

As this reconstruction of Adams's character suggests, life for
him was difficult even during those times when it was fulfilling.
His life began on October 29, 1735, in the North Precinct of
Braintree, which in 1792 became Quincy, Massachusetts. The
family was an old one, and respected in Braintree. The founder,
Henry Adams, arrived in America in 1638, the victim, according
to family legend, of religious persecution. John Adams's father was
Deacon John Adams, a farmer and cordwainer, as shoemakers
were called, who was a genuine force in the town, serving for many
years as a selectman, tithingman, constable, or tax collector—not
a popular assignment in New England towns—and militia officer.
John Adams said at the time of his father's death in 1761 that his
father had managed the town's business for twenty years and in
his *Autobiography* declared that his father was "the honestest man
I ever knew."[7]

Not much is known about Susanna Boylston Adams, his
mother. The Boylston family lived in Brookline and had a prominence the Adamses lacked. Susanna Adams outlived her husband
by a quarter of a century, dying in 1797 at eighty-eight. John Adams remembered her fondness for reading, but he reported little
about her in his *Autobiography*. Nor does she appear often in his
Diary. Two entries indicate that her son sometimes looked at her
with dispassion. In one he noted her "very confused, blundering
Way of asking Questions." He thought she never really understood what she wanted to know. Hence the questioning he de-

scribed as "random." His mother also remembered names only with difficulty, a characteristic many shared with her, he thought. The reason was a natural "Hurry and Impatience" of thought, a description which might also have applied to himself.[8]

Recapturing the texture of John Adams's life as a boy is not possible, but there are revealing episodes described in his *Diary* and *Autobiography*. His mother could be emotional, even fiery, in confronting his father over some lapse. On a visit to the family home in December 1758, he was the unwilling witness to a quarrel between his father and mother over the boarding of two girls, taken on at the behest of the town because of their poverty. Deacon Adams had apparently agreed to give them shelter and board because as a selectman it was expected of him. Susanna Adams, who would be put to extra work even though the town paid something toward the expenses of the girls, objected. " 'I wont have all the Towns Poor brought here, stark naked, for me to clothe for nothing. I wont be a slave to other folks folk for nothing.'—And after the 2 Girls cryed.—'I must not speak a Word [to] your Girls, Wenches, Drabbs. I'le kick both their fathers, presently. [You] want to put your Girls over me, to make me a slave to your Wenches.' "[9]

Such eruptions occurred only infrequently if we may trust the young Adams in his *Diary* and the old Adams many years later in his *Autobiography*.

As a boy he played and hunted and rambled about like any of those of his age in Braintree. He later remembered the great pleasure that shooting gave him. Life for a boy of parents of comfortable means was good. Yet he was not an easy child, for there was a streak of rebelliousness in him from an early age. When he was ten years old and resisting the requirement to go to school, his father asked him what he wanted to be, perhaps hoping to hear that John aspired to the ministry, a calling Deacon Adams coveted for his son. John, however, replied that he would be a farmer. His father decided that the most effective way of stifling such an ambition was to give his son a taste of a farmer's life. We will go to Penny Ferry tomorrow, he told John, to cut thatch, and the next day the two repaired to the nearby marsh for a long, difficult, and muddy labor. When the day ended, the father asked the son how he liked the work. The reply was "I like it very well Sir." Deacon Adams did not like the reply or his son's defiance, and back to school John went. School was a sore spot too. Young Adams thought the master, Mr. Cleverly, was lazy; and indeed it seems to have been the dullness that a very bright boy encountered in school that had made him a truant. Cleverly did not demand much, and young Adams had not done much except avoid school in favor of outdoor diversions. Now, back in school, he showed his rebelliousness in still another way—by studying arithmetic rather than the Latin that Harvard College demanded of all who would enter its classes. Young Adams knew that his studies under Cleverly were inadequate and soon persuaded his father to send him to Joseph Marsh, a private schoolmaster who prepared him for Harvard. He entered in 1751 when he was sixteen.[10]

Harvard College at mid-century was still a provincial institution, though scientific study had been added to the classics, which had, since its founding, provided the center of the curriculum. Adams joined his class better prepared than most of his fellows, and he seems to have used himself well at Harvard. Whether his studies bit deeply into his mind is not clear; we do know that under the influence of John Winthrop, Hollis Professor of Natural Philosophy and Mathematics, he became interested in science. Winthrop was the most distinguished scholar on Harvard's faculty, and his lectures stimulated Adams to summarize them in his diary. Adams found science interesting, perhaps fascinating, but not so fascinating as to lead him to consider its study as a lifetime calling.

In fact when he was graduated in 1755, he did not know what he was going to do.[11]

For the moment, the commencement exercises at which he received his bachelor's degree answered the question. Adams took part in the exercises and attracted the attention of the minister of the town of Worcester who had been sent to Cambridge to hire a master for the town grammar school. Harvard graduates often spent their first few years out of college leading boys through the intricacies of Cicero and Caesar. Adams accepted Worcester's offer and soon found himself in the town, boarding with a local family and drumming Latin grammar into young minds. The school received younger children as well as the boys preparing for Harvard, some apparently sent there to learn to read. Adams occasionally surveyed his pupils with wryness, if not detachment, and concluded that his "little school like the great World, is made up of Kings, Politicians, Divines, LD [LL.D's?], Fops, Buffoons, Fidlers, Sycophants, Fools, Coxcombs, chimney sweepers, and every other Character drawn in History or seen in the World." If the school could amuse him occasionally, he did not really like the work; and though the town was friendly enough, he knew he would have to decide soon what he was going to do with himself.[12]

Deacon Adams wanted his son to choose the ministry, but he was a reasonable man, a good father, and he did not attempt to force the young man to agree. John Adams decided on the law a little more than a year after going to Worcester. His choice may have been affected by suggestions of his classmates that among his talents was one for public speaking. Adams did not disagree, for his vanity was touched by anyone who listened to what he said and who liked the way he said it. He knew he was not cut out for the clergy—observing the theological knots clergymen tied themselves up in and the sectarian squabbles that disfigured a religion that claimed the meek would inherit the world was enough for him. As for medicine, it offered few attractions.[13]

So it was the law. James Putnam, only a few years older than Adams but the most impressive lawyer in the vicinity, agreed to take him on as a legal apprentice. The study of the law with Putnam consumed two years, and in the autumn of 1758 he left Worcester for Braintree to put the final edge on his knowledge and to present himself to the court in Boston for admission to the bar. Not much can be learned of these two years—his diary, if he kept one, seems not to have survived—and he wrote few letters. He evidently read intensively and widely, though he did not master the technicalities of the day-to-day business of legal work—the form and filing of writs for example. Putnam did not hold him grimly to his studies, and Adams found time to drink his tea and see his friends. He also daydreamed, with his attention often wandering off into visions of Hannah Quincy, the daughter of Colonel Josiah Quincy of Braintree. Hannah, who appeared in Adams's letters as "Orlinda," or "O," broke the hearts of more than a few romantic swains in Braintree, and for a time Adams seems to have thought of marrying her. It was a bedazzled young man who wrote of his attempts to study while love was all that he could see: "If I look upon a Law Book and labor to exert all my Attention, my Eyes tis true are on the Book but Imagination is at a Tea Table with Orlinda, seeing that Face, those Eyes, that Shape, that familiar friendly look, and [hear]ing Sense divine come mended from her Tongue."[14]

The requirements of the law displaced that "familiar friendly look" as Adams made his way through "the traditional masters of the common law."[15] At the end of this period of study, in October 1758, he presented himself to Jeremiah Gridley in Boston, one of the masters of the Suffolk County Bar. Gridley advised him to read widely in all kinds of law, including civil law, natural law, and admiralty law, to add to his store of legal knowledge. The profession in America differed from that in England, where specialization prevailed; in America, Gridley told Adams, a lawyer had to do the work of a counselor, an attorney, a solicitor, and even a scrivener. Gridley also suggested that Adams "pursue the Study of the Law rather than the Gain of it," advice he did not need but never forgot.[16]

Adams went from the interview with Gridley deeply impressed. Two weeks later Gridley presented him to the Suffolk County Inferior Court where he was sworn an attorney. He now had a recognized profession and work, if he could get it.

While he was building his legal practice, Adams began to court Abigail Smith, the young woman who would become his wife. Abigail, born in 1744, was nine years younger than John, the second child and the second daughter of William Smith, the minister in Weymouth, and his wife, Elizabeth, a Quincy who had been born there. The year William Smith was asked to lead Weymouth's church was also the year he married Elizabeth Quincy, a very good marriage for him, for the Quincys had status and money.[17]

Abigail Smith had two sisters—Mary, three years older than she, and Elizabeth, six years younger. Her brother, William, born in 1746, is an elusive figure, a son in a prominent family who never amounted to much. The Smith girls, however, were made of different stuff—all were bright—and Abigail proved to be the strongest of the three.

She was not the family pet. None of the children were in fact, for Parson Smith and his wife, though loving parents, believed in training and disciplining their children. As the oldest of the children, Mary was expected to help with her sisters and her brother. A quiet and thoughtful girl, she apparently did so without complaint. Abigail, anything but quiet, also did her part in the house, though servants did most of the work of cleaning and cooking. None of the girls was sent to school, but each was taught to read, and with the assistance of others in and out of the family learned much more than young women in New England ordinarily did.

Within the family, both parents played a part, each providing instruction in reading. Religion was the parson's responsibility, and the atmosphere in the Smiths' house was devout, but not oppressively so.

Abigail would have been hard to oppress. She was spirited, at times stubborn, with a lively mind and a wide-ranging curiosity. One of those from outside the family who contributed to her education also, in a way, gave John Adams to her. He was Richard Cranch, who married her sister Mary. Cranch was a neighbor of the Smiths, and sometime in 1762, after he began calling on Mary, he brought John Adams along. John had met the Smith sisters three years earlier when Abigail was fifteen. He was not taken with them, in part, perhaps, because he was smitten with Hannah Quincy at this time, Hannah of the wonderful eyes and shape who he said was "Loving and compassionate." She also possessed "Frankness and Candour" and "Fondness" in contrast to the Smith girls, who were "not fond, not frank, not candid."[18]

He was to change his mind after he came to know Abigail. She was a lovely young woman, though not beautiful by eighteenth-century standards. Her eyes were interesting, her skin clear, her body slender but, as people of her time said, "comely." John Adams felt a physical attraction, but it would not have held him had Abigail not had a quickness of mind and a passionate nature equal to his own.

When they declared their love for one another is not known, but late in 1762 John Adams addressed her in a letter as "Miss Adorable" and demanded a "prodigious" number of kisses. They did not marry for another two years—Adams had a legal practice to establish, and Abigail's parents wanted her to wait until she was older before marrying. They were frequently together in these years, and frequently apart. The times of separation saw them write letters—some teasing, some openly passionate, and others restrained by the knowledge that those delivering them would doubtless also read them. She was "Diana" in many of these letters, he "Lysander." The letters reveal that they wanted badly to be together and that they were very comfortable, very sure, in their love. As lovers have always done, they appealed to one another—lightly—for an accounting of their faults. Such appeals were really requests for testimony about the perfections each saw in the other. From their letters, one can see that they were well matched.[19]

The marriage of John and Abigail Adams proved much more satisfying than their courtship. From its beginning more was left to Abigail than to John. He was absorbed by his law practice and soon by the crisis with Britain. She was occupied by the coming of children—John Quincy Adams, the first, was born in 1767. Three more followed, two sons and a daughter. These children and the management of the household, including its finances, fell to her. But she did not allow the demands of her life to subdue her interest in public matters, and in the 1760s and 1770s she eagerly followed the course of American resistance.

By 1774, when John Adams went to the First Continental Congress, he, like Abigail, believed that no reconciliation with Britain was possible. In the Congress he found some who agreed but more who did not. Franklin, still in England as the Congress met, would have confirmed Adams's judgment that harmony within the empire could not be achieved.

Adams did not meet Benjamin Franklin until May 1775, when Franklin, after his return to America, took up his seat in the Second Continental Congress. Franklin's reputation had long been

known to Adams of course. In 1756 when Adams presided over
the Worcester school he had referred to Franklin as a "prodigious
genius."[20] The awe expressed in this comment soon wore off in
Congress, so soon in fact that he said little about Franklin in his
letters home to Abigail. Naturally curious, she asked about Franklin. Her husband's reply in late July showed that an old familiar
process was at work in his psyche. He had already grown a little
suspicious of Franklin—or at least suspicious that Franklin would
receive credit for leading the opposition to Britain and for giving
Congress its very character. John Adams did not say so in this
letter, but he knew that he, John Adams, led the opposition and
infused the Congress with his own spirit. Franklin, he told Abigail,
was not a forceful leader in the Congress, though he had not been
"backward." As for the leadership the English attributed to him,
"there cannot be a greater Mistake." All Franklin had done was "to
cooperate and assist." Still Adams was impressed, though hardly
bowled over, and he ended this report by remarking that Franklin
was a "great and good Man."[21]

The months that followed until Franklin sailed for France late
the next year brought no reasons to qualify that assessment. And
as far as we know, the two men worked amiably together in Congress on behalf of the American cause. Their work included service on the committee to draft the Declaration of Independence.
Thomas Jefferson did most of the composition, with both Franklin and Adams gladly conceding that Jefferson's prose style was
more appropriate to the work than their own. Adams took the lead
soon after in drafting the Model Treaty, the plan which provided
the essential terms for the diplomacy to be practiced in France.

When John Adams arrived in Paris in April 1778, he was a mature man, well educated by American standards, learned in law,
history, and political theory, but still uneasy and concerned about
himself and his reputation. He was courageous yet full of fears

about his abilities and alternately naive and suspicious. But about one matter he was secure and solid—his country's national interest.

Though John Adams was a magnificent patriot, for all his learning and his intellect, he was not quite prepared for what he found in Paris. In the next four years he was to learn much and was to contribute to his country's interest despite his temperament, which was unsuited to the obliqueness and slow rhythms of European diplomatic life.[22] What Adams brought with him roughened the course he traveled in Europe but also enabled him to reach his destination. For he was still the Puritan, one who felt profoundly those old impulses that led Puritans to regard men different from themselves with suspicion and often to find them corrupt and untrustworthy. In particular his cast of mind led him frequently to mistake the actions French diplomats took in the interests of their country for treachery and betrayal. And Adams's impatience colored his perceptions of delay and slowness, and made inaction seem sinister.

These same qualities brought him to a harsh condemnation of Benjamin Franklin. Sometimes they found expression in action as well as speech that made Franklin's life miserable. And on occasion they made the conduct of American affairs, which were already difficult, even more so.

Adams's early reports home to Abigail reveal, not unexpectedly, that he did not really know at first what to make of France and of Franklin. His first impressions of the two were entangled and to some extent remained that way. The aristocratic French women shocked him by their speech and dress. He had hardly arrived in Bordeaux when he was invited to a glittering dinner party. There, amidst the splendor of lovely women in surroundings that sparkled with fine silver and china, a young French lady suggested to him that because his name indicated that he was descended from the original pair, he might be able to answer a question that had always baffled her—"How the first couple found out the Art of lying together." The wit of the questioner, whom he described even years later as brazen, could not be matched, but he gamely tried by invoking "the Power of Electricity or of the Magnet, by which when a Pair approached within a striking distance they flew together like the Needle to the Pole or like two Objects in electrical Experiments." The explanation, heavy and clumsy, was immediately topped by the lady's response: "Well I know not how it was, but this I know it is a very happy shock."[23]

The ladies of Paris were even bolder. Adams first wrote Abigail that "I admire the Ladies here" and that he envied Franklin the "Priviledge" they granted him of kissing them as often as he pleased. And the ladies, he noted, were "perpetually embracing" Franklin. For a short time Adams was titillated by these women, and he was surprised and impressed by the "delights" of France. His letters of spring 1778 burst with exclamations about the "Magnificence" of the physical environment—the buildings, public and private; the furniture; the dress of the French he encountered; and especially the "Entertainments," that is, the dinners and evening gatherings of the learned and the mighty. But the astonished reports were only a part of his reaction; unease prevented him from really enjoying what he saw, the unease and guilt of one saturated with the austerities of the Protestant ethic. His moral nature asserted itself immediately, for he recognized that the style and opulence of the French court could not be reconciled with the republican simplicity of the new nation across the seas. His disapproval was clear in his judgment that "the more Elegance, the less Virtue in all Times and Countries."[24]

That Franklin accepted and enjoyed the elegance did not at first draw Adams's disapproval. He still regarded Franklin with awe in these first months in Paris. Living in the same house with Franklin in Passy may also have kept him from saying all that he felt, and it was not until summer 1778 that he ventured to criticize his older colleague. At that time he was fully informed of the bad blood between Franklin and Arthur Lee—Franklin had given him an account of his troubles soon after Adams's arrival, and Lee seems not to have waited much longer. Adams did not take sides during these months—both Lee and Franklin were "honest men," he told Samuel Adams, though Franklin "may be too easy and good natured upon some occasions" and Lee "too rigid, and Severe on some occasions." He thought the conflict ugly, but he resolved to stay out of it yet not "trim" his principles.[25]

Adams seldom showed much tact in his life, but he managed not to offend either party to the conflict; indeed, during the entire year he got on well with both men. Part of the reason for his success may simply have been his hard work. He had found little to do at first—the treaties of alliance and commerce were completed shortly before the ship carrying him put into Bordeaux, and most of the "business" of the commission was in Franklin's hands. Temporarily let down and dogged by a feeling that he had come too late to be of service, Adams looked for something to do. He soon discovered that the papers of the commission were in confusion, and he set about putting them in order. Before long he had in effect made himself the secretary to the commission.[26]

In early autumn Adams and the others heard that the commission might have been abolished by Congress—and indeed it had, in September. He now began once more to wonder what the Congress had in mind for him, if anything. In February 1779 Franklin received official notification that the commission had been dissolved and that he, Franklin, had been appointed minister plenipotentiary. Arthur Lee was to be the minister to Spain, and as for John Adams, well, he would hear later. For the moment there was nothing for him.[27]

Periods of uncertainty were harder for John Adams to bear than for most men. To some extent he had been in such a period since his arrival in France. His usual emotional state included some anxiety, and now the level had been raised. Not knowing what Congress intended for him, he fumed at his treatment and despaired of his future. But he put the best face on Congress's actions, telling friends that he had long believed that the American commission needed only one minister—not three virtually autonomous creatures. Franklin, because of French affection for him, should fill the post and the others be put to fresh tasks. There is little doubt that Adams really believed this—he was honest and he was smart.[28]

But he did not share the regard of the French for Franklin. His disapproval of Franklin on just about every conceivable score had begun shortly after he joined the commission in Paris, though at first it was muted by the awe he still felt. Now with the transformation of the commission he could at least say privately what he really thought about the old man. What he thought—or what he disapproved of—received intense expression in the anger and misery he felt at his own fate. It was Abigail to whom he laid bare his soul. Of the change in the commission and his own lack of assignment he wrote in February: "The Scaffold is cutt away, and I am left kicking and sprawling in the Mire, I think. It is hardly a state of Disgrace that I am in but rather of Total Neglect and Contempt."[29] There was more along this line in his letter, which exposed the rawness of his nerves.

His old complaints about Franklin now took on a sharper edge, particularly because about this time he read Silas Deane's attack on Arthur Lee, published in the *Pennsylvania Packet* and reprinted in England and France. Deane had not mentioned Adams, but almost inevitably, it seems, Adams expected a similar blast. When he thought of Deane, he thought of Franklin, Deane's associate in the struggle with Lee, and his concern for his own reputation intensified, especially since he suspected that Franklin had encouraged Deane.[30]

Awaiting word of his fate in Paris, he proceeded to let his friends in America know his assessments of his colleagues. Lee was "an honest Man: faithful and zealous in our Cause," but there was an "Acrimony" and a "Jealousy" [suspiciousness], and "an Obstinacy, and a Want of Candor at times, and an Affectation of Secrecy the Fruit of Jealousy, which renders him disagreable often to his Friends, makes him Ennemies." Izard was also difficult because of his indulgence of his passions and because of his inexperience. Franklin, Adams thought, had "a Monopoly of Reputation here, and an Indecency in displaying it."[31]

The remaining months of his stay in France did nothing to soften this judgment. He soon decided that he would go home, with or without the permission of Congress. Not long after reaching this decision, he learned that he might sail on the *Alliance*, an American-built frigate that had recently brought Lafayette back to France. Sartine, the French minister of marine, soon dashed this hope by asking Franklin to place the ship under the command of John Paul Jones, who was in France and had already demonstrated his ability to strike fear into English hearts. Franklin had little choice—no point in biting the hand that fed American mouths—and in April wrote Adams, then at Nantes, of the change. Adams would sail on the *Sensible*, which had been assigned the duty of carrying Luzerne, the new French minister, to his post in America. Unfortunately the *Sensible* would not sail for several months, and consequently Adams would have no choice but to cool his heels until she did. Despite the distinction of the passenger who would accompany him, Adams felt slighted. He did not care for Jones, suspecting that he was being given preferential treatment and that he, Adams, was simply a sacrifice to Jones's ambition. A darker thought soon presented itself: the reassign-

ment of ships was more than the "cruel disappointment" he had
first thought it; in fact he now suspected that it was a plot by
Franklin and Chaumont, an important merchant trading to
America and still Franklin's landlord, who wished to delay Adams's departure to prevent his telling "some dangerous Truths,"
presumably about their profiteering at the expense of the American public. The thought of this conspiracy unsettled Adams but
also comforted him, for it attested to his importance, and more—
to his virtue. His satisfaction at this recognition is clear in the
question posed in his *Diary*—"Does the old Conjurer dread my
voice in Congress? He had some Reason for he has often heard it
there, a Terror to evil doers."[32]

The "old Conjurer" gave no evidence in his letters to Adams in
these early months of 1779 that he was aware of how tainted he
was in Adams's eyes. At the beginning of their relationship in
France he had confessed to the heartburn produced by frequent
doses of Arthur Lee, but he seems not to have pressed Adams
to join him in opposing Lee. Franklin indeed had treated Adams
with his usual thoughtfulness almost from the day of Adams's
arrival. Adams noted in his *Diary* the day after he reached Paris
that Franklin had taken him to dinner "in Company with the
Dutchess D'Anville, the Mother of the Duke De Rochefoucault,
and twenty of the great People of France." Grateful for this hospi-
tality, Adams recorded his satisfaction at the "Magnificence of the
house, Gardens, Library, Furniture, and the Entertainment of the
Table." That evening the two men supped together on cheese and
beer.[33]

For the remainder of Adams's service outward relations seem
to have been correct and even cordial, at least on Franklin's part.
He invited Adams and his son, John Quincy, to live with him in
Passy and made them as comfortable as possible. Franklin always
liked children and he seems to have gone out of his way for the

young Adams—"Master Johnny," as he sometimes called him. He
also accepted John Adams's offer to serve as de facto secretary to
the commission. He consulted Adams on a variety of problems,
including measures to relieve the sufferings of American sailors
held in English prisons. The two men worked well together on
most of these matters and sometimes found themselves together
disagreeing with Arthur Lee. In these months of 1778 and early
1779 Franklin went his own way in the cultivation of influential
French officials, and he never curtailed his social life—the visits,
the dinners, and the flirtations with the ladies of Paris. It was during this period that Madame Brillon rejected him as a lover but
accepted him as *mon cher Papa*. While this was going on, he discovered Madame Helvetius and began spending time at Auteuil. He
must have sensed Adams's fascination with this part of his life,
though he may not have recognized the disapproval Adams expressed in his *Diary*.[34]

If Franklin worked comfortably with Adams, he also took care
not to tell Adams everything about diplomacy in Europe. In particular, at Vergennes's request he kept information from Adams
and from Congress about the mediation Spain undertook in 1778
to bring the war to a close. Spanish diplomats approached the
English with several possibilities to end the war, at least two of
them involving a truce during which, with some face-saving by the
English, American independence would in effect be recognized.
Franklin proved receptive to these proposals, especially the two
that would produce de facto independence for his country. Adams
learned of the Spanish mediation only after the British had rejected all offers of peace.[35]

Because Franklin knew that Adams would feel disappointment
when his return to America was delayed in spring 1779, he tried
to let him down gently. Earlier in the spring he had given him
considerable discretionary authority to spend money in French

ports. But nothing helped, and Adams left France in June full of suspicion and anger.

Adams returned to Paris in February 1780 in a better frame of mind, but rather than take up his old quarters with Franklin in Passy, he set up his own establishment in the Hôtel de Valois. He had been appointed by Congress as minister plenipotentiary, charged to make peace and to establish commercial relations with Britain. He was on his own, not beholden to Franklin or any other American in Paris. Though his temper was better, he did not at first share the details of his assignment with Franklin or even bother to see him. For the old suspicions lingered, now joined to a determination to do things his own way, unencumbered by the deceptions of a man he believed to be in the pocket of the French. In the two years that followed he resumed relations with Franklin, keeping them correct, though never warm or intimate.

For the moment Adams was free of his old rival and meant to stay that way. He could not, however, completely ignore the French government or, for that matter, Franklin. Congress indeed intended that he keep in close touch with both, and for more than a year the money he needed to maintain himself and his household would be paid by Franklin.

Adams soon saw and wrote Vergennes of his desires. He wanted to proceed by informing the English government of his commission, even though the chances of peace and resumption of trade remained bleak in 1780. His purpose was to smoke out the English, discover their intentions, and probably—though he did not admit this—to do something and thereby give his own restless soul some satisfaction. Vergennes opposed the action Adams contemplated, thereby making him an even more implacable enemy. And Adams, never easily subdued, proceeded to give Vergennes advice on how to run the war in America. There is no evidence that Vergennes solicited Adams's opinion, but he now received letters telling him that the war in America could not be won without a permanent naval presence there. Send fleets to the West Indies and to the coasts of America, Adams advised. American efforts on land would surely succeed if they were supported on the sea.[36]

Vergennes replied that a French fleet commanded by Ternay was on its way—it would reach Rhode Island even as the two men argued—but Adams remained unsatisfied. What the French had sent, he insisted, was not large enough to bottle up the British. More ships were needed.

This exchange between Adams and Vergennes was only one point of friction. Money provided another, in particular the currency devalued by Congress in the spring. French creditors held much of this paper, and Vergennes protested and attempted to draw Franklin to his side. Franklin deflected this attempt at capture, and Adams defended American action in every detail. By late July Vergennes had had enough and sent Adams's correspondence to Franklin with the request that he forward it to Congress. Franklin delayed, but he complied. He also reported to Congress that Adams had given "offence to the Court here," adding that Adams apparently disapproved of his conduct of negotiations. It was a fair judgment, but one that should not have been expressed to Congress.[37]

Vergennes wanted Adams silenced or, better yet, recalled. More than personal offense at being challenged by a rude American who seemed bumptious and even a little out of control to sensibilities formed by the indirections of European diplomatic style, Vergennes feared Adams represented an anti-French party in Congress and feared also that Adams might find a way to peace before French interests were satisfied.[38]

No anti-French party existed in Congress and Adams had no intention of betraying American obligations incurred by the French alliance. Franklin knew this, but he disapproved of Adams's style and suspected that Adams in his eagerness might offend Vergennes so deeply as to cost America French support. His own values were clear in the argument he and Adams conducted through their letters during Adams's dispute with Vergennes. Two assumptions lay at the base of his position on how to deal with European powers. The first and most basic was simply that France and other European states acted in ways determined by self-interest. The second was that American actions were far more important than American words, and argument for assistance, or begging, would return nothing. "Our Credit and Weight in Europe," he told Adams, "depend more on what we do than what we say: And I have long been humiliated with the Idea of our running about from Court to Court begging for Money and Friendship, which are the more withheld the more eagerly they are sollicited, and would perhaps have been offered if they had not been asked." As if to clinch this argument, Franklin, citing the old proverb about God helping those who help themselves, observed that "the World too in this Sense is very Godly."[39]

Adams agreed that European states acted only to serve their own interests, but he did not agree with Franklin's estimate of how the French defined their interests. Throughout the Revolution, Adams tried, at least at times, to think well of the French. He never freed himself of the awe that French society and its rich surroundings inspired, and there were moments during which he recognized French enlightenment and tolerance. These moments of clarity—or romanticism—soon passed, replaced by a grim suspicion.

The events of the next two years added to Adams's bleakness: when he heard of Vergennes's dealings with the Spanish, or the Russians and Austrians, he feared a sellout of America. When negotiations commenced with England in 1782, his suspicions grew in intensity. Franklin, in contrast, concealed whatever wariness he felt and seemed to trust Vergennes on every issue. Some of Franklin's reactions undoubtedly arose from a sense of gratitude to the French for agreeing to make the treaties of alliance and commerce. He had of course taken the leading part in making these agreements, and his success gave him a stake in thinking well of the French. Equally important in the formation of his attitude was the adulation he received from the French people, including the nobility governing the nation. He enjoyed the praise and the fame that were his even as he used them in representing the United States in France. All this—success, recognition, popularity—reinforced an inclination to avoid conflict, to avoid making unpleasant judgments and decisions until he was forced to.[40]

Franklin brought a hard intelligence to all he did, and that intelligence told him to proceed cautiously in dealing with a powerful ally. There was also his role or, more accurately perhaps, his responsibility as minister of the United States to France. Once the alliance fell into place, the chief problem he faced was money—money for a poor and young republic at war. He did not wish to risk causing a rich friend to tighten purse strings or to close the purse altogether.

By late July Adams had had his fill of Vergennes and took himself off to the Netherlands in search of recognition for the United States and a loan for his country from Dutch bankers. He was to obtain both in 1782, a vindication of his style of diplomacy. Franklin, though he had adopted something of the same diplomatic practice when he first arrived in France, opposed Adams's mission to the Dutch and deplored his style. That style, which has been called "militia diplomacy," entailed pressing foreign governments to act in the new republic's favor—first by recognizing it—whatever their relations with Britain, and to act forthwith.[41]

Shortly after Adams arrived in Amsterdam, Franklin confessed again to his disapproval of Adams's methods of dealing with foreign powers. But formal relations remained correct between the two men throughout Adams's stay in the Netherlands, though Adams may have muted slightly his own firm opinions about diplomatic practice out of a concern that Franklin might refuse to provide the money needed to conduct his business with the Dutch. Franklin did not deny Adams's calls on his purse, though he complained, sometimes with bitterness, about them.[42]

But Franklin had done Vergennes's bidding in his dispute with Adams, who could not forgive him once he learned that his letters had been sent to Congress. Adams returned to Paris only once before serious discussions with Britain began over the recognition of American independence and an end to the war. Vergennes asked him to come to Paris in summer 1781, when an offer of mediation was made by Russia and Austria. Adams found the offer unsatisfactory, told Vergennes of his objections, and returned to his Dutch headquarters. He did not bother to seek out Franklin and did not see him again until October 1782.[43]

By that time John Jay, recently arrived from an unsuccessful mission in Spain, had joined Franklin in Paris. He, Franklin, Adams, Henry Laurens, and Thomas Jefferson now made up a commission appointed by Congress to negotiate peace. French influence, always feared by Adams, had won its way to an enlarged commission replacing the one-man effort of John Adams. Laurens appeared in Paris only at the end of the process that produced the preliminary articles of peace, and Jefferson, deep in grief over the death of his wife, Martha, did not appear at all.

Almost all the negotiations leading to the preliminary articles, signed on November 30, were carried by Franklin and Jay. Franklin started the deliberations on the American side, but it was Jay who drove them home to a satisfactory conclusion. During a part of the summer only Jay could have represented the American interests, with Franklin confined to a sickbed in Passy and John Adams, now at The Hague, deeply enmeshed in talks with the Dutch. Adams indeed did not reach Paris until October 26 and seems to have delayed his arrival—it took him almost three weeks to make the trip—out of an aversion even to seeing Franklin.[44]

Once on the scene, Adams resisted the notion that he should call on Franklin. Matthew Ridley, an American merchant in Paris on business and a friend of both men, urged him to go to Franklin. According to Ridley, Adams replied that after the treatment he had received from Franklin, "he could not bear [to] go near him." Ridley reminded him that the "differences" he had with Franklin should not be exposed "to the world" because they might have "a bad effect on our Affairs at this time." Adams then said that Franklin might come to him. Ridley pointed out that this would violate the usual custom that "the last comer always paid the first visit." Adams still held out until Ridley asked how Franklin could know Adams was in Paris unless Adams went to him. Adams capitulated because of this logic and began to put on his coat preparatory to a visit but then stopped, saying that "he could not bear to go where the Doctor [Franklin] was." In the end, after this anguished exchange, Ridley prevailed and Adams called on Franklin.[45]

It is a revealing episode in its exposure of Adams's revulsion from Franklin. Nothing apparently could remove it, but the two men managed to get along in November, at least until the preliminary version of the treaty was signed at the end of the month. But Adams could not resist opportunities to abuse his colleague behind his back; nor could he apparently avoid posturing in his letters to Abigail. In one description of the negotiations to persuade the British to recognize American independence before a treaty of peace was made, he struck a pose of fierceness on behalf of his country. He and Jay, he boasted to Abigail, "peremptorily refused to Speak or hear, before we were put upon an equal foot." Franklin, in contrast, "as usual would have taken the Advice of the

Comte de Vergennes and treated without, but nobody would join him."[46]

Near the end of November Franklin put an end to Adams's posing by giving him a taste of reality. The reality by this time was that Franklin agreed with Jay and Adams on the major issues of the negotiations—American access to the Newfoundland fisheries and the Mississippi River as America's western boundary. Franklin's fierce opposition to compensation for the Loyalists—he called them Royalists—came as a pleasant surprise to Adams, who reported that Franklin was even more implacable in his hatred than either Jay or himself. The day before the preliminary treaty was signed, Adams brought himself to praise Franklin to Ridley, saying that on matters of substance Franklin had "behaved well and nobly." Adams offered this judgment in the euphoria of the moment. He had reason to be delighted, as his colleagues on the commission did, and their remarkable success led him to this generous recognition of Franklin.[47]

In January 1783 Britain, France, and Spain signed preliminary articles of peace, and two weeks later the British issued a proclamation officially ending military and naval combat. As fighting ended in the Revolution, aggression revived in the heart of John Adams. Unable to forget, let alone forgive, his old enemy, he once more began to belittle him. One of the reasons for the resurgence of his bile was his concern about his own future. With peace, he was adrift, perhaps to return to Abigail and Massachusetts or perhaps to travel to London as the first American minister to Britain. He speculated and fretted over his future for more than a year until his appointment came through early in 1785. The worst of it was that he wanted the appointment but feared that Franklin and Vergennes—equal devils in his pantheon of the satanic—also wanted him to receive it to prevent him from returning to America, where he might make "Mischief" for them. His feelings resembled those of 1779, when because of the reassignment of the *Alliance* to John Paul Jones he had smelled a plot to keep him in Europe.[48]

The second reason for the resurgence of the old hatred of Franklin was his fear that his own achievements in the negotiations would be obscured once more by Franklin's shadow. This feeling characteristically brought out his self-pity, his sense of himself as a martyr to the animus of others. He was "hated," he told Abigail; he was "a Man running a race upon a right line barefooted treading among burning Plowshares, with horrid Figures of Jealousy Envy, Hatred Revenge, Vanity Ambition, Avarice Treachery Tyranny Insolence, arranged on each side of his Path and lashing him with scorpions all the Way, and attempting at every Step to trip up his Heels."[49]

Concern about "Franklinian Politicks" filled his thoughts in these months before his appointment to London. During this period Francis Dana, a friend and fellow New Englander who had been sent to Russia to gain recognition for the United States, gave up his assignment, conceded failure, and returned home. Somehow Franklin was responsible, though Adams could not say exactly how he had managed to defeat Dana's purposes. But the conclusion was clear—"Never was a country more imposed on by Finesse." The finesse extended to Congress and its secretary for foreign affairs, Robert R. Livingston, who Adams believed had been "a mere Puppet danced upon French wires electrified from Passy."[50]

This dismissal of Livingston's independence followed a letter to Livingston himself that paraded most of Adams's grievances, including his resentment of Franklin: the burden of his indictment of Franklin—a characterization that perhaps does not do justice to his poisonous feelings—was that Franklin was in French hands. In the recent negotiations Franklin, Adams insisted, was "always easy, quiet, never advising any thing, never asking anything, doing al-

ways as they [the French] would have him." But in the same letter
Adams also insisted that the French lacked "confidence" in Franklin and never did "from first to last, consult with him, or communicate anything to him, more than any other Minister with few
exceptions." Somehow, presumably, the French made Franklin do
their bidding without telling him—this is the implication of Adams's assessments. But he was so angry at Franklin as to be unable
to think through the implications of what he charged. Finally, he
professed to feel only contempt for Franklin:

> Sir I must say, that I can lay no stress upon the Opinion of
> this unintelligble Politician. If I was in Congress, and this
> gentleman and the Marble Mercury in the Garden of Ver-
> sailles were in Nomination for an Embassy, I would not hesi-
> tate to give my Vote for the Statue, upon the principle that it
> would do no harm.[51]

The feeling expressed in this statement never left Adams,
though it quieted and with the passage of time and Franklin's
death in 1790 lost its power to trouble him deeply. Franklin may
not have ever learned how unyielding Adams's hatred was, but
he recognized that his colleague distrusted him. What concerned
Franklin most during the negotiations for peace was Adams's reck-
lessness in announcing his disgust with Vergennes and the French.
For Adams had not withheld any of his invective, even in discussions with the British negotiators. Franklin feared that Adams
would harm the chances for a peace, perhaps even leave the impression with the British that the French and the Americans could
be divided. Yet he respected Adams's devotion to the American
cause, and he knew that Adams brought a fierce determination to

defend national interests. Therefore, although he wrote Congress of Adams's excesses, he also praised him. But his most effective, indeed famous, assessment of Adams was damaging to that worthy's reputation and damaging to his vanity. For inevitably Adams read this appraisal of himself a few months after it was written by Franklin in a letter to R. R. Livingston: "I am persuaded however, that he means well for his Country, is always an honest Man, often a Wise One, but sometimes and in some things, absolutely out of his Sences."[52]

Thomas Jefferson delivered an equally corrosive estimate of Adams at about the same time. Jefferson had known Adams in the Second Continental Congress, and he had heard the stories of the conflicts within the American commission in Paris. In February 1783 James Madison, then a member of Congress, wrote him from Philadelphia that Congress had recently received letters from Adams "not remarkable for any thing unless it be a display of his vanity, his prejudice against the French Court and his venom against Doctr. Franklin." Jefferson, who had read in the newspapers that Adams on his return to Paris had taken quarters with Franklin, speculated that this information was wrong and confessed that he was "nearly at a loss" to imagine how Adams would conduct himself in the negotiations. "He hates Franklin, he hates Jay, he hates the French, he hates the English. To whom will he adhere?" But Jefferson also remarked that Adams had "a sound head on substantial points," and he also thought that Adams had "integrity." On balance, he was "glad" that Adams was a member of the peace commission and expected Adams to be "useful in it." The basis of this judgment was Jefferson's belief that Adams's "dislike of all parties, and all men, by balancing his prejudices, may give the same fair play to his reason as would a general benevolence of temper. At any rate honesty may be extracted even from poisonous weeds."[53]

Adams was not a "poisonous weed," but neither was he sweet-smelling honeysuckle—unless the plant grew abundant thorns. Jefferson was right about honesty, just as Madison and a score of others since the Revolution were about Adams's vanity. What has not been seen clearly is that the two—his vanity and his honesty—were connected. Vanity led John Adams to define himself against others—adversaries were desirable and enemies better. The misreading of others' motives, the self-deceptions, the propensity to see immorality where none existed all served his inflated, yet fragile, sense of himself. In some perverse way these tortured qualities made action possible.

All these unhealthy aspects of his vanity struggled against his honesty—his determination to see things as they really were. Honesty did not always win out in the struggles enacted within his psyche, but it did keep him from degenerating into futility and irrelevance. Adams was, as Franklin said, sometimes completely out of his senses. He was absurd in his fears and his preenings. But he could also be "wise," as Franklin acknowledged, and as Jefferson said, he had "a sound head on substantial points."

Epilogue:
No Love for Franklin's Enemies

Throughout his stay in Paris Franklin had persevered in the face of both trivial and important opposition from his enemies in Paris. At times he betrayed his annoyance in an outburst of temper, almost always contained in letters he wrote but did not send. Tormenting the likes of Lee and Izard by acting with civility toward them gave him satisfaction and perhaps some ease, since he suspected that such courteous behavior was upsetting. But whatever these small private victories gave him, or did not give him, he persevered.

He might have resigned and gone home. He threatened to do just that when he learned of Congress's displeasure in 1779. That response, however, was to Congress, not to the enemies in Paris. Still, he might have given up, though surrender to those who hated him would have been uncharacteristic behavior. Blasting them openly in letters to Congress or in the newspapers was simply out of the question. Franklin's instincts were always to keep the existence of struggle to himself. And in the case of the commission a great cause was at stake and not to be damaged by yielding to anger.

There were still other reasons for holding steady in the face of his enemies' worst. These were the enemies themselves, a far different lot from the Penn family and its American agents. There was no one like Thomas Penn, who could deliver snubs from his superiority as an English gentleman. Ralph Izard came the closest and evidently gave himself airs that both amused Franklin and set his social sensitivities fluttering. Most of the time he hid whatever annoyance he felt. But in "The Petition of the Letter Z," he had Z claim to be "of as high extraction" with "as good an Estate as any other Letter of the Alphabet." Franklin, not content to allow his enemy to expose his social pretensions unassisted, added in the margin that Izard "was always talking of his Family and of his being a Man of Fortune." No possibility here that a reader would escape noting that in Franklin's judgment, at least, Izard was a snob. Still, Izard was an American like Franklin, and, like Franklin, only recently free of a colonial's status. Full of himself as Izard was, he could not really make Franklin uneasy or unsure of himself. Besides, his defects were so prominent—a vile temper, a dreadful impatience, a smugness that no one could dismiss as simple self-confidence—that he could be discounted.[1]

Arthur Lee possessed some of the same qualities, but his fanaticism overbore everything else, so much so in fact that Franklin thought it might carry Lee into insanity. Lee came from a family Franklin respected; Richard Henry Lee, Arthur's older brother, had proposed that Congress declare independence, and Congress had accepted his advice. Arthur Lee's patriotism burned as bright as his brother's. To be sure he was as vain as Izard was, and his insecurities revealed an unhealthy self-absorption. Franklin sympathized with him—occasionally—but even though he could not sustain this sympathy, neither could he really despise Lee. More important, he soon recognized that for all the trouble Lee could make, he could be handled or safely ignored. No more than Izard could he really deflect Franklin from his course.

Franklin seems never to have feared John Adams or even disliked him in the way he disliked Izard and Lee. Certainly Adams brought no claims of social prominence to the commission. He was a provincial and unable to come to terms with the larger sophisticated world. Although Paris dazzled him at first, it never softened him, and his virtue remained hard and true. Some of his rough edges may have been smoothed off, but they were only edges. The core of the man could not be touched.

Adams proved most troublesome to Franklin in 1780, early in his second mission to Europe. For a time he felt the bit between his teeth on this mission, and he ran like the thoroughbred he was. Unfortunately, he failed to recognize that the diplomatic race would go, not to the swift, but to those who conserved their energies—and French goodwill. The end of the war was farther away than he realized, and his efforts to bring about the peace he was commissioned to make would take time. His rough tactics did not please Vergennes and put Franklin in the middle. All parties survived the encounters that rubbed tempers raw in the summer of 1780, but had Franklin demanded Adams's recall, he might have persuaded Congress.

Franklin was a quiet man who did not easily reveal what he wanted. Adams complained of Franklin's reserve a number of times. It surprised him, and it alarmed him, because he read into it disagreement rather than caution. One of Adams's weaknesses was making up his mind quickly, an aptitude Franklin never cultivated in himself. Besides, remaining silent armed him, for others' chatter exposed their real purposes.

John Adams's purposes in Paris were transparent. He did not conceal his hatred of Tories or his sympathy for Americans held prisoner in England. He made his convictions clear about the Newfoundland fisheries and the western boundary of the United States. He loved his country—not naively but still passionately, just as he hated England with a passion equal to Franklin's.

Adams's disapproval of Franklin on moral grounds could never

be erased. Nor would he ever fully persuade himself that Franklin
was not in the hands of the French. In the negotiations that produced the Treaty of Paris, though Franklin went a long way toward disabusing Adams of his suspicions, he never banished them.
Had John Jay not been such a firm advocate of American interests,
Adams and Franklin might have clashed. But Jay was there, firm
and clearheaded. In the end the basic agreement of the three men
on what served America best prevailed over any personal conflicts.
All were "big men" who put aside whatever divided them in style
and approach.

All this helps explain Franklin's evenhandedness in dealing with
his American enemies in Europe. That he was wiser than they was
also important, wiser in that he recognized more clearly than any
of the Americans that they all wanted to serve their country, and
that with few exceptions they all agreed on what its interests were.
Important as this recognition was, no more than any other circumstance does it account for his adroitness amidst all his difficulties.

Finally his years and his experience made him clear-sighted. He
was seventy years of age when he arrived in Paris and almost
seventy-eight when the permanent articles of peace were signed
in 1783. His years: he had, by the time the Revolution began, seen
almost everything an American—or a European—could have seen;
and he had done almost everything as well. Whatever ambitions
drove him in the struggle with Thomas Penn had long since died.
Perhaps in the 1750s and 1760s he had hoped to be appointed
governor of the royal colony of Pennsylvania. Perhaps for a few
moments he had even fancied himself cutting a figure in English
politics. Failure in Pennsylvania and the smashup at Wedderburn's hands had shattered those dreams. In Paris from 1776 on
he discovered that a great people loved him; or so he interpreted
the fuss they made over him, with his portrait painted on almost

every inanimate object and the ladies of Paris drawn to him as butterflies were to camellias.

Franklin's head was not turned by the attention of the fashionable people and the kindness of the French court. In fact his cynicism served him well. He was no fool; he knew that in case of conflict between France and America, national interests would brush aside affections, and protestations of admiration would mean nothing. But if he was not a fool, neither was he a stiff-neck, a prig whose overdeveloped sense of virtue disabled him from enjoying the surface of social life as well as genuine friendship. So he relaxed and accepted the adulation of the French world, not as if it came to him by merit or right, but in the recognition that there was nothing he could do about it.

The surface of life seemed to be enough as long as he could represent American interests effectively. He soon realized that he could do much for his country and that his service was profoundly important. He was old; his self-regarding ambitions had dissipated; he wished now only to do what he could to make his country independent. And he would have a good time while doing it—attempting, weakly, to seduce Madame Brillon; courting, persistently, Madame Helvetius; and learning all he could about the European world in science, politics, and diplomacy.

The old passion still lived within him, however. The desire to learn was part of it and would be as long as Franklin lived. But within Franklin the hatred of Britain, his new enemy, and the desire to serve his country burned with the greatest intensity.

Living with enemies in the American peace commission was easier, Franklin discovered, than living with one in his family.

Franklin's last enemy, the one causing him the most sorrow, was his son William Franklin. His son was illegitimate, but Benjamin Franklin reared him and apparently loved him until the break between them. The break occurred with the American Revolution. For when the war began, William Franklin, governor of New Jersey, remained loyal to Britain.[2]

Most of their lives the two Franklins had agreed politically, but at the opening of the Revolution, William Franklin served as a royal appointee and a faithful servant of the Crown. In June 1776 Congress ordered his arrest and had him sent to Connecticut, where for a time he was free on parole. He was in effect under house arrest and lived a comfortable life. Under this arrangement he promised to take no action in the service of royal forces. He soon broke his parole and provided information to nearby units of the British army and also issued certificates of protection to loyalists in Connecticut and New Jersey. When his action was uncovered, he was thrown into a filthy jail in Litchfield and held in solitary confinement, where he suffered horribly. He was exchanged in November 1778 but went to England only after it was clear that the war was lost.

Benjamin Franklin had not attempted to do anything for his son during his imprisonment and had no communication with him. In 1784, still in Paris, he let William know that he was willing to receive a letter from him. "Dear and Honoured Father," William wrote. "Ever since the termination of the unhappy contest between Great Britain and America, I have been anxious to write to you and to endeavor to revive that affectionate intercourse and connection which, till commencement of the late troubles had been the pride and happiness of my life." He did not apologize for his actions during the Revolution, but asked that all that had happened be "forgotten." He wanted only to see his father again.[3]

The reply from Benjamin Franklin gave little promise that the old relationship could be revived. Although Franklin wrote that he wanted affectionate relations with William, he reproached him for his conduct. Few men, he wrote, would have censured William for doing nothing in the war. But of course William had acted in a way hateful to his father, who reminded him of his conduct. Then came these words—"There are natural duties which precede political ones and cannot be extinguished by them." Franklin's meaning was clear: his son should have put aside his principles in favor of his father's, because he was his father's son. After imparting this message, Franklin refused to see his son.[4]

The next year, as Franklin was leaving France for America, he relented. The two men met briefly in England, where Benjamin Franklin had gone to see old friends. There was a strained meeting or two, and they then avoided one another. Benjamin Franklin had brought his grandson, William's son, with him. A few days after their arrival in England, sailing conditions were right for the voyage to America. The old man woke early, roused his grandson, and boarded ship. Benjamin Franklin did not wake William, and no good-byes were exchanged before the ship sailed. The two men, father and son, never laid eyes on one another again.

Several general propositions can be extracted from this history of Franklin's relations with his enemies. Benjamin Franklin, this man of extraordinary talent of a range unsurpassed in the eighteenth century, made enemies, with few exceptions, only in politics. The break with his son was more complicated and must have had sources besides their political disagreements. What they were is not clear, although Franklin's insistence that "natural duties" take precedence over political allegiances suggests that his conception of fatherhood was somehow at stake. There is not much evidence to speculate on further. The main contests of Franklin's life arose from political conflict—especially over questions of how free men should be governed and how they should conduct their public lives. The early enemies of Franklin, the Penns and the governors they sent to America, all had an understanding of the rights of Americans that differed from Franklin's. There was something else involved in the disdain the Penns felt for Benjamin Franklin. He was an American colonial, an upstart who by his challenge to proprietary authority crossed the boundaries of good taste and trespassed on the territory of the English governing class.

The later enemies, most notably Adams and Lee, were as determined as Franklin to protect America's freedom but did not believe that he really shared their concern or thought that his means were inappropriate. There was something else involved in the appearance of these enemies: they all had a narrower vision of the world than he, and both Adams and Lee were given to translating questions of politics into questions of morality. Both disapproved of Franklin's surface behavior, which they thought was most revealing of the inner man.

There was an important issue separating the later enemies from Franklin: how the young republic should deal with European states. Franklin publicly played the role of the American innocent, full of respect for the sophisticated courts of Europe. In fact he was full of guile. His advice to Arthur Lee and John Adams not to roam around Europe like lovesick swains—"suitoring" after recognition of American independence—was rooted in a deeper understanding of power and the role of interest in diplomacy than either of them possessed.

But why did such differences—over the uses of power, diplomatic strategy, policy, and procedure—arouse such animosities, such hatreds in John Adams, Arthur Lee, and other Americans

who served with Franklin in Paris? These colleagues, who thought
him without principles, who described him as debauched, not only
hated him but at times seemed to feel a physical revulsion from
him.

The fact that the French loved him did not help matters, did
not reassure Adams and Lee. Many of the French thought Franklin an innocent, the classic natural man from the wilderness of
America. He was to them Benjamin Franklin, simple, honest, uncorrupted: he of the fur cap and the spectacles that gave his face
an owlish, wise look. He was a plain man, apparently free of the
worst of old-world vices.

Both Franklin's American enemies and the French who made
him something of a cult hero were wrong about him. He was not
corrupt; but neither was he simple and innocent. He was the only
American sent by the Continental Congress to Paris who felt at
home there. His American enemies sensed that he was comfortable in France and assumed that he had embraced all the worst of
the Old World: the luxury and the idleness and the sexual license
of the French aristocracy. Franklin certainly accepted that world;
he usually accepted the circumstances of his life. But acceptance
did not imply approval, a point John Adams could never grasp.
Adams and Lee condemned what they saw in aristocratic French
life; Franklin accepted what he saw, sorted out what was relevant
for the American commission, and used it for American interests.

In a limited sense Franklin's enemies were right. He had long
since given up the kind of morality cherished by Lee and Adams.
He was growing old and tired in these years in France, and he was
a little cynical, and certainly skeptical of most conventional beliefs
about religion and politics. So he was different in style and in
moral perceptions from his American enemies. They recognized
the difference and, misunderstanding what it meant, hated him for
it. Part of the hatred came out of differences in temperament and

culture, part had a connection to genuine disagreements on policy, and part is simply mysterious, and perhaps defies explanation.

Franklin was proud of his achievements and generally pleased with his world. Although his papers offer little evidence of his deepest feelings about his enemies, he seems, on the surface at least, to have regarded several of them with some serenity, much as he might have regarded wayward children. Thomas Penn did not fall in this category. He was a special case: Franklin loathed him. Occasionally there was an eruption of anger at Lee, or Adams, but almost never were they made to feel it. Franklin buried his anger in his papers, in those letters he wrote but never sent. He probably would have admitted to feeling pride in such restraint; yet he proved incapable of taking the advice he had offered others years before in *Poor Richard's Almanac:* "Love your enemies, for they tell you your faults."[5]

He was not proud of his relations with his son William—nor did he understand his son's conduct, which, he said, gave him more "grief" than anything in the world. The loss of William may have reminded him of an earlier time. Almost fifty years before, in 1736, his son Francis Folger died of smallpox. Franky, as he was called, was four years old. The sadness of that loss seems never to have left his father, who many years afterward said that he could not think of the boy "without a Sigh."[6]

Franklin did not reveal his affectionate side easily. He usually expressed it in some slightly disguised form—in his advice to his friends, his concern for their welfare, and his generosity to them and to his family and relatives. His public spirit, evident in so much of what he did, had its enlightened—or rational—side. But it also grew from a genuine affection for humankind. To be sure, Franklin's enlightenment had bleakness as well as hope at its core. He did not really have much faith in human nature, despite his splendid commitment to making human life better.

There was, if his writings may be trusted, little rhapsody in his life, probably little, if any, passionate love. He said he loved Deborah, his wife, and he surely cared about her. But he also neglected her in her last years, remaining in England from 1764 until just before war began in 1775, though he knew she wanted him to come home. His letters to her in this period are barren of deep feeling, almost dull, and surely perfunctory.

Franklin's affections found expression most fully with children. He doted on them, listened to them carefully, told them stories, teased them mildly, and indulged them in their fancies. He grew especially fond of his grandson, Temple (as he was familiarly called), in his years in Paris. He indulged Temple and proved blind to his faults, faults that seemed obvious to everyone else. With the estrangement of William Franklin, Temple became more than a grandson; he became a surrogate son.

The break with William was another matter—William had refused to separate himself from the hated enemy Britain. What Franklin called "Moral or Prudential Algebra" may not have been consciously used when he decided to reject his son, but the disposition to calculate, to weigh motives and perhaps interests against feelings, must have entered into his decision. His "understanding" and his "reason," to use those words in their eighteenth-century meaning, served him in dealing with his son. Reason told him to separate himself from William, a Tory, a traitor to America. But his affections—we would say his heart—which might have led him to another conclusion about William—failed him.

Abbreviations and Short Titles

Adams Family Correspondence
Adams Family Correspondence. Edited by L. H. Butterfield and others. 6 vols. to date. Cambridge: Harvard University Press, 1963.

AHR
American Historical Review

APS Proc.
American Philosophical Society Proceedings

BF
Benjamin Franklin

BF *Autobiography*
The Autobiography of Benjamin Franklin. Edited by Leonard W. Labaree and others, New Haven, Conn.: Yale University Press, 1964.

BF Mss, Yale
Benjamin Franklin Papers, Yale University Library. Includes photocopies from collections and holdings all over the world.

BF *Papers*
The Papers of Benjamin Franklin. Edited by Leonard W. Labaree, William B. Willcox (from vol. 15), Claude-Anne Lopez (vol. 27), Barbara B. Oberg (from vol. 28), and others. 30 vols. to date. New Haven, Conn.: Yale University Press, 1959–.

HSP
Historical Society of Pennsylvania

JA
John Adams

JA *Diary and Autobiography*
Diary and Autobiography of John Adams. Edited by L. H. Butterfield; Leonard C. Faber and Wendell D. Garrett, assistant editors. 4 vols. Cambridge: Harvard University Press, 1961.

JA *Earliest Diary*
The Earliest Diary of John Adams. Edited by L. H. Butterfield; Wendell D. Garrett and Marc Friedlaender, associate editors. Cambridge: Harvard University Press, 1966.

JA *Papers*
Papers of John Adams. Edited by Robert J. Taylor, Greg L. Lint (from vol. 6), and others. 8 vols. to date. Cambridge: Harvard University Press, 1977.

NEQ
New England Quarterly

PMHB
Pennsylvania Magazine of History and Biography

TP
Thomas Penn

TP Mss, HSP
Thomas Penn Papers: Official Correspondence and Letterbooks, Historical Society of Pennsylvania.

Wharton
The Revolutionary Diplomatic Correspondence of the United States. Edited by Francis Wharton. 6 vols. Washington: Government Printing Office, 1889.

WMQ
William and Mary Quarterly (3d series)

Notes

1. "The Late Benjamin Franklin" (1870), reprinted in Mark Twain, *Collected Tales, Sketches, Speeches, and Essays, 1852–1890* (New York: Library of America, 1992), 425–27; all quotations from these pages.
2. D. H. Lawrence, *Studies in Classic American Literature* (New York: Penguin Books, 1977; first published in 1924), 15–27; all quotations from these pages.

1. Thomas Jefferson to Ferdinand Grand, Apr. 20, 1790, in Julian P. Boyd, ed., *The Papers of Thomas Jefferson*, 25 vols. to date (Princeton, N.J.: Princeton University Press, 1950–), vol. 16, 369; vol. 19, 113. Rodolphe-Ferdinand Grand was the commissioners' banker. Quotations throughout the book retain the spelling and punctuation of the sources.
2. Carl Van Doren, *Benjamin Franklin* (New York: Viking, 1938), is still the best biography. Indeed, it is a great biography. Esmond Wright, *Franklin of Philadelphia* (Cambridge: Harvard University Press, 1986), is superior to all recent biographies of Franklin.
3. BF *Autobiography*, 60, 64–65. Franklin would have known Xenophon's *Memorable Things of Socrates* in the translation by Edward Bysshe (London, 1712).
4. Franklin tells of the unhappy results of Governor Keith's interest in

him in the *Autobiography*. For the Junto, see BF *Autobiography*, 116–18, and passim; BF *Papers*, vol. 1, 255–69; Van Doren, *BF*, 73–80.

5. For the White Oaks, see James H. Hutson, "An Investigation of the Inarticulate: Philadelphia's White Oaks," *WMQ* 28 (Jan. 1971): 3–25.

6. The most perceptive account of Margaret Stevenson's relationship with BF is in Claude-Anne Lopez and Eugenia W. Herbert, *The Private Franklin: The Man and His Family* (New York: Norton, 1975), especially 78–91.

7. Many of the letters Franklin and Mary (Polly) Stevenson wrote each other are in the BF *Papers*; James M. Stifler, ed., *"My Dear Girl": The Correspondence of Benjamin Franklin with Polly Stevenson, Georgiana and Catherine Shipley* (New York: George Doran Co., 1927); and Whitfield J. Bell, Jr., " 'All Clear Sunshine': New Letters of Franklin and Mary Stevenson Hewson," *APS Proc.* 100 (1956): 521–26.

8. For a short sketch of Wilson, see BF *Papers*, vol. 4, 391n. There are informed accounts about the controversy between BF and Wilson over the relative merits of pointed lightning rods and round spherical knobs in J. L. Heilbron, *Electricity in the Seventeenth and Eighteenth Centuries* (Berkeley and Los Angeles: University of California Press, 1979); and I. Bernard Cohen, ed., *Benjamin Franklin's Experiments* (Cambridge: Harvard University Press, 1941).

9. Details about Collinson's life are provided by a friend, John Fothergill, in *Some Account of the Late Peter Collinson* (London, 1770). See also E. G. Swem, ed., *Brothers of the Spade: Correspondence of Peter Collinson, of London, and of John Custis, of Williamsburg, Virginia, 1734–1746* (Worcester, Mass.: American Antiquarian Society, 1949).

10. Strahan to Deborah Franklin, Dec. 13, 1757, BF *Papers*, vol. 7, 296.

11. J. A. Cochrane, *Dr. Johnson's Printer: The Life of William Strahan* (Cambridge: Harvard University Press, 1964), is excellent. See Lopez and Herbert, *Private Franklin*, 76–77, for the two men's plotting of their children's marriage.

12. For Price and Shipley, see Caroline Robbins, *The Eighteenth-Century Commonwealthman* (Cambridge: Harvard University Press, 1959). See also Carl B. Cone, *Torchbearer of Freedom* (Lexington: University of Kentucky Press, 1952), for Price; and for Shipley, BF *Papers*, vol. 18, 136 (headnote), and the correspondence in that volume and

those following. *The Art of Procuring Pleasant Dreams* is in BF *Writings* (New York: Library of America, 1987), 1118–22.

13. Verner W. Crane, "The Club of Honest Whigs: Friends of Science and Liberty," *WMQ* 23 (Apr. 1966): 210–33.

14. Frank Brady and Frederick A. Pottle, eds., *Boswell in Search of a Wife, 1776–1779* (New York: McGraw-Hill, 1956), 167.

15. BF *Papers*, vol. 6, 88. The volumes covering the years 1757–62 of the BF *Papers* are rich in information about members of the Club of Honest Whigs. See also Robbins, *Eighteenth-Century Commonwealthman*.

16. BF *Papers*, vol. 11, 244–46; vol. 12, 220–21.

17. Crane, "Club of Honest Whigs," 224–27, is helpful on Priestley's life, as is Robbins, *Eighteenth-Century Commonwealthman*, 347–53. For Franklin and the attempts to have the Copley Medal awarded to Priestly, see BF *Papers*, vol. 14, 311, 324–26; vol. 15, 68–71.

18. BF *Papers*, vol. 21, 526n.

19. Joseph Priestley, *An Address to Protestant Dissenters of All Denominations* (London, 1774), 11.

20. Boyd, *Papers of Thomas Jefferson*, vol. 1, 117–37.

21. Priestley, *Address*, 13.

22. Priestley, *Address*, 16, for the quotations from Price.

23. Price resisted all attempts to persuade him to leave England during the war. See American commissioners to Price and his reply, Dec. 7, 1778, Jan. 18, 1779, BF *Papers*, vol. 28, 200, 393.

24. BF *Papers*, vol. 20, 489–91; BF to Condorcet, Mar. 20, 1774, BF *Papers*, vol. 21, 151.

25. Lavoisier to BF, June 8, 1777, BF *Papers*, vol. 24, 142; Denis I. Duveen and Herbert S. Klickstein, "Benjamin Franklin (1706–1790) and Antoine Laurent Lavoisier (1743–1794)," *Annals of Science* 2 (Dec. 1955): 103–28. For mesmerism, see Robert Darnton, *Mesmerism and the End of the Enlightenment in France* (Cambridge: Harvard University Press, 1968).

26. Duveen and Klickstein, "Benjamin Franklin and . . . Lavoisier," 125–26.

27. Evidence of Franklin's dealings can be found in his papers of the period. See especially BF *Papers*, vols. 24–30; and for related activities, Ja-

cob M. Price, *France and the Chesapeake*, 2 vols. (Ann Arbor: University of Michigan Press, 1973), vol. 2, 681–727.
28. Claude-Anne Lopez, "Benjamin Franklin, Lafayette, and *The Lafayette*," *APS Proc.* 108 (June 1964): 181–223.
29. Claude-Anne Lopez, *Mon Cher Papa: Franklin and the Ladies of Paris* (New Haven, Conn.: Yale University Press, 1966; new edition, 1990), is essential; see especially 29–121. Madame Brillon was Madame Brillon de Jouy, née Anne-Louise d'Hardancourt.
30. Lopez, *Mon Cher Papa*, 30.
31. Ibid., 92–96.
32. Ibid., 243–301.
33. Ibid., 244–47.
34. Ibid., 249–55.
35. Ibid., 246–90.
36. Ibid., 273–80.
37. BF *Writings* (cited in note 12), 925–26.
38. Ibid., 924–25.

CHAPTER 2

1. For biographical details about Thomas Penn, see Howard M. Jenkins, "The Family of William Penn," *PMHB* 20 (1896): 1–29, 158–75, 370–90, 435–55; and 21 (1897): 1–19, 137–60, 324–46, 421–44. For William Smith, see Horace W. Smith, *Life and Correspondence of the Rev. William Smith, D.D.*, 2 vols. (Philadelphia, 1879–80); and Albert F. Gegenheimer, *William Smith: Educator and Churchman, 1727–1803* (Philadelphia: University of Pennsylvania Press, 1943).
2. *Historical Statistics of the United States: Colonial Times to 1970*, Bicentennial edition (Washington, D.C., 1975), 1168.
3. Information in this paragraph and the next is drawn from Joseph E. Illick, *Colonial Pennsylvania: A History* (New York: Scribner, 1976); James T. Lemon, *The Best Poor Man's Country: A Geographical Study of Early Southeastern Pennsylvania* (Baltimore: Johns Hopkins University Press, 1972); Sally Schwartz, *"A Mixed Multitude": The Struggle for Toleration in Colonial Pennsylvania* (New York: New York University Press, 1987).

4. Stephanie Grauman Wolf, *Urban Village: Population, Community, and Family Structure in Germantown, Pennsylvania, 1683–1800* (Princeton, N.J.: Princeton University Press, 1976), chap. 4, especially 131–32.

5. Ibid., chap. 1.

6. For this and the following paragraph see Lemon, *Best Poor Man's Country*, 150–217; Thomas M. Doerflinger, *A Vigorous Spirit of Enterprise: Merchants and Economic Development in Revolutionary Philadelphia* (Chapel Hill: University of North Carolina Press, 1986), 76–82.

7. Doerflinger, *A Vigorous Spirit of Enterprise*, 11–20. See also Frederick B. Tolles, *Meeting House and Counting House: The Quaker Merchants of Colonial Philadelphia, 1682–1763* (Chapel Hill: University of North Carolina Press, 1948).

8. The discussion of politics in this paragraph and in those following in this section is based on the following: James Hutson, *Pennsylvania Politics, 1746–1770* (Princeton, N.J.: Princeton University Press, 1972), a perceptive study; William Hanna, *Benjamin Franklin and Pennsylvania Politics* (Stanford, Calif.: Stanford University Press, 1964); G. B. Warden, "The Proprietary Group in Pennsylvania, 1754–1764," *WMQ* 21 (July 1964): 367–89; Alan Tully, *William Penn's Legacy: Politics and Social Structure in Provincial Pennsylvania, 1726–1755* (Baltimore: Johns Hopkins University Press, 1977); William Robert Shepherd, *History of Proprietary Government in Pennsylvania* (New York: Columbia University Press, 1896); Gary Nash, *Quakers and Politics; Pennsylvania, 1681–1726* (Princeton, N.J.: Princeton University Press, 1968); Mary Maples Dunn, *William Penn: Politics and Conscience* (Princeton, N.J.: Princeton University Press, 1967); Herman Wellenreuther, "The Quest for Harmony in a Turbulent World: The Principle of Love and Unity in Colonial Pennsylvania Politics," *PMHB* 107 (Oct. 1983): 537–76; Allan Tully, "Quaker Party and Proprietary Policies: The Dynamics of Politics in Pre-Revolutionary Pennsylvania, 1730–1775," in *Power and Status: Officeholding in Colonial America*, ed. Bruce C. Daniels (Middletown, Conn.: Wesleyan University Press, 1986).

9. Hanna, *Benjamin Franklin and Pennsylvania Politics*, 25–26; Esmond Wright, *Franklin of Philadelphia* (Cambridge: Harvard University Press, 1986), 73–76.

10. BF *Autobiography*, 173–75, 194–96, 199–207.

11. Jenkins, "The Family of William Penn" (cited in note 1), 21:6.

12. Ibid., 21:12.

13. Ibid., 21:324–30.

14. Ibid., 21:341.

15. BF *Papers*, Library Company to TP, July 29, 1747, vol. 3, 164.

16. TP to James Hamilton, Feb. 12, 1749, Thomas Penn–James Hamilton correspondence, TP Mss, HSP.

17. Ibid.

18. BF *Papers*, vol. 3, 180–88 (headnote).

19. Ibid., vol. 3, 180.

20. Ibid., vol. 3, 17, notes on Assembly debates.

21. BF, *Plain Truth* (Philadelphia, 1747), reprinted in BF *Papers*, vol. 3, 188–204.

22. BF *Papers*, vol. 3, 184, 205.

23. Ibid., vol. 3, 184.

24. Ibid., vol. 3, 184–85; Carl Van Doren, *Benjamin Franklin* (New York: Viking, 1938), 184–87.

25. BF *Papers*, vol. 3, 224.

26. TP to Lynford Lardner, Mar. 29, 1748, TP Mss, HSP.

27. BF *Papers*, vol. 3, 186; TP to Richard Peters, Mar. 30, 1748, TP Mss, HSP.

28. TP to Richard Peters, June 9, 1748, TP Mss, HSP.

29. BF *Papers*, vol. 3, 188.

30. The background of Penn's attitudes is clear in his papers. For an acute analysis, see Hutson, *Pennsylvania Politics* (as in note 8), 6–40.

31. Hutson, *Pennsylvania Politics*, 13–24; *Votes and Proceedings of the House of Representatives, 1754–1755* (Philadelphia, 1755) in BF *Papers*, vol. 5, 527–34.

32. James Hutson, "Benjamin Franklin and Pennsylvania Politics, 1751–1755: A Reappraisal," *PMHB* 93 (July 1969): 303–71, is a helpful discussion of Penn's purposes.

33. BF *Papers*, "Pennsylvania Assembly Committee: Report on Proprietors' Answer," Sept. 11, 1753, and editorial notes, vol. 5, 42–47, 51–56.

34. Horace W. Smith, *Life and Correspondence of the Rev. William Smith, D.D.*, vol. 1, 18–21. H. W. Smith says that Smith took a degree at Aberdeen in 1747.

35. William Smith, *A General Idea of the College of Mirania* (New York, 1753), 15.

36. BF to William Smith, Apr. 19, May 3, 1753, BF *Papers*, vol. 4, 467–70, 475–76.
37. Collinson to BF, Aug. 12, 1753, and Jan. 26, 1754, ibid., vol. 5, 20, 193.
38. Richard Jackson to BF, March 17, 1754, ibid., vol. 5, 242.
39. JA, *Diary and Autobiography*, vol. 2, 115.
40. By 1762 Penn was complaining of the cost of the subsidy paid Smith—"The allowance made to him is very great"—to James Hamilton, Mar. 6, 1762, Thomas Penn–James Hamilton correspondence, HSP.
41. BF to Peter Collinson, June 26, 1755, BF *Papers*, vol. 5, 120, 263.
42. Ibid. For BF's early hopes for the academy, see his *Proposals Relating to the Education of Youth in Pensilvania* (Philadelphia, 1749), reprinted in BF *Papers*, vol. 3, 395–421.
43. BF to Peter Collinson, June 26, 1755, BF *Papers*, vol. 6, 86.
44. BF *Autobiography*, 216–17; BF *Papers*, "Memorandum on Wagon Accounts," vol. 6, 13–22.
45. Israel Pemberton to John Fothergill [May 19, 1755], BF *Papers*, vol. 6, 55.
46. BF to Richard Partridge, Nov. 27, 1755, ibid., vol. 6, 273.
47. [William Smith], *A Brief State of the Province of Pennsylvania* (London, 1755); BF to Peter Collinson, June 15, 1756, BF *Papers*, vol. 6, 457.
48. Quotations from *Brief State*, 3.
49. *Brief State*, 40, 27, for the quotations.
50. *Brief State*, 32–42; quotation from 41.
51. [William Smith], *A Brief View of the Conduct of Pennsylvania for the Year 1755* (London, 1756), 86.
52. Ibid., 61.
53. William Smith to TP [Sept. 1755?], BF *Papers*, vol. 6, 211.
54. *Brief View*, 32.
55. BF *Papers*, vol. 6, 138.
56. Ibid., vol. 6, 138.
57. Ibid., vol. 6, 129–38, 140–66, 193–210, 238–44, 245–71, 279–84.
58. Isaac Norris identifies Smith as the author of the pamphlet in a letter to R. Charles, June 16, 1756, Isaac Norris Letterbooks, HSP.
59. *Pennsylvania Journal*, Mar. 11, 1756; Mar. 25, 1756 (Supplement),

mentions Smith's ambition to be a bishop and accuses him of writing pastoral letters.

60. *Pennsylvania Journal,* June 10, June 17, 1756, where the Smith-Roberdeau affair is laid out.

61. *Pennsylvania Journal,* June 10, 1756, for Smith's deposition; June 17, Roberdeau's and George Sharpless's deposition (dated June 12) in support of Roberdeau, along with still others that included sixty-six signatures. "NQ" in the *Journal,* June 17, charged Smith with attempting an insurrection.

62. *Pennsylvania Journal,* Mar. 11, 1756.

63. *Pennsylvania Journal,* Apr. 22, 1756.

64. BF to Collinson, June 15, Nov. 5, 1756, BF *Papers,* vol. 6, 457; vol. 7, 12.

65. The newspapers suggest that for many in Pennsylvania Smith was a reprehensible figure. See issues cited in notes 59–63.

66. BF *Papers,* vol. 7, 109–11.

CHAPTER 3

1. BF *Autobiography,* 88.

2. Richard Jackson to BF, Nov. 12, 1763, BF *Papers,* vol. 10, 371–72. Franklin responded on Jan. 16, 1764, BF *Papers,* vol. 11, 19–20. Franklin sometimes reduced his method of judging and reading conclusions to "Moral or Prudential Algebra": he would write down reasons or motives for action on either side of a question "in opposite Columns on a Sheet of Paper"; then he would observe "what Reasons or Motives in each Column are equal in weight, one to one, one to two, two to three, or the like; and when you have struck out from both Sides all the Equalities, you will see in which Column, remains the Ballance" BF to Jonathan Williams, Jr., Apr. 9, 1779, BF *Papers,* vol. 29, 283. See also BF to J. Priestley, Sept. 19, 1772, BF *Papers,* vol. 19, 299–300 ("my Way is, to divide half a Sheet of Paper by a Line into two Columns, writing over the one *Pro,* and over the other *Con*"). Franklin then describes a process similar to the one described above in this note.

3. Franklin's first attempt to see Pitt is described in BF to William

Franklin, Mar. 22, 1775, "Journal of Negotiations in London," BF *Papers*, vol. 20, 546–47. Michael G. Kammen, *A Rope of Sand: The Colonial Agents, British Politics, and the American Revolution* (Ithaca, N.Y.: Cornell University Press, 1968), 69–70, provides insightful analysis.

4. James Hutson, *Pennsylvania Politics, 1746–1770* (Princeton, N.J.: Princeton University Press, 1972), 41.

5. For a helpful short biographical note, see BF *Papers*, vol. 3, 187n.

6. Richard Peters to TP, Peters Papers, Nov. 8, 1755, HSP.

7. Ibid.

8. Ibid., Nov. 12, 1755.

9. Ibid., Nov. 13, 1755.

10. Ibid., Nov. 20, 1755.

11. Ibid., Apr. 28, 1756.

12. Ibid., Apr. 26, June 5, Dec. 26, 1756.

13. Robert Morris to TP, Oct. 23, 1755, TP Mss, HSP.

14. Robert Morris to TP, Oct. 23, 1755; William Smith to TP, Nov. 27, 1755, TP Mss, HSP.

15. William Smith to TP, Nov. 27, 1755, TP Mss, HSP.

16. [William Smith], *A Brief State of the Province of Pennsylvania* (London, 1755), 5–7.

17. For the "Heads of Complaint," see BF *Papers*, vol. 7, 248–52; quotation from 251.

18. Hutson, *Pennsylvania Politics*, 42.

19. The notes in BF *Papers*, vol. 6, 248–51, are helpful in establishing the context; Hutson's full account, 41–44, is insightful.

20. BF to Isaac Norris, Jan. 14, 1758, BF *Papers*, vol. 7, 361.

21. Ibid.

22. Ibid., vol. 7, 362.

23. Ibid.

24. Ibid. for all quotations in this paragraph.

25. The *OED* gives examples of eighteenth-century meanings of "jockey," including "to play the jockey," "play tricks," to "manipulate in a tricky way."

26. BF to Joseph Galloway, Feb. 17, 1758, BF *Papers*, vol. 7, 374, for the quotation.

27. Ibid.

28. "Documents on the Hearing of William Smith's Petition," William Smith's Petition, BF *Papers*, vol. 8, 28–51.

29. Paris directed his answer to the Pennsylvania Assembly, Nov. 27, 1758, BF *Papers*, vol. 8, 178–83; quotations from 182.

30. Thomas and Richard Penn to the House of Representatives of . . . Pennsylvania, Nov. 28, 1758, ibid., vol. 8, 184–86; quotation from 185. Franklin comments on Penn's message in a letter to Isaac Norris, Jan. 19, 1759, ibid., vol. 8, 233.

31. Quotations are from ibid., vol. 8, 187. Franklin learned from John Fothergill of Penn's reading the letter in which the term "low Jockey" was used. See BF to Isaac Norris, Mar. 19, 1759, ibid., vol. 8, 292.

32. Indian affairs, the statutes, and parliamentary appropriations may be followed in BF *Papers*, vols. 8–10.

33. Indian affairs can be reconstructed from the "Report on the Easton Conference," Jan. 29, 1757, BF *Papers*, vol. 7, 111–14, and from documents reprinted in vol. 7, especially 15–17, 18–23. See also Anthony Wallace, *King of the Delawares: Teedyuscung, 1700–1763* (Philadelphia: University of Pennsylvania Press, 1949; rpt. Syracuse, N.Y.: Syracuse University Press, 1990).

34. "Petition to the King in Council," by BF [Sept. 20, 1758]; BF *Papers*, vol. 8, 269, for quotation.

35. For Penn's comment, TP to Benjamin Chew, Dec. 9, 1758, TP Mss, HSP.

36. For background, see BF *Papers*, vol. 8, 6–27; and vol. 9, 125–31 (headnote).

37. "Report to the Lords of the Committee of the Council upon 19 Acts passed in Pennsylvania in 1758 and 1759," June 24, 1760, ibid., vol. 9, 131–73; quotations from vol. 9, 169, 170.

38. "Order in Council," Sept. 2, 1760, ibid., vol. 9, 196–211; quotations from 206.

39. Ibid., vol. 9, 241–46, 392–94; vol. 10, and passim for various stock transactions.

40. TP to James Logan, Dec. 9, 1758; to Richard Peters, Feb. 10, 1759; to Dr. Graeme, Apr. 10, 1759, TP Mss, HSP.

41. (London, 1759).

42. BF to Isaac Norris, June 9, 1759, BF *Papers*, vol. 8, 402, quotations;

and to Joseph Galloway, Apr. 7, 1759, vol. 8, 313, comment on "low jockey" and Penn's liver.

43. BF to Isaac Norris; Mar. 19, 1759, ibid., vol. 8, 293. Granville was John Carteret, first Earl Granville.

44. Ibid., vol. 8, 294. Halifax was Philip Yorke, first Earl of Hardwicke.

45. Ibid., vol. 8, 295.

46. BF to Israel Pemberton, Mar. 19, 1759, ibid., vol. 8, 297–300; quotations from 300.

CHAPTER 4

1. BF to Richard Jackson, Dec. 2, 1762, BF *Papers*, vol. 10, 160–61.

2. The background may be studied in Howard Peckham, *Pontiac and the Indian Uprising* (Chicago: University of Chicago Press, 1961).

3. BF *Papers*, vol. 11, 51, 53–54.

4. Reprinted in BF *Papers*, vol. 11, 47–69.

5. BF *Papers*, vol. 11, 70–74. For a careful account of events of frontier actions, see Brooke Hindle, "The March of the Paxton Boys," *WMQ* 3 (Oct. 1946): 461–86.

6. BF to John Fothergill, Mar. 14, 1764, BF *Papers*, vol. 11, 101–5; quotations from 103.

7. Ibid., vol. 11, 103–4.

8. Quotation, BF *Papers*, vol. 11, 85. For the lighthouse and supply bill, vol. 11, 104–5, 116–21. James Hutson, *Pennsylvania Politics, 1746–1770* (Princeton, N.J.: Princeton University Press, 1972), 80–121, provides a superb account of Indian affairs and the struggle with the governor.

9. BF to John Fothergill, Mar. 14, 1764, BF *Papers*, vol. 11, 104, 105.

10. Jack D. Marietta, *The Reformation of American Quakerism, 1748–1783* (Philadelphia: University of Pennsylvania Press, 1984), 107–201.

11. BF *Papers*, vol. 11, 126–33, for the resolves of Mar. 24, 1764. The editors' commentary, as usual, is perceptive and informative. The Board of Trade's report, June 24, 1760, is reprinted in ibid., vol. 9, 131–73; criticism of the proprietors for not insisting on their authority—indeed for their "Supineness"—is given on 171–73.

12. BF *Papers*, vol. 11, 130, for quotations.

13. Franklin referred to the resolves as the "Necklace of Resolves" in a letter to William Strahan, Mar. 30, 1764, ibid., vol. 11, 149.

14. This account of the petitioning effort is based on BF *Papers*, vol. 11, 135–44; the resolves and the exchanges with the governor are in *Pennsylvania Gazette*, Mar. 29, 1764. Hutson, *Pennsylvania Politics*, 122–27, is very helpful.

15. For Galloway, see the biographical note in BF *Papers*, vol. 7, 29n; Benjamin H. Newcomb, *Franklin and Galloway: A Political Partnership* (New Haven, Conn.: Yale University Press, 1972), 5–36. Studies of loyalists discuss his later career and sometimes are helpful in understanding his prerevolutionary politics. See especially John E. Ferling, *The Loyalist Mind: Joseph Galloway and the American Revolution* (University Park: Pennsylvania State University Press, 1977); Robert M. Calhoon, *The Loyalists in Revolutionary America, 1760–1781* (New York: Harcourt Brace Jovanovich, 1973); and Mary Beth Norton, *The British-Americans: The Loyalist Exiles in England, 1774–1789* (Boston: Little, Brown, 1972).

16. *The Plain Dealer No. 1* (Philadelphia, 1764), 4. This tract was followed by two others of the same title, but with No. 2 and No. 3 indicated.

17. Hutson, *Pennsylvania Politics*, 127–33.

18. For the petition, BF *Papers*, vol. 11, 193–200. John Dickinson, *A Speech Delivered in the House of Assembly of the Province of Pennsylvania, May 24th 1764*, 2d ed. (Philadelphia, 1764), 15, 13, 14 for the quotations.

19. Joseph Galloway, *The Speech of Joseph Galloway, Esq.'s One of the Members for Philadelphia County: In Answer to the Speech of John Dickinson, Esq; . . . May 24, 1764 (Philadelphia, 1764)*. For Dickinson's charge that it was "a *pretended* speech," see BF *Papers*, vol. 11, 195n.

20. Galloway, *The Speech*, 40, 41.

21. Ibid., 27.

22. BF *Papers*, vol. 11, 196–97 (headnote).

23. One of the strongest attacks on Thomas Penn was *The Scribbler: Being a Letter from a Gentleman in the Town to His Friend in the Country* (Philadelphia, 1764), which called him an "avaricious master," 2. *The Scribbler* also attacked William Smith, 19–24.

24. Hutson, *Pennsylvania Politics*, 164–68; BF to Richard Jackson, July

12, 1764, BF *Papers*, vol. 11, 256.

25. Reprinted in BF *Papers*, vol. 11, 267–311.

26. Ibid., vol. 11, 272, 275 for the quotations.

27. Ibid., vol. 11, 286.

28. Ibid., vol. 11, 294.

29. Ibid., vol. 11, 294–95, 297, 287 for the quotations in this and the preceding paragraph.

30. Hugh Williamson, *What is Sauce for a Goose is also Sauce for a Gander* (Philadelphia, 1764), reprinted in BF *Papers*, vol. 11, 380–84; quotations from 383–84; and *An Answer to the Plot* (Philadelphia, 1764), a broadside.

31. For Smith's charge that Franklin failed to acknowledge Ebenezer Kinnersley's contributions to his own discoveries, see the *American Magazine and Monthly Chronicle for the British Colonies* 1 (1757–58), Supplement, 639. Kinnersley's response of Nov. 30, 1758, originally printed in the *Pennsylvania Gazette*, Nov. 30, 1758, is reprinted in BF *Papers*, vol. 8, 189–90. J. A. Leo Lemay, *Ebenezer Kinnersley: Franklin's Friend* (Philadelphia: University of Pennsylvania Press, 1964), is excellent. On Franklin's Oxford degree and Smith's attempt to have it denied, BF *Papers*, vol. 10, 76–78. Hugh Williamson, in *What is Sauce for a Goose is also Sauce for a Gander*, cited in note 30, attacked Franklin for a lack of originality in his electrical experiments and also accused him of buying the Oxford degree. *The Scribbler*, cited in note 23, defended him on both scores.

32. *Pennsylvania Journal*, Supplement, Sept. 27, 1764.

33. See above, Chapter 3, especially note 39.

34. "Palatine Boors" appeared in *Observations Concerning the Increase of Mankind*, written in 1751 but not published until 1755 in Boston. It is reprinted in BF *Papers*, vol. 4, 227–34. BF was attacked for this usage in *Pennsylvania Journal*, Supplement, Sept. 27, 1764; and defended in *The Plot* (Philadelphia, 1764).

35. William Smith, in the preface to John Dickinson's *Speech* (cited in note 18), iv–v.

36. Ibid., v.

37. See above, Chapter 2, notes 26–28.

38. BF *Papers*, vol. 11, 390–94; Hutson, *Pennsylvania Politics*, 173–76.

39. John Penn to TP, Sept. 22, 1764; TP to Benjamin Chew, June 8, 1764; TP to James Hamilton, June 13, 1764; William Allen to TP, Sept. 25, 1764, TP Mss, HSP. Hyde was Thomas Villiers, 1st Baron Hyde.

40. John Penn to TP, Oct. 19, 1764; Benjamin Chew to TP, Nov. 5, 1764, TP Mss, HSP.

41. BF *Papers*, 407–12.

42. Ibid., vol. 11, 448.

43. BF, *Remarks on a Late Protest Against the Appointment of Mr. Franklin an Agent for this Province* (Philadelphia, 1764), reprinted in BF *Papers*, vol. 11, 430–41.

44. Ibid., vol. 11; quotations from 431.

45. Smith's tract was printed in Philadelphia in 1764 and reprinted in BF *Papers*, vol. 11, 488–516; quotations, in order, are from 488, 497, 497, 498, 498, 504, 506, 510, 505, 505, 504.

46. Israel Pemberton to David Barclay, Nov. 6, 1764, Pemberton Papers, HSP.

47. John Penn to TP, Mar. 16, 1765, TP Mss, HSP.

48. TP to Benjamin Chew, Jan. 11, 1765, TP Mss, HSP.

49. TP to William Allen, July 13, 1765; TP to John Penn, Dec. 7, 1764, TP Mss, HSP.

50. TP to John Penn, Nov. 9, Nov. 30, 1765, TP Mss, HSP.

51. TP to William Allen, June 6, 1766, July 31, 1767; to Richard Penn, Nov. 8, 1766, TP Mss, HSP.

52. BF to Joseph Galloway, Jan. 13, Oct. 11, Dec. 13, 1766, BF *Papers*, vol. 13, 35, 448, 522; June 13, Aug. 8, vol. 14, 184, 230–31, 1767. Shelburne was William Petty, Earl of Shelburne.

53. BF to Joseph Galloway, Aug. 20, 1768, ibid., vol. 15, 189–90. Hillsborough was Wills Hill, Earl of Hillsborough.

54. Pennsylvania Assembly Committee of Correspondence to BF and Richard Jackson, Oct. 17, 1769, ibid., vol. 16, 219.

55. Richard Peters to TP, Dec. 26, 1756, Richard Peters Papers, HSP.

56. BF *Papers*, vol. 2, 370.

57. BF *Autobiography*, 50, for "obscure."

58. Ibid., 56, and 75, 197 for quotations in the following paragraph.

59. TP to John Penn, Jan. 11, 1765, TP Mss, HSP.

CHAPTER 5

1. On Catherine Ray (who married William Greene in 1758), see William G. Roelker, ed., *Benjamin Franklin and Catherine Ray Greene: Their Correspondence, 1755–1790* (Philadelphia, 1949). See Chapter 1, above, for Madame Brillon and Margaret and Mary (Polly) Stevenson.
2. BF to William Strahan, Aug. 23, 1762, BF *Papers*, vol. 10, 149.
3. BF to William Strahan, Dec. 7, 1762, ibid., vol. 10, 169.
4. BF to Mary Stevenson, Mar. 25, 1763, ibid., vol. 10, 232.
5. "Observations Concerning the Increase of Mankind, Peopling of Countries, etc.," in ibid., vol. 4, 227–34, reveals the basis of his beliefs about America. For an expression of the imperial idea with America at the center, see BF to Lord Kames, Jan. 3, 1760, BF *Papers*, vol. 9, 6–7.
6. The essential studies of Franklin's part in the crisis of the Stamp Act are Verner W. Crane, "Benjamin Franklin and the Stamp Act," *Proceedings of the Colonial Society of Massachusetts* 32 (Feb. 1934): 56–77; and Edmund S. Morgan and Helen M. Morgan, *The Stamp Act Crisis* (Chapel Hill: University of North Carolina Press, 1953), 63–66, 244–48.
7. "N.N.": First Reply to Vindex Patriae, BF *Papers*, vol. 12, 413–16; quotation from 414.
8. BF *Papers*, vol. 12, 255, writing as "A Virginian," in *Lloyd's Evening Post, and British Chronicle*, Sept. 9–11, 1765.
9. Verner W. Crane, *Benjamin Franklin's Letters to the Press, 1758–1775* (Chapel Hill: University of North Carolina Press, 1950).
10. The quotation is from BF *Papers*, vol. 12, 414. For Franklin's testimony before the Commons, see BF *Papers*, vol. 13, 124–59.
11. The quotation is from the Declaratory Act, reprinted in Merrill Jensen, ed., *English Historical Documents: American Colonial Documents to 1776* (New York: Oxford University Press, 1969), 695–96.
12. BF expresses an early and typical regard for the king in a letter to John Whitehurst, June 27, 1763, BF *Papers*, vol. 10, 302.
13. BF to William Strahan, Dec. 19, 1763, and Strahan to BF, Aug. 18, 1763, ibid., vol. 9, 407, 325.
14. See William Strahan's letter of Aug. 18, 1763, ibid., vol. 10, 325.
15. BF to Joseph Galloway, Dec. 1, 1767, ibid., vol. 14, 331.

16. BF to William Franklin, Jan. 9, July 2, 1768, ibid., vol. 15, 16, 159–64; quotation from BF to J. Galloway, Mar. 21, 1770, ibid., vol. 17, 117.

17. BF to Samuel Cooper, Feb. 5, 1771, ibid., vol. 18, 24.

18. BF to Thomas Cushing, Jan. 13, 1772, ibid., vol. 19, 21.

19. Franklin's humiliation in the Cockpit—the chamber of the Privy Council's Committee for Plantation Affairs—has been described many times. The relevant documents are reprinted in ibid., vol. 21, 37–70, 86–96, and passim.

20. Ibid., vol. 21, 47.

21. For the Hutchinson-Oliver letters, see Bernard Bailyn, *The Ordeal of Thomas Hutchinson* (Cambridge: Harvard University Press, 1974), 221–56.

22. BF *Papers*, vol. 2, 8.

23. Ibid., vol. 21, 48–49 (bracketed insertion in quoted text). The Latin passage quoted by Wedderburne is from Plautus, *Aulularia*, II, 325: "Tun, trium litterarum homo me vituperas? fur" (Do you find fault with me? You, a man of three letters—thief!).

24. BF to Thomas Cushing, Feb. 15 [–19?], 1774, ibid., vol. 21; quotations from 92, 93–94.

25. BF to Lord Kames, Feb. 25, 1767, ibid., vol. 14, 65.

26. To Cushing, Feb. 15, 1774, ibid., vol. 21, 94.

27. To William Franklin: "Journal of Negotiations in London," Mar. 22, 1775, ibid., vol. 21, 540–99; quotation from 572.

28. Ibid., vol. 21, 589–90.

29. Ibid., vol. 21, 576–85, and passim in this volume.

30. BF to William Franklin, Mar. 3, 1768, ibid., vol. 15, 75, 78.

31. "Journal of Negotiations," ibid., vol. 21, 581–82, 594–96; BF to Joseph Galloway, Feb. 25, 1775, vol. 21, 510.

32. BF to William Franklin, July 14, 1773, ibid., vol. 20, 308.

33. To William Strahan, July 5, 1775, ibid., vol. 22, 85.

34. To David Hartley, Sept. 12, 1775, ibid., vol. 22, 196. George Guttridge has written a valuable study that, among other things, describes Hartley's friendship with BF. See George Herbert Guttridge, *David Hartley, M.P., an Advocate of Conciliation, 1774–1783* (Berkeley: University of California Press, 1926).

35. To David Hartley, Sept. 12, 1775, BF *Papers*, vol. 22, 196. Lord Dunmore was John Murray, Earl of Dunmore.

36. To David Hartley, Oct. 3, 1775, ibid., vol. 22, 216.

37. To Priestley, Jan. 27, 1777, ibid., vol. 23, 238.

38. To James Hutton, Feb. 1, 1778, ibid., vol. 25, 562.

39. To David Hartley, Feb. 12, 1778, ibid., vol. 25, 651.

40. To James Hutton, Feb. 12, 1778, ibid., vol. 25, 653.

41. To John Jay, Jan. 27, 1781, BF Mss, Yale.

42. The standard treatment of Franklin and prisoners of war in England is Catherine M. Prelinger, "Benjamin Franklin and the American Prisoners of War in England during the American Revolution," *WMQ* 32 (April 1975): 261–94. See also Larry G. Bowman, *Captive Americans: Prisoners during the American Revolution* (Athens: Ohio University Press, 1976).

43. The letters of prisoners may be read in BF *Papers*, vols. 22–30.

44. Prelinger, "Benjamin Franklin and the American Prisoners," 262–67, and passim.

45. Franklin and Deane to Stormont, Apr. 2, 1777, BF *Papers*, vol. 23, 549; Stormont's reply is quoted in Prelinger, 263. The appraisal by a captive of Mill Prison is from BF *Papers*, vol. 24, 31.

46. BF to James Lovell, Mar. 16, 1780; Sept. 13, 1781, BF Mss, Yale.

47. BF to R. R. Livingston, Mar. 4, 1787, BF Mss, Yale.

CHAPTER 6

1. For this sketch of the European diplomatic background, I have relied upon H. M. Scott, *British Foreign Policy in the Age of the American Revolution* (Oxford: Clarendon Press, 1990); three studies by Jonathan R. Dull: *The French Navy and American Independence: A Study in Arms and Diplomacy, 1774–1787* (Princeton, N.J.: Princeton University Press, 1975), *A Diplomatic History of the American Revolution* (New Haven, Conn.: Yale University Press, 1985), and *Franklin the Diplomat: The French Mission* (Philadelphia: American Philosophical Society, *Transactions* 72, part 1, 1982); Felix Gilbert, *To the Farewell Address: Ideas of Early American Foreign Policy* (Princeton, N.J.: Princeton University Press, 1961); Orville T. Murphy, *Charles Gravier, Comte de Vergennes: French Diplomacy in the Age of Revolution, 1719–1787* (Albany: State University of New York Press, 1982); James H. Hutson, "Intellectual Foun-

dations of Early American Diplomacy," *Diplomatic History* 1 (Winter 1977): 1–19. The subtitle to this chapter—"Wedderburnes in France"—appears in BF to William Carmichael, June 2, 1779, BF *Papers*, vol. 29, 601.

2. Durand Echeverria, *Mirage in the West: A History of the French Image of American Society to 1815* (Princeton, N.J.: Princeton University Press, 1957), 46 and passim. Franklin described his appearance in a letter to Emma Thompson, Feb. 8, 1777, BF *Papers*, vol. 23, 296–99. Charles Coleman Sellers, *Benjamin Franklin in Portraiture* (New Haven, Conn.: Yale University Press, 1962), 101, says that the French ladies thought he wore "cracked lenses"—his bifocals—"as an emblem of economy and a white hat as an emblem of innocence."

3. On the Plan of Treaties or the "Model Treaty," see James H. Hutson, *John Adams and the Diplomacy of the American Revolution* (Lexington: University Press of Kentucky, 1980), 26–32, and "Early American Diplomacy: A Reappraisal," in *The American Revolution and "A Candid World*," ed. Lawrence S. Kaplan (Kent, Ohio: Kent State University Press, 1977), 40–68; William C. Stinchcombe, "John Adams and the Model Treaty," in ibid., 69–84.

4. Dull, *Diplomatic History*, 13–25, and *French Navy and American Independence*, 3–29.

5. John Ferling, "John Adams, Diplomat," *WMQ* 51 (Apr. 1994): 227–52; Hutson, *John Adams*, 29–32.

6. American purposes and ideas at the beginning of the Revolution were best expressed in the Model Treaty. See note 3, above, for studies of the treaty.

7. This sketch of Deane is based on H. James Henderson, *Party Politics in the Continental Congress* (New York: McGraw-Hill, 1974); Julian P. Boyd, "Silas Deane: Death By a Kindly Teacher of Treason," *WMQ* 16 (Apr., July, Oct. 1959): 165–87, 319–42, 515–50; and Jack Rakove, *The Beginnings of National Politics: An Interpretative History of the Continental Congress* (New York: Knopf, 1979).

8. The letters written and diary kept by Deane while in Congress can be seen in Paul Smith, ed., *Letters of Delegates to Congress, 1774–1789*, 19 vols. to date (Washington, D.C.: Library of Congress, 1976–), vols. 1 and 2.

9. Boyd, "Silas Deane"; Thomas P. Abernethy, "Commercial Activities of Silas Deane in France," *AHR* 39 (Apr. 1934): 477–85. Two books devoted to public finance in the Revolution are helpful in understanding Deane's activities and his relations with Robert Morris: Clarence L. Ver Steeg, *Robert Morris: Revolutionary Financier, with an Analysis of His Earlier Career* (Philadelphia: University of Pennsylvania Press, 1954); and E. James Ferguson, *The Power of the Purse: A History of American Public Finance, 1776–1790* (Chapel Hill: University of North Carolina Press, 1961).

10. Evidence regarding Jonathan Williams's financial dealings is scattered through vols. 23–29 of BF *Papers*.

11. Louis W. Potts, *Arthur Lee: A Virtuous Revolutionary* (Baton Rouge: Louisiana State University Press, 1981), is the only modern biography.

12. Ibid., 20–23, 59–63.

13. Two of Lee's best efforts in presenting the American cause are *An Appeal to the Justice and Interests of the People of Great Britain* (London, 1774) and *A Second Appeal to the Justice and Interests of the People on the Measures Respecting America* (London, 1775). Lee writes in these tracts as if he were an Englishman with an interest in American affairs.

14. The quotation is from JA *Papers*, vol. 7, 256.

15. Potts, *Arthur Lee*, 40–42.

16. Michael G. Kammen, *A Rope of Sand: The Colonial Agents, British Politics, and the American Revolution* (Ithaca, N.Y.: Cornell University Press, 1968), 133, 148–51.

17. Ibid., 149.

18. For Lee's and Franklin's letters while Lee was on his Spanish mission, see BF *Papers*, vol. 23, 309, 318–19, 329–30, 339–42, 356–58, 388–89, 416–19, 430–31, 477–79, 498–500, 508–11. Franklin mentions Ludwell Lee in his letter of Mar. 2, 1777, BF *Papers*, vol. 23, 419. On Lee's unsuccessful mission to Spain, see Potts, *Arthur Lee*, 167–72.

19. "American Commissioners to Commanders of American Armed Vessels," Nov. 21, 1777, BF *Papers*, vol. 25, 174 and headnote; and "American Commissioners to Committee on Foreign Affairs," Nov. 30, 1777, BF *Papers*, vol. 25, 207–8 (headnote).

20. Abernethy, "Commercial Activities of Silas Deane in France" (cited in note 9), 477–85; Potts, *Arthur Lee*, 183–86, and passim.

21. Boyd, "Silas Deane" (cited in note 7), 306–7, and the documentation there; Ferguson, *The Power of the Purse* (cited in note 9), 90–93.

22. Richard Henry Lee, *Life of Arthur Lee*, 2 vols. (Boston, 1829), vol. 1, 363.

23. "American Commissioners to Simeon Deane," Dec. 20, 1777; "William Stevenson and American Commissioners: An Exchange of Three Letters," Jan. 4, 1778; and Arthur Lee to BF and Silas Deane, Jan. 7, 1778, all in BF *Papers*, vol. 25, 322–23, 406–8; quotation from 433. The editors' notes, as always, are valuable.

24. Arthur Lee to BF, Apr. 2, 1778, BF to Arthur Lee, Apr. 4, 1778, ibid., vol. 26, 220–22, 231–35.

25. Ibid., vol. 26, quotations 221, 222.

26. Rakove, *Beginnings of National Politics* (cited in note 7), 246–55.

27. Arthur Lee to BF, Apr. 2, 1778, BF *Papers*, vol. 26, 222.

28. BF to Arthur Lee, Apr. 3, 1778, ibid., vol. 26, 223; BF to Lee, Apr. [4], 1778, also not sent, ibid., 231–35.

29. For Izard, see Mark M. Boatner III, *Encyclopedia of the American Revolution*, Bicentennial edition (New York: David McKay Company, 1974); and Dull, *Diplomatic History* (cited in note 1).

30. Izard to BF, Jan. 28, 1778, BF *Papers*, vol. 25, 537, 538 for the quotations. The entire letter should be read for Izard's argument.

31. BF to Ralph Izard, Jan. 29, 1778, ibid., vol. 25, 539.

32. For Izard's complaints, Izard to BF, Apr. 25, June 17, 1778, ibid., vol. 26, 342, 343, 640–53.

33. JA, *Diary and Autobiography*, vol. 4, 87.

34. Wharton, vol. 2, 711.

35. "To the Free and Virtuous Citizens of America," *Pennsylvania Packet*, Dec. 5, 1778, was the most controversial essay published by Deane. There were various plays on the word "innuendo." James Lovell in a letter of Aug. 6, 1779, to Arthur Lee reported that Richard Henry Lee referred to Deane as an *"Innuendo Man,"* Smith, ed., *Letters of Delegates* (cited in note 8), vol. 13, 335.

36. BF to Arthur Lee, Feb. 18, 1779; Lee to BF, BF *Papers*, vol. 28, 565, 585, 586 for the quotations.

37. BF to Arthur Lee, Mar. 13, 1779; Arthur Lee to BF, Mar. 19, 1779, ibid., vol. 29, 110, 168.

38. For a sample of the exchanges between the two in this affair, see ibid., vol. 29, 111–12, 130–34, 218–19.

39. BF to William Carmichael, July 29, 1778, ibid., vol. 27, 176.

40. Izard's letters to Henry Laurens, president of Congress, of June 28, July 25, and Sept. 12, 1778, reveal much about his opinions and ambitions; see Wharton, vol. 2, 629–32, 661–63, 710–14. Franklin's son-in-law, Richard Bache, informed him of Lee's and Izard's attacks at home; Bache to BF, Oct. 22, 1778, BF *Papers*, vol. 27, 599–602.

41. BF to William Carmichael, June 2, 1779, BF *Papers*, vol. 29, 601; and see BF's letter to James Lovell, ibid., vol. 29, 608, same date.

42. To Carmichael, June 2, 1779, ibid., vol. 29, 601.

43. "The Petition of the Letter Z" is reprinted in ibid., vol. 28, 517–21, with informed and perceptive notes.

44. Ibid., vol. 28, 520.

CHAPTER 7

1. What follows in the text about John and Abigail Adams's personal development is based largely on JA *Earliest Diary*, JA *Diary and Autobiography*, JA *Papers*, and *Adams Family Correspondence*. But I owe much to other historians who have studied John and Abigail Adams, especially Page Smith, *John Adams*, 2 vols. (Garden City, N.Y.: Doubleday, 1962); Peter Shaw, *The Character of John Adams* (Chapel Hill: University of North Carolina Press, 1976); John Ferling, *John Adams: A Life* (Knoxville: University of Tennessee Press, 1992); Joseph J. Ellis, *Passionate Sage: The Character and Legacy of John Adams* (New York: Norton, 1993); Lynne Withey, *Dearest Friend: A Life of Abigail Adams* (New York: Free Press, 1981); Edith B. Gelles, *Portia: The World of Abigail Adams* (Bloomington: Indiana University Press, 1992); Paul C. Nagel, *Descent from Glory: Four Generations of the John Adams Family* (New York: Oxford University Press, 1983), and *The Adams Women* (New York: Oxford University Press, 1987); Bernard Bailyn, "Butterfield's Adams: Notes for a Sketch," *WMQ* 19 (April 1962): 238–56; E. S. Morgan, "John Adams and the Puritan Tradition," *NEQ* 34 (Dec. 1961): 518–29.

2. JA *Diary and Autobiography*, vol. 1, 67–68 for the quotations.

3. Ibid., vol. 1, 68 for the quotations.

4. Ibid., vol. 1, 31 for the quotations.

5. Ibid., vol. 1, 35.

6. Ibid., vol. 1, 78.

7. Smith, Shaw, and Ferling (all cited in note 1) provide excellent accounts. The quotation is from JA *Diary and Autobiography*, vol. 3, 256.

8. Nagel, *Adams Women*, 18–19; quotations from JA *Diary and Autobiography*, vol. 1, 79.

9. JA *Diary and Autobiography*, vol. 1, 65.

10. Ibid., vol. 1, 257–58; quotation from 258.

11. JA *Earliest Diary*, following 42, photographs of pages, and passim.

12. JA *Diary and Autobiography*, vol. 1, 13–14; quotation from vol. 3, 263.

13. Ibid., vol. 3, 262–63.

14. JA *Earliest Diary*, 70, for the quotation (bracketed addition in quoted text).

15. L. Kevin Wroth and Hiller B. Zobel, eds., *Legal Papers of John Adams*, 3 vols. (Cambridge: Harvard University Press, 1965), vol. 1, xiv.

16. JA *Diary and Autobiography*, vol. 1, 54–55, for the recommended reading; quotation from vol. 1, 55.

17. Withey, *Dearest Friend*, 1–4; Nagel, *Adams Women*, 8–9.

18. Withey and Nagel are excellent on matters discussed in this paragraph and the one preceding. For the quotations, see JA *Diary and Autobiography*, vol. 1, 108, 109.

19. *Adams Family Correspondence*, vol. 1, for letters of courtship and the details of their love. John Adams addressed his letter of Oct. 4, 1762, to "Miss Adorable," vol. 1, 2. Withey, *Dearest Friend*, 14–22, provides perceptive comment on the courtship.

20. JA *Diary and Autobiography*, vol. 1, 13.

21. JA to Abigail Adams, July 23, 1775, *Adams Family Correspondence*, vol. 1, 243.

22. For assessments of the older Adams, see Smith, Shaw, Ferling, Ellis, Bailyn, and Morgan (cited in note 1); and Edmund S. Morgan, *The Meaning of Independence* (Charlottesville: University of Virginia Press, 1976), 3–25.

23. JA to Abigail Adams, Apr. 12, Apr. 25, 1778, *Adams Family Corre-*

spondence, vol. 3, 9–10, 17; JA *Diary and Autobiography*, vol. 4, 36–37 for the quotations and the encounter with the brazen French lady.

24. *Adams Family Correspondence*, vol. 3, 17, 10 for the quotations. See JA to Abigail Adams, June 3, 1778, vol. 3, 31–32.

25. JA to Sam Adams, Aug. 7, 1778, JA *Papers*, vol. 6, 354. For JA's retrospective account of his first days with his colleagues in Paris, JA *Diary and Autobiography*, vol. 4, 86–88.

26. JA *Diary and Autobiography*, vol. 4, 118–19.

27. BF *Papers*, vol. 28, 509; James H. Hutson, *John Adams and the Diplomacy of the American Revolution* (Lexington: University Press of Kentucky, 1980), 45–48.

28. JA to Richard Henry Lee, Feb. 13, 1779, JA *Papers*, vol. 7, 407.

29. JA to Abigail Adams, Feb. 28, 1779, *Adams Family Correspondence*, vol. 3, 181.

30. Silas Deane, "To the Free and Virtuous Citizens of America," *Pennsylvania Packet*, Dec. 5, 1778; reprinted in the Deane Papers, New-York Historical Society *Collections*, vol. 21 (1858), 66–76. For Adams's reactions, see his letters to Vergennes, Feb. 11; James Lovell, Feb. 13, Feb. 20; James Warren, Feb. 25; Samuel Cooper, Feb. 28, 1779, JA *Papers*, vol. 7, 401–3, 408–9, 419, 427–28, 432–33.

31. JA to James Lovell, Feb. 20, 1779, JA *Papers*, vol. 7, 419–20.

32. Franklin feared Adams's reaction to the cancellation of the voyage to America in the *Alliance* and asked Sartine to write the letter. For the quotations in this paragraph, see JA *Diary and Autobiography*, vol. 2, 369. Adams's letter to BF of Apr. 29, 1779, BF *Papers*, vol. 29, 394–95, is less revealing.

33. JA *Diary and Autobiography*, vol. 2, 297.

34. BF to JA, Apr. 3, 1779 ("Master Johnny"); JA *Papers* (letters by the American commissioners), vol. 7, 44–45, 54–55, 194–95; 334–35; JA *Diary and Autobiography*, vol. 4, 58–59, 119.

35. Hutson, *John Adams*, 51–52; Orville T. Murphy, *Charles Gravier, Comte de Vergennes: French Diplomacy in the Age of Revolution, 1719–1787* (Albany: State University of New York Press, 1982), 264–76.

36. Hutson, *John Adams*, 66–67.

37. Hutson, *John Adams*, 59–66; Albert H. Smyth, ed., *The Writings of Benjamin Franklin*, 10 vols. (New York: Macmillan, 1907), vol. 8, 127.

38. Hutson, *John Adams*, 68–69.
39. BF to JA, Oct. 2, 1780, BF Mss, Yale.
40. Adams's regard for the French was highest early in his first mission. See, e.g., JA to James Warren, Aug. 4, 1778, JA *Papers*, vol. 6, 347–49. For his suspicions, see Hutson, *John Adams*, 86, 96–97.
41. BF to JA, Oct. 2, Oct. 8, 1780, BF Mss, Yale. On "militia diplomacy," see Samuel F. Bemis, *The Diplomacy of the American Revolution* (Bloomington: Indiana University Press, 1957; first published 1935, American Historical Association), 114n, 157; Gerald Stourzh, *Benjamin Franklin and American Foreign Policy*, 2d edition (Chicago: University of Chicago Press, 1969), 126, 159–61.
42. JA to BF, Feb. 15, 1781, and BF to JA, Feb. 22, 1781, Charles F. Adams, ed., *The Works of John Adams* 10 vols. (Boston: Little, Brown, 1850–56), vol. 7, 369, 371.
43. Hutson, *John Adams*, 96–97.
44. Shaw, *The Character of J 'n Adams* (cited in note 1), 164–67.
45. Herbert E. Klingelhofe "Matthew Ridley's Diary during the Peace Negotiations of 1782," *WMQ* 20 (Jan. 1963): 95–133; quotations from 123.
46. JA to Abigail Adams, Nov. 8, 1782, *Adams Family Correspondence*, vol. 5, 28–29.
47. Klingelhofer, "Matthew Ridley's Diary," 132.
48. JA to Abigail Adams, Apr. 16, 1783, *Adams Family Correspondence*, vol. 5, 125–27.
49. Ibid., vol. 5, 127.
50. Adams uses the term "franklinian Politics" twice in the letter of Apr. 16, 1783, to Abigail, ibid., vol. 5, 125, 126. The remarks about Dana and Livingston are in JA to Abigail Adams, Sept. 1, 1783, ibid., vol. 5, 232.
51. JA to Robert R. Livingston, May 25, 1783, BF Mss, Yale. Adams also complained that although he had "suffered much in public life in America [it was] but little, in comparison of what I have suffered in Europe, the greatest and worst part of which has been caused by the ill Dispositions of the c de Vergennes, aided by the Jealousy, Envy & selfish Servility of Dr. Franklin."
52. BF to R. R. Livingston, July 22, 1783, BF Mss, Yale.

53. James Madison to Thomas Jefferson, Feb. 11, 1783, Julian P. Boyd, ed., *The Papers of Thomas Jefferson*, 25 vols. to date (Princeton, N.J.: Princeton University Press, 1950–), vol. 6, 235; Jefferson to Madison, Feb. 14, 1783, ibid., 241.

EPILOGUE

1. BF *Papers*, vol. 28, 519, for quotation.
2. Sheila L. Skemp, *William Franklin: Son of a Patriot, Servant of a King* (New York: Oxford University Press, 1990), is a first-rate biography.
3. William Franklin to BF, July 22, 1784, BF Mss, Yale.
4. BF to William Franklin, Aug. 16, 1784, BF *Writings* (New York: Library of America, 1987), 1097.
5. BF *Papers*, vol. 6, 321.
6. Ibid., vol. 19, 29.

Index

Designer:	Ina Clausen
Compositor:	Maple-Vail Book Manufacturing Group
Text:	11/14.6 Janson
Display:	Adobe Garamond
Printer and Binder:	Maple-Vail Book Manufacturing Group